Joe Girard's
13 Essential
RULES OF
SELLING

From "The World's Greatest Salesman"
–*Guinness Book of World Records*

Joe Girard's
13 Essential
RULES OF
SELLING

How to Be a Top Achiever and Lead a Great Life

WITH TONY GIBBS

New York Chicago San Francisco Lisbon London Madrid Mexico City
Milan New Delhi San Juan Seoul Singapore Sydney Toronto

1 2 3 4 5 6 7 8 9 0   QFR/QFR   1 8 7 6 5 4 3 2

ISBN   978-0-07-179905-8
MHID   0-07-179905-2

e-ISBN   978-0-07-179906-5
e-MHID   0-07-179906-0

McGraw-Hill books are available at special quantity discounts to use
as premiums and sales promotions or for use in corporate training
programs. To contact a representative, please e-mail us at
bulksales@mcgraw-hill.com.

Library of Congress Cataloging-in-Publication Data

Girard, Joe.
  Joe Girard's 13 essential rules of selling : how to be a top achiever and
lead a great life / by Joe Girard with Tony Gibbs.
     p. cm.
  Includes index.
  ISBN 978-0-07-179905-8 (alk. paper) -- ISBN 0-07-179905-2 (alk. paper)
  1. Selling. I. Title. II. Title: Joe Girard's 13 essential rules of selling.
  HF5438.25.G574 2013
  658.85--dc23
                              2012016578

To the select group who commit to realizing
their full potential in life

CONTENTS

INTRODUCTION

Many of life's failures are people who did not realize how close they were to success when they gave up.

— Thomas Edison, inventor and scientist

They weren't really buying a shoeshine; they were being sold Joe Girard.

The purpose of this book is to establish the foundation you need to help realize your most important goals and expectations in life. Whether you're in sales or service, a different kind of profession, or just searching for a way to make your life more fulfilling and meaningful, *My 13 Rules* will get you on the winning track to *health, happiness, and success.*

I've had the privilege of writing four very successful books that have sold millions of copies over the years. The book you have in your hands right now goes a step further. It not only captures the essence of what made me the world's greatest salesperson but, more important, it describes how I overcame difficult obstacles as I powered my way through life. By following my 13 rules, I put a set of gold keys in my hands that not only unlocked the doors to a rewarding and satisfying life, but also gave me a richer experience. *They changed who I was as a person and how I lived my life!*

My success came making a living in the toughest retail selling game of them all: automobiles. While I certainly had my share of good fortune, there was no luck involved. Since I'm not a superstitious person, I don't believe in luck. In fact, for me a number like 13 is fantastic! I sold 13,001 brand-new retail vehicles over a 15-year sales career (and threw in one more to remind everyone I was #1 in what I did). I became the world's greatest salesperson (as attested in the *Guinness Book of World Records,* audited by the accounting firm Deloitte & Touche) by applying *My 13 Rules.* I sold more retail big-ticket items, *one-at-a-time,* than any other salesperson in any retail industry in history including houses, boats, motor homes, insurance, and automobiles. It's a record that has never been broken!

If you're browsing this book for the first time in a bookstore, look at some of the other books on the shelves that surround this one. Some of them will have flashy titles that promise you the world, with "secret" steps and formulas to untold wealth and rewards. Others will claim to be written by "experts." Whenever you see books like these, begin by asking yourself these questions:

» "Were they written by people who have actually had *real-life experiences*?"

» "Are the claims just armchair psychologists' theories, or *do they really work*?"

In other words, "How credible are they?" I call people who make those claims ATANAs because they're "All Talk and No Action." Before you tell somebody to do something, it's a good idea to have first *lived the part* and *walked the talk* yourself. Don't get me wrong. I have nothing against psychologists. I do have a problem with smug-sounding theories that are hawked as solutions for serious decisions in life.

Many of the books you see on these shelves were written by educated people who studied or learned a few things from other people and then decided to take their message to the street by writing a book. Me? I did it in just the opposite way. I got my *street smarts* first on the front lines, and *then* I wrote a book. What approach makes the most sense to you? In the end, it's all about credibility. That's exactly what you get with Joe Girard: CREDIBILITY.

I put my foundation for success together when I first got started selling cars and trucks. I analyzed and organized everything I did. I was mainly looking for things I did or had done that might have an impact on the success or failure of a typical workday. I studied the various processes and approaches I used. I compared my methods with others in similar retail businesses. *I wanted to know what other successful people were doing.* Before long, I had a pile of different ideas. I was basically looking for a success pattern. And I finally found it— the first step up the steep climb to success!

I realized that anything that had to do with a process—like the flow of paperwork, or the order of explaining detailed product features and benefits to a customer—was not where the edge would be that I was looking for. I figured anyone could do that. We all had the same paperwork flow and the same products and information (training manuals, videos, and catalogs). There was clearly *no advantage to be gained* there. I quickly discarded anything process- or product-related, or anything that had to do with how the dealership operated. At that point, it was very clear there was only one thing left—ME.

By narrowing my focus on me and how I did things, I was able to pinpoint some very special characteristics—*13, to be exact*. But I was in for a pleasant surprise:

They would apply to everything I did in life, not just work-related things!

I discovered that these 13 traits would form the foundation for (and become) something much bigger. They became *My 13 Rules.*

I Overcame Adversity and You Can, Too!

The reason I'm so confident you will find this book useful (especially when compared to other books) is because it represents the experience of somebody who is probably a lot like you: struggling to find a way to succeed in life. I know how depressing and discouraging that can be. There will always be intimidating roadblocks in life. The question is, "Do you see them as *obstacles* or *opportunities*?"

If you want to become successful, the first rule in life is to build a foundation. That's what these rules will be focusing on: getting your future planted on some solid ground so you can properly launch your efforts on a targeted course for success.

Looking back, I wish I had gotten my future on solid footing earlier in life. For many years, I found myself "spinning my wheels." I must have had 40 jobs in a variety of fields. I had no idea what I wanted to do or how to do it. I got absolutely no encouragement at all from my father. It seemed as though the only time he ever talked to me was to remind me I'd never amount to anything. The rest of the time, I was subjected to his beatings. Without knowing it, he actually lit a spark of energy inside me because I so resented his treatment of me. But through her love and encouragement, *my mother was the gasoline in my engine.* "Show him, Joey. Show him," she used to whisper to me. Although I didn't realize it at the time, that was the birth of my burning desire to be somebody.

As luck would have it, even with my rough childhood, I discovered something early on about myself that really helped me. From the time I shined shoes as a nine-year-old kid, trolling the local bars on Detroit's lower east side where the factory workers would go after work, I had pretty good instincts about "how to make the sale." I got quite creative in my approach. Even pleading and begging, but with style, became an art form with me. Sure enough, I noticed an increase in customers. I began to believe that a good salesperson could sell anything— because people don't buy *products*, they buy *people* they like and trust who can solve their problems. They weren't really buying a shoeshine; they were being sold *Joe Girard.*

I quickly learned the most important thing to sell was the world's *number-one product*—YOU! It was a "game-changing" discovery that would prove itself right on the mark years later when I became the world's number-one salesperson. To this day, in my office, I have a framed picture of me when I was nine years old, on my knees shining a shoe. I keep it there as a constant reminder of where I came from. It was a childhood I wouldn't wish on anyone, but it's one I'm also proud of. *It was truly where it all started for me.*

I couldn't have been more depressed and disillusioned about life than when I was growing up. As a result, I took a lot of left turns early on, hanging around with the wrong crowds. But for my mother and a special friend, Abe Saperstein, who took me under his wing in his home-building business early on in my working years, I might well have finished up getting into serious trouble.

Although my start was shaky, as I grew older I learned from my failures and experiences. I soon realized that unless I had some idea of what things I should be focusing on to be successful, I was going nowhere. And on top of it all, I had a young family of my own. Nothing will motivate you any faster than a wife and child who need something to eat. *Motivation to me meant survival*—a bag of groceries for the next couple of days for the ones I loved who were counting on me.

Through many years of trial and error, I eventually did develop a foundation for myself. It wasn't easy, but I did accomplish it. In fact, I've been improving and perfecting it my entire life. My foundation for a successful life has been to continuously sharpen the skills and traits that were major contributors to my success. The result is *My 13 Rules*. Everything I am about to tell you came from the front lines of life, not from some university term paper or theory. This is how it REALLY is.

Forget About a Magic Formula

If you're looking for a book on Joe Girard's "secrets" to success, forget it. Put the book down now. I've got a news flash for you:

THERE ARE NO SECRETS!

The elevator to Health, Happiness, and Success is "out of order." You'll have to use the stairs, one step at a time, just like I did—a kid expelled from high school with a bad attitude. How about that for a place to launch your future? But it can be done. I am living proof. *In spite of setback after setback, whatever the world threw at me, I made it to the top just the same!* IF I CAN DO IT, ANYONE CAN!

I never thought for one moment there was a magical set of secret steps or a shortcut to success. I had seen and read about too many of these scam artists who deliberately took people's money when they were down by promising them a way to the top. I always felt there was something suspicious about that. I never bought into it. Whenever I saw something like that, I always asked myself, "Why? Why the hell would anyone who claimed to have the 'secret' to success want to give it away by sharing it with others?" If you had something like that, you'd probably hide it and keep it to yourself. Wouldn't you? In my mind, these promises are no different than the books that claim to pick winners at the racetrack or beat the blackjack table. Believe me, I know from my delinquent days as a teen how easy it is to fall prey to the lure of "easy money" gambling.

As I said up front, there are no shortcuts and no secrets. I will show you how to become successful by using your *smarts*. If you think there's another way, forget it. You're dead. There is no other way.

Let's be clear about one thing. There's nothing magical about putting a list together of things you should do to give a good impression. Anyone can do that (and many have). That's not what this book is about at all. I'm going to take you beyond that kind of shallow thinking and drive into your mind and heart principles that are to be *lived by*, not just memorized.

What I'm talking about is a cycle of actions you put into motion every day of your life automatically, from the moment you get up in the morning. These principles become who you are. They are what people see whenever you are present. They will see YOU, living and breathing *My 13 Rules*. You are going to transform yourself starting right now! THAT will be your foundation for success.

How This Book Is Organized

So what are the 13 things I did (and still do) every day that made a positive difference in my performance and in my life? They are *My 13 Rules*.

If you look carefully at the rules in the Contents, you'll notice they are grouped into a sequence of four logical categories that follow a very natural cycle and flow:

1. **Prepare.** *Rules 1 to 6* focus on making healthy choices with a positive attitude, having a well-organized plan, being ready to work, and being ready to make the right impression. Be fully prepared before seeing anyone.

2. **Interact.** *Rules 7 to 10* deal with how you *interact* positively with the people you come in contact with. The emphasis on this group of rules is being sharp, sensitive, and aware. In other words, at your very best.

3. **Close the deal.** *Rules 11 and 12* are all about succeeding in getting your desired outcome. Winning the customer's confidence is the primary target. Learning to sell yourself is the main objective. Closing the deal will follow naturally from that.

4. **Reenergize.** Finally, *Rule 13* focuses on *reenergizing* yourself with a reward for a job well done. And believe me, I'm not all work and no play. Whenever I reached or exceeded my goals (which was often), I would reward myself and my wife. You should, too. Celebrate your hard work because you'll soon be ready to restart the cycle all over again by preparing for your next challenge.

From the moment I got out of bed in the morning until I came home, my day was "locked" into this cycle of *My 13 Rules*. By preparing well for the day ahead of time, and by demonstrating sharp but caring traits whenever I interacted with customers, I was able to produce a positive environment to help me close the deal practically every time. A reward at the end of it all was how I reenergized myself to remain motivated to do it again and again and again. In fact, when I returned home from one of our trips, I'd be so enthusiastic the next morning that, by the time I actually got to work, I was primed, pumped, and ready to go, with the energy of a conquering lion. That's how I approach everything I do in life.

I worked hard, often putting in many long hours perfecting my approach to becoming successful. My dedication and commitment to winning was fueled even more when I began to see positive improvements in my performance. The key to all of this was simple—follow the rules. That's exactly what I did.

How to Read This Book

Each one of the *13 Rules* has some very specific things you will need to pay attention to. As you read each of the 13 chapters, the goal is not to memorize the 13 rules, but rather to become them. That's right—*become* them. When you "become the rules," that's when you've really succeeded in understanding them at the highest level. You've finally arrived! You're a changed person. You're on your way to a rich, rewarding, and personally fulfilling life.

With these rules, I was able to set in motion a positive cycle of actions that would serve me well throughout my sales career and beyond into my personal life. Before long, I found my interactions with family, friends, and others rising to a new level of satisfaction and fulfillment. And it was all because of the principles behind the rules. They're not just for the office. Take them home with you and be the person you appear to be. That's when you know you really have something: when you become a better person by *living the part.*

When you begin to see positive changes start to happen, then (and only then) will you realize that I have succeeded in equipping you with the right tools and values to reach the mountain summits in your life. I'm not just talking about success on the job. I'm talking about success as a spouse, success as a parent, success as a citizen in your community, success as a complete person.

I want to unleash the *real* you that's been locked up and blocked from moving forward by your past. I didn't write this book to entertain you. I wrote it so you could become a more complete, a more fulfilled, and, above all, a better person—in other words, a success. The way to get the most out of this book is to go about reading it the same way you would sit down to a well-prepared meal. You'd want to enjoy and savor the taste of each course from beginning to end. You wouldn't rush through it because you'd get indigestion. You'd take your time. This book is the same way.

Each course (chapter) has been well prepared and designed to be digested slowly, carefully, and thoroughly. After you read a chapter, put the book down. Think about what you just read. Don't go on to the next chapter. Speed-reading doesn't work here. Go slow and soak it up! Meditate on the ideas and concepts. Ask yourself, *"How can I make them work in my life?"*

You might see something right away you need to change in the way you're doing things. Don't wait until you've read the entire book to act on my advice. It might even be a few days before you get back to the next chapter. That's okay. If something isn't clicking, go back and reread the chapter again until it makes sense to you. When you understand it, then you're ready to go on to the next chapter.

You'll be amazed at how much your learning ability will improve if you use this approach to reading this book. The idea is to *digest* what I'm telling you so you can *apply* it. Take your time. Unlike the great meal I used as an example, the nice thing about this book is that when you're finished with it, it's always there for you to reread again and again. What if you forget something or start slipping back into old habits? Go back and reread the book. Maybe it's a specific chapter you need to bone up on. Go back again and again as often as you like. Get refreshed and reenergized! If you do this, you will have discovered a dynamic way of learning from a powerful reference book. Keep it near you. You'll find it especially helpful when you're experiencing some of life's "speed bumps" both at home and at work (which happens to all of us from time to time). These rules will provide the spirit-lifting boost and guidance you need at just the right time.

As long as you make an honest effort to adopt the principles of *My 13 Rules*, you'll set yourself in motion on a course for success unlike anything you've ever experienced before in your life! *You'll never go back* to who you were! You've done your time! Focus on the future. After all, it's where you're going to spend the rest of your life.

In the End, It's All About You

Now, if you think these rules are very basic, you're right. They're supposed to be. That's the whole point. Most people fail in life not because they don't know how to perform certain steps in a task. They fail because they don't know how to REACT in a situation that requires some thought and judgment before actually doing something. Suddenly, they're on shaky ground. This is where good judgment comes into play—*thinking smart*, as I like to put it.

Thinking smart has everything to do with perfecting basic skills. Once these 13 rules become second nature to you, you'll be able to cope with situations professionally, sensibly, and, most important, successfully, in a way unlike anything you've ever experienced before. Disciplined habits are the only way to succeed over the long haul. If you make a sincere effort to embrace and live the rules every day, you will see positive results.

Never play down the importance of sharpening your basic skills. That's where the critical mistakes are almost always made. That's where the success edge lies. That's what separated me from other salespeople. I never made or lost a sale because I did or didn't know what all the steps in the paper trail of our dealership were. For a salesperson, that was something you either knew or could easily find out. It wasn't that complicated. You're focusing on small stuff if you think that's where the winning edge is. *My ability to influence* the outcome by how I went about doing things is what closed the deal.

I knew how to do the basics better than anyone else. That has also helped me tremendously to better understand people and see things *as they* see them—not only as I see them. That's the edge, and that's what these 13 rules are all about—the basics.

No matter what you do professionally, sooner or later, the things that are going to differentiate your performance from the person in the office next to you will center on how you, as an individual, go about executing the basics in whatever it is you do. It won't be about the process. It won't be about how the dealership, the hospital, or the factory operates. It's going to be ALL ABOUT YOU AND HOW YOU OPERATE. Sound simple? It is. If your reaction to that statement is, "Well, that's easy for him to say; he doesn't have to deal with so-and-so, or the politics in the office, etc., etc., etc. If only they'd make these adjustments, then I could be successful." *STOP!*

You'll never reach the top (you won't even get out of the basement) if all you ever do is take on the role of *victim*. Forget about blaming other people for your failures and shortcomings. If you do, you're a LOSER! You'll never get out of jail! *There will always be obstacles and people like that.* Think smart. They're just another mountain that needs to be conquered. You must get your mind off of dwelling on the negative side of things. Slowly but surely, you'll get sucked into the pit of adversity, and you'll be like all the other losers. You'll be just like one of them—"behind bars." Get off that trip NOW.

There's nothing mystifying about *My 13 Rules.* They're all about discipline and repetition. **You cannot win if you attempt to do it any other way.** You're doomed if you try. Unfortunately, conquest and winning aren't for everybody.

Many people are satisfied with just a so-so existence—nothing too challenging and nothing too difficult. Just an ordinary life will do. You and I both know there are lots of people out there like that. But they all have to ponder the sobering thought, "Imagine what I *could* have been," as they look in the mirror one day at the end of their working days. What will you see?

The saddest part of all is that you will be haunted by that question for the rest of your life—never knowing what you could have done or achieved, not just for yourself but for your family too. I know what I committed myself to do for just a bag of groceries so my family could eat for one more day. I'll never forget it.

Let's be honest here and face the truth—make all the excuses you want, but in the end, you decide where your life is going. Living with the guilt of failure for not even trying will drive you mad. It's been said that the only real failing in life is the failure to try. When you come to the full realization that you, and you alone, make the difference in your quest for success, you will have taken that critical first step to understanding what it *really* takes to get to the top! *Joe Girard's 13 Rules* will help you get there. **We both *know* what YOU have to do now. I also know that YOU CAN DO IT. When you're ready to take that first step up the mountain, I'll be the first one to greet you when you reach the top.**

It's a new day. Let this book be the key that unlocks your future. Are you ready to get out of jail? If the answer is "yes," then let's unleash the *real* you now! **Here's to your health, happiness, and success!**

PART I
PREPARE

RULE ONE
MAKE A HEALTHY CHOICE

Use your health, even to the point of wearing it out.
That is what it is for. Spend all you have before you die;
do not outlive yourself.

—George Bernard Shaw, playwright

I went from 207 pounds down to 156 and a 34-inch waistline.

A WORD ON PREPARATION

As I mentioned in the Introduction, my first six of the *13 Rules* focus on how you PREPARE—the things you do before you ever get in front of anybody who's counting on you for something, like a customer, for example. *Preparation* is critical to your success.

No matter how many times a seasoned high-altitude mountain climber attacks a mountain peak like, say, Mt. Everest, the process always begins the same way—with *preparation*. Not one step is taken up that mountain until all preparations are thoroughly checked out. This means a detailed going over of all planning and equipment to make sure the strategy is sound and that everything works. Climbers spend weeks and months getting used to the climate in the area before ever venturing up the mountain. There are many stories of failed and tragic expeditions up high mountains because the planning wasn't right or the equipment didn't perform properly.

In life, failing to prepare is where most people fall short of the mark, especially on the job. They don't think they need to prepare because they've done something so many times they believe they can practically do it in their sleep. Or they think that it really doesn't make any difference. They let their egos get in the way of good judgment. Don't be one of these statistics. Get on the right track with thorough preparation before you start your day. By the time you walk in the front door of your office or place of work you should be primed and ready to "hit the bricks running." If you don't latch onto this basic idea about the importance of preparation YOU ARE DOOMED. Period.

We don't climb anything until we know what we're doing and with what. *Nothing happens in our day until everything is checked out first.* If you're not prepared, you might as well stay home. Your performance will always reflect how well prepared you are. It's true in sports, in how you make investments—even in your personal life with family, where it really counts big and, of course, obviously where you work. It's true about everything in life. If you're counting on luck to get you through, remember this: *Luck is for losers. Winners play it smart and plan ahead.*

D eciding where to begin with *My 13 Rules* was actually quite easy. When you review the list of rules in the Introduction, it's pretty obvious that nothing positive is going to happen, even with the best of intentions, if you're not up to the task—and that means being as fit as you can be. That's why I'm talking about my first rule, *Make a healthy choice*, right up front. Without a healthy mind, a healthy spirit, and a healthy body, you are not as complete a person as you could be. Mental, emotional, and physical stability are the three pieces to the puzzle of maintaining your good health.

Your Good Health—Life's Starting Point

To me, good health is not about a race to become smarter or stronger than the next guy or gal. It's not about being healthier than someone else. *The contest I'm talking about is only between you and yourself.* God didn't make us all the same. Each one of us is unique. We weren't all blessed with the same good health any more than we have the same gift of smarts. But that's okay. I'm talking about *making the most of what you do have!* That's the only yardstick you need. Ask yourself, "Am I all that I can be?" If you answered, "No," you've got the right book in your hands.

If you don't think you're a particularly healthy person, I could spend hours talking to you about people I know who are not (and never have been) in good health. Yet, somehow, through sheer grit and determination, they were bound to succeed and live as complete and healthy lives as they possibly could. While they may not have been in the best of health, they all decided they would control what attitude they would wear when they woke up each morning to start their day. That might not be easy for many, but it is the secret to living a full and successful life. Let me share examples of two very special people who figured that out and succeeded in life in spite of severe health obstacles.

A case in point is Lance Armstrong, the winner of a record seven consecutive Tour de France races that recognize the world's greatest cyclist. If you would've seen him three years before he won the first of those seven races, you wouldn't have given him a chance in hell of surviving what he faced back then. Lance was stricken with a cancer that spread to his lungs, abdomen, and brain. His outlook was not good. He was given less than a 40 percent chance of survival following surgery and therapy. But survive he did! Following his illness, his astounding rise to dominance as the world's greatest cyclist was almost unbelievable. But his victories on a bicycle were nothing compared to his triumph over death. He has since gone on to champion the cause for treatment and support for those afflicted with cancer. He is a model of determination, fitness, and survival—all marks of a true champion.

Another example that comes to mind is the late Steve Jobs, CEO of the consumer electronics giant, Apple, who battled pancreatic cancer for more than seven years before finally succumbing to the disease. During this time, and in spite of this painful form of cancer, Apple designed and launched some of its most successful and imaginative products under Jobs's innovative and inspiring leadership. It is a testament to his courage, his work ethic, and his love of the company he founded. There are many more individuals I could go on and on about.

These real winners in life never took the easy path, even when faced with poor health. Instead of looking for pity, they accepted their situations and then made the courageous decision to *be everything they could possibly be in this life before checking out.* Nothing was allowed to get in the way of their achieving what they set out to do. When faced with a challenge to their health, they all said, "Bring it on." And because they did, we now have inspiring examples of what each of us has the potential to be—regardless of what health obstacles are thrown in our path.

To get into the right frame of mind mentally and emotionally to take on life, start by taking care of yourself physically. For most of us the problem is not a condition, a disease, or illness—it's *neglect!*

Listen up! Listen to your body—it's trying to tell you something!

A Mirror Always Tells the Truth

The key to being as healthy as you can be is, in a word, discipline. That brings us to the biggest culprits of why many people aren't healthy (and don't look healthy)—*diet and exercise.* Nothing makes an overweight person feel more uncomfortable and guilty than these two subjects. The vast majority of people don't like talking about them, and it shows. I KNOW. I WAS ONE OF THEM.

During the early years of my sales career success, I admit to being a workaholic. I was there night and day making calls, closing deals, and preparing for the next day. I think remembering my days as a kid with nothing was the biggest reason I would stop at nothing to make as much money as I could. As a result, I had very little time for myself and my family. I spent most of it in a chair, on the phone, or with customers. I never exercised. I never took the time for that. I was "too busy" to be healthy. I ate the wrong kinds of food, and I smoked three packs of cigarettes a day. What a combination—no exercise, fatty foods, and cigarettes. And I looked the part. But I was making money and lots of it. I was getting recognition all over the country for what I was achieving in sales. Still, when I got home at night and looked in the mirror, the truth of my identity was all too clear—a fat-bellied salesman who ignored his own good health for money. Something would have to change. Even though I was making plenty of money, deep down inside I didn't like myself.

When I was in my forties, I met a man who had a major impact on my life. It was Jack LaLanne, the renowned health and fitness pioneer. We were both receiving Golden Plate awards and national recognition in our respective fields from the prestigious American Academy of Achievement. Mine was for sales, and Jack's was for preaching the gospel of physical fitness. Jack was all muscle. I was all polyunsaturated fat. He said to me after the banquet, "Joe, I admire your philosophy. And I like what I see— from the neck up. But, frankly, I can't stand what I see from the neck down." He looked with disdain at my larded belly. "You're the world's greatest salesman," he continued, "but here's a sale I'll bet you can't close successfully." He then challenged me to lose all that weight and *keep it off*. He even told me how to do it, by eating sensibly: more fruits and vegetables and less starches. He also put me on a fitness program of three simple daily exercises (sit-ups, push-ups, and bicycle kicks). He told me, "Do it slowly, but stick to it." I'll never forget how I finally got started. All it took was one glance in the mirror. BOOM. I was going to make my body obey my mind no matter how hungry I was or how much my muscles ached until I succeeded. It was tough at times, but I stuck to my guns. *My mind was in total control of my body.* That was the key. How did I do? Just look at the photo at the beginning of this chapter. As the old saying goes, "One picture is worth a thousand words."

A year later, I sent Jack a letter telling him he had lost the bet. I went from 207 pounds down to 156 with a flat and hard belly and a 34-inch waistline. I got a letter back from Jack with a new challenge. "But can you *keep it off*?" A year later he lost that bet too. And I've been under 160 pounds ever since. Thanks for the push, Jack. You got me off the couch.

Now I'm challenging all of you to do the same thing. I tell everybody I see, "If I can do it, anyone can!" And that means YOU can too. MAKE YOUR BODY OBEY YOUR MIND. You're the captain of your ship. Don't be the *Titanic*. Don't let any icebergs get in the way of your good health and take you down. GET HEALTHY AGAIN AND STAY HEALTHY! I'm also throwing you a life preserver in life's stormy seas—*My 13 Rules*. Grab onto them and never let go. Stay the course and you'll reach your destination safely.

Now I know that some people have medical conditions that make weight control difficult, but let's be honest: most people are overweight because they choose to be. They choose to eat cholesterol-filled fast foods. They choose sitting on the sofa instead of doing sit-ups. They refuse to commit to change. Any excuse for inactivity will do. Some of them are so fat, they can hardly bend over to tie their shoelaces. Their great companions sitting on the sofa with them are LAZINESS and SELF-PITY. It's pathetic.

According to research conducted by both the Centers for Disease Control and Prevention and Duke University, by the year 2030, 42 percent of Americans will be obese! Are you in that crowd? ONCE UPON A TIME, I WAS! I can tell you right now, you're gonna have one helluva time getting on board with *Girard's 13 Rules* if you are. The people who are healthy and fit are not lucky. They *choose* to care about their health and their appearance. They want to feel good about themselves, so they do something about it and stick to their routines every day. They're disciplined. They conquer adversity whenever it rears its ugly head. *People aren't born that way; they choose to be that way.*

One of the most successful television personalities of all time is Oprah Winfrey. For years she has battled weight control due to a thyroid condition. But through her ups and downs, her busy schedule never kept her from trying relentlessly to take off the pounds and keep them off. Oprah has always felt an obligation to be a good example for others even when the will-power wasn't there. It is particularly difficult for her because of her medical condition. But that doesn't keep her from going the extra mile. Even with occasional setbacks, she is a winner and a model of determination because she never gives up. That's who you want to be! Don't you? THEN DO SOMETHING ABOUT IT! I DID!

It's been said that a person's health can be judged by which they take two-at-a-time—pills or stairs. If you *should be* taking two stairs at a time *but don't,* you will soon be taking two pills at a time, as sure as night follows day. Get control of your health now before it gets control of you. If you don't, you will find recapturing it will be one of the most difficult things you will ever do in your life. And it gets more difficult with each passing day. No matter what your condition or circumstance, talk to your doctor about getting on a physical fitness program that's tailor-made for you. You'll not only look better. You'll feel better about yourself. And that's where positive mindsets are born. More about that in our next chapter. Whatever you do, *don't give up before you even get started.*

Control Your Habits—Before They Control Your Career

Earlier in this chapter, I mentioned that I smoked three packs of cigarettes a day. It was a nasty habit that I was glad to escape from once I realized what it was doing to my overall health. I think if I could have drawn a chart with two lines on it—one representing the growth of my sales success and one representing the state of my health during those years—you would have seen two lines going in opposite directions as they crossed in the middle forming the letter "X." Now I don't want you to get the idea that you have to ignore your health in order to be a success in life. In fact, just the opposite is true. But I had to learn that the hard way, as I have so many things in my life. Fortunately for me, I was able to recognize and do something about both my eating and smoking habits before they took hold of me forever.

During my sales career, practically everyone I knew at work smoked. We weren't the most health conscious society when it came to food content either. That's the way things were back then. That's not the case today. We know a lot about what cigarettes and food with bad cholesterol levels can do to you. A well-known television news anchor's life was cut short because of lung cancer brought on by heavy cigarette smoking. Had he known better, I'm sure Peter Jennings would have made some better decisions about his health. There's no excuse for those choices today! NONE! So why do we do it?

I believe that when you're doing well at something, it's quite normal to want to continue doing that, and maybe more of it, even if it means sacrificing common sense. Why? Because it's a routine that works. That's my story right there. I kept doing what I was doing because it worked. The more I did of something, the more money I seemed to be making. The problem was, I was ignoring the basic attention my body needed. So I paid the price. All I did was cough all day long in my chair. Cigarettes were killing me, and I didn't even know it. Besides, I had no time for that. I had to focus on making the next call—closing the next deal—grabbing the next buck before someone else tried to take it from me. Except for the ties we wore, the business of retail selling might as well have been a contest between wild animals in the jungle fighting over a piece of raw meat. I always felt I was in a game of *survival of the fittest*. Except fittest, in this case, didn't apply to Joe Girard's health. That took a backseat. I became a *prisoner of my own success*.

But it didn't stop there. Once I achieved the top sales spot in the world, there was no one else left to beat—except, of course, myself. My only challenge was to beat my previous year's sales record. And I did that on a number of occasions. Once I became number one, I never looked back ever again. I remained the number-one salesperson in the world for the rest of my career. There was a lot to celebrate. And I did. I rewarded myself with frequent trips to Las Vegas for my wife and me. And that's where I met the devil; I discovered gambling.

At first it was small-time. A few hundred bucks here and there. Pretty soon it became thousands. Eventually I had a personal marker (in the gambling world, that's like a line of credit) in certain hotel casinos that I simply signed my name to. Although I was not a big-time gambler with a disease or anything like that, I know I had run up gambling debts of at least $11,000 on occasion. My problem was, I didn't see it as gambling. I saw it as enjoying my success. I liked the action; I liked the recognition I would often get; I liked being in the limelight of Las Vegas. Life was "good." But this, too, was ruining my health. The track was fast, but I didn't want to get off. Once I came to my senses (and it didn't take long to realize I was "giving away" my hard-earned money), I jumped off that train to nowhere. I didn't want to follow in the footsteps of people like PGA golfer John Daly (read John's book, *John Daly: My Life In and Out of the Rough*), whose promising career has been plagued with distracting personal problems including losing tens of millions of dollars gambling. That's not where I wanted to be.

My wife and I still enjoy going to Vegas. The difference is, we're in total control of what we do—common sense rules—and it's a lot more fun that way.

Here's the lesson: One of the most difficult things to do once you've reached the top of the mountain is to be careful you don't "dance" too much up there. You might slip and come crashing down to the bottom. What you'll see on the way down, in a few seconds as you plunge to your demise, is just a blurry picture of the path you worked so hard to climb up for months and years—soon to be snuffed out in a moment of bad judgment. Gone—just like that—game over. We've all seen and heard about this kind of thing happening too often to star athletes and movie idols. I'll be talking more about that later in

Rule #4, *Work when you work*. Take a tip from Joe Girard: You don't have to drink the whole bottle in order to enjoy the wine.

Somewhere along the way, I must have developed a nagging awareness for knowing when something I was doing wasn't quite right. I'm convinced my mother and The Man Upstairs had a hand in this. Whatever it was, in spite of my success, I didn't like how I looked, how I felt, or how I was living my life. I didn't like the direction my life was headed in—self-destruction. I was at an important crossroads in my life, and I knew it.

Thanks in part to Jack LaLanne, who got me started on the right track, I soon made several changes to my life. I decided to "cash in my chips" on the life I had been living and "trade up" for a life of health, happiness, and prosperity for myself and my family, as well as developing a more compassionate awareness of others.

My 13 Rules have their roots in my story about that walk through life on the road to an awareness and fulfillment I knew all too little about when I first got started.

Quitters Never Win—Stay the Course

Have you ever noticed how much physical fitness equipment is sold around the beginning of each new year? It's mind-boggling. We all know why—everyone's making New Year's resolutions to make improvements in their physical appearance and eating habits. They all want to make a change for the better. We've all seen the ads that run during the college football bowl games on TV at that time of year—Jenny Craig, Weight Watchers, Nutrisystem, etc. Everyone's pumped up to make a change, right? Wrong. After a few weeks of "pumping iron" and getting used to eating the "right" kind of food, one by one they fall off the wagon and slip right back into their old habits. The statistics are not good for success stories here. While everyone starts out the same way with the right intentions, only the strong-willed seem to survive to experience noticeable change. By the time the summer rolls around, that stair-stepper or treadmill machine is either in a garage sale or waiting at the curb for trash pick-up. Why? What happened? What's missing?

In a word, what's missing is *commitment*. Another way of putting it is, that "healthy person" they were trying to become wasn't worth the effort needed to get there, plain and simple. *The willpower to change just wasn't there.* It had nothing to do with understanding the benefits of good health or the risks of bad health. People just have a way of justifying decisions even if they're not in their best interest. I know that sounds odd, but it's true. Since they hadn't had their first heart attack—yet—and since they couldn't "see" the fat in their body and what it was doing to them, this whole idea of getting in shape and being healthy was something they could do "down the road." It didn't apply to them. That's how doing nothing about good health is rationalized in people's minds. Can you believe it? It's true. Isn't it?

What you've just witnessed is the birth of *commitment's* ugly cousin in the opposite corner: *laziness*, the easy way out, anything to avoid taxing yourself physically. *Inactivity rules.* The truth is that is not the easy way—it's the devil in disguise.

You'd think only someone with both eyes closed would make this choice if he or she knew what they were doing to themselves. Wouldn't you? Amazingly, there are plenty of people like that out there. And I know where they all are. They're all making appointments at the same places—the emergency rooms of our hospitals. Conservative estimates suggest that obesity-related problems already account for at least 9 percent of the nation's yearly health spending, or $150 billion annually. Because of their gluttonous stupidity, they're now clogging up hospitals everywhere (as well as their arteries) and stealing beds from people who really need the attention. Now they want mercy and attention. It's so pathetic, it's hard to feel sorry for them. *You're not one of them, are you?*

What don't they understand about what I just said? **They're killing themselves and yet they choose to ignore the repeated warnings about obesity and smoking!** People like that have to actually see death *staring* them in the face before they believe, and then it's a whole new ballgame. By then, it's often too late. How many times has a doctor had to utter these words? "I'm sorry, Mr. Jones, but you have untreatable lung cancer." Still want to "Light up a Lucky"? A physical fitness program seems like a breeze now, doesn't it? What has to happen to get you off your butt and moving? Do you have to be told by a doctor that your arteries are filled with cheese and sugar first? Use common sense!

Still think you can't do it? You'd be absolutely amazed at the hidden reserves your body has just waiting to be unleashed in a good physical fitness program. You have no idea how much speed and endurance you could generate if you were being chased by a tiger or grizzly bear in an open field and were running toward the safety of a small enclosed shed just ahead. How long do you think you could hang suspended from an exercise bar with one arm? Thirty seconds? A minute? I'll bet you could easily break your record if you were hanging from a tree branch with one arm and letting go meant falling to your death over a gorge. Adrenaline is an amazing thing. When it kicks in, it's the fuel of survival. *Pain disappears rather suddenly when it comes to matters of life and death.* That's the mindset you need to get yourself in shape.

Still think you can't do a few sit-ups or push-ups? Still think smoking is a cool idea? Still think what you eat is right for your body? We're talking about your health here! C'mon! If you can't do it on your own, then get help. Look, I'm not asking you to do anything stupid. Check with your doctor before you do anything. BUT DO IT NOW! Don't let procrastination take you down. There may not be as many tomorrows as you think. And yesterday is a cancelled check.

Making the Change—Wanting It Bad Enough

Have you ever heard of someone losing something because *they wanted* it too much? It's an interesting question. I know I've been disappointed whenever I lost a sale. But the reason I lost it was not because I wanted it so much. There was almost always a very clear reason, including something I did that could have been done a little bit better. Now let me ask you the same question with a slightly different twist: Have you ever heard of somebody getting something because they wanted it bad enough? Now the answer is a resounding "YES!" I'm living proof of that. What are you living proof of?

How badly do you want to be in the best health of your life?

How badly do you want your family to have the very best life has to offer?

How badly do you want to be a success in life?

How badly do you want to say to yourself in your old age from a rocking chair, *"Yes, I gave life everything I had. I was the very best I could have been"?*

If you want any of these things as badly as Joe Girard did, you'll do something about it. **GET IN SHAPE!** Time is the enemy of all of us. We have only a limited amount of it. As you'll hear me say more than once in this book, "If I can do it, anyone can!" *Make the change now!*

RULE TWO
HAVE A POSITIVE ATTITUDE

Any fact facing us is not as important as our attitude toward it, for that determines our success or failure.

Dr. Norman Vincent Peale, author,
The Power of Positive Thinking

In 1973 I sold 1,425 cars and trucks, setting a world record that still stands.

Besides having good health, having a positive attitude is the other important rule for getting your day off on the right foot. It's gonna be a rough one without it. A positive attitude is the logical partner of good health. When you've got them both going for you, you've got an unbeatable combination in your corner. But if your head's not screwed on right before your day gets started, good health isn't going to be enough to get the job done. You need to be mentally sharp, focused, and in a positive frame of mind. As that great jazz composer, Duke Ellington, used to say, "It don't mean a thing if it ain't got that swing." If you want to swing with the winners, you've got to know how they play the game—what makes them successful. If you look at the real success stories in any business, you'll notice that, in almost all cases, they look the part—fit, neat, and wearing a confident (not arrogant) smile. Just being in good health isn't enough. You need the whole package. So let's meet Rule #2: *Have a positive attitude.*

Motivation and Attitude—the Difference

I remember when I first got into the business of selling, it seemed as though all I ever heard was that you couldn't be successful without first being motivated. Everything was about motivation, motivation, motivation. It was as though motivation were based only on what someone would give you in exchange for your accomplishing something. I disagreed with that idea then, and I disagree with it now. That view of motivation is incomplete at best and ignores what really drives someone to achieve goals and exceed expectations. I always felt there was something else needed that was far more important and fundamental to actually becoming successful. While we are all basically motivated by a need or want for something, how successful we are in attaining it is driven by something very special. And that's the key—WHAT DRIVES YOU. Before I tell you what that special something is, let me give you a little bit of background first.

In a perfect world, we'd all work for companies that had phenomenal compensation plans with fantastic, high-quality, competitively priced products or services all the time; success would pretty much be guaranteed to all of us. Most of us have been burned too many times or are smart enough to know that companies like that don't exist in the real world. They either aren't that way to begin with or can't maintain that level of perfection without being forced to change from time to time in order to remain competitive. And if they don't, then the unthinkable can happen—they either declare bankruptcy or go out of business altogether. Who would have thought we'd see this happen to blue chip companies like Lehman Brothers on Wall Street or the mighty General Motors in Detroit. But it did. When changes happen for the worse in the corporate world, that's when the cutbacks begin, and we all know who's affected first: the employees.

Lesson number one: you can't always control what goes on around you. If you're relying only on what someone else can give you to motivate you, you're basically putting your future in someone else's hands. That's the *kiss of death*. I don't like that plan at all. I want *my* future in *my* hands.

Don't get me wrong. There's nothing wrong with working for a large company and enjoying the benefits that come with that. Just make sure you are motivated to succeed by what YOU are doing for yourself rather than *only* by what someone else is doing for you. *Nobody* can guarantee where you'll wind up in this life, not even General Motors. Your best shot is YOU.

When I was selling cars and trucks, there were many times when I didn't have the greatest compensation plan in the world. There were also times when the new products weren't the greatest either. Sometimes the market conditions were lousy. But that never stopped me. Ever since I became the world's number-one salesperson, I was always challenging myself to improve. I had no one else to beat. First I would try to top my previous week's record, then the previous month's, then the previous year's. I never stopped trying to get better and better. For the rest of my sales career, I remained the number-one salesperson in the world; that's 12 consecutive years! No matter what was thrown at me, *I believed* I was unstoppable, and *I was.*

Try selling cars and trucks during the oil embargo of 1973–74. I did. The last thing on earth you'd want to be selling when there's a gas shortage is a car or truck. Right? Salespeople were dropping like flies. They said it couldn't be done! Get this. I had my best year in 1973 when I sold 1,425 cars and set a world record that was recognized by the *Guinness Book of World Records*! The following year was really rough when we saw rationing at the pumps.

Not only did the oil embargo almost paralyze showroom traffic, but we also experienced attempts to unionize all auto salespeople in the Detroit area. The dealers in metro Detroit got together and made a deal with the salespeople: stay away from the union and we'll give you Saturdays off by closing all our stores that day. "What? Are they nuts or something?" I used to ask myself.

How the hell were we gonna sell someone a car when the door was slammed shut? I wanted no part of that crazy idea, but that's exactly what happened. My best selling day, Saturday, when it was convenient for many of my prospects and customers to come in and see me, was tossed out into the trash heap of "great" decisions in January 1974, and for the rest of my sales career. Fifty-two of my best selling days in a year—gone just like that. The capital of the auto industry, Detroit, was the only place you couldn't buy a car on Saturday in the entire country! How pathetic is that? So that shut down Joe Girard's sales express in a hurry. Right?

WRONG! I just pressed down on the "accelerator" a little bit harder and *fired up my attitude machine* with the same *gasoline* my mother filled me with as a kid!

1. I made additional calls to offset the slow market.
2. I followed up on my contacts with more vigor.
3. I stepped up my direct mail with additional mailings.
4. I expanded my contacts with local banks to try and get better credit terms.

Nobody was going to get off "Girard's hook" without a fight!

The result: while others were barely surviving, I had my second-best year ever in 1974 with sales of 1,376 units—only 49 short of my all-time record the previous year! NO GASOLINE and NO SATURDAYS? Girard says, "NO PROBLEM!" How about that for in-your-face audacity!

Even though I barely missed breaking my own world record, I still think I am most proud of what I accomplished that year, mainly because of the rotten conditions I was faced with. I did something that others said couldn't be done. I decided to ignore the mobs of losers out there and choose the path of conquest! I could have panicked too and given up like all the others. But then what? Now what happens? I don't have anything. Do I throw in the towel? Not in my world, pal. I've got mouths to feed at home. People are counting on me. We're talking about my family here! I don't need someone to "motivate" me. I'm already motivated! I have to count on ME to get over the top! But how? What do I reach for now?

I believe that something more basic than just being motivated by a want or need is required to succeed. What I'm looking for is that thing that *drives* motivation to insure you successfully achieve your goal or objective at the end of the day. I'm after the weapon I need to get me there! That weapon is simply ATTITUDE. Yes, *attitude*. And that's what drives Joe Girard.

I focused on *having a positive attitude.* I figured I could control that. I decide whether or not to let circumstances dictate how I behave or react to something. I control the actions of my mind, not someone else who's already been beaten into the ground. If you throw an oil embargo in my way, I'll mop your face in it. You'll be steamrolled in my tracks! I thrived on those situations!

It's not just how I look at things. It's the right way to look at things. It's the *positive* way to look at things. I never put my emphasis on motivation. In my world, that comes automatically. I know what my needs and wants are. Just wanting something isn't enough. You need the weapon to get it. With me, it's all about *attitude.* This is where motivation really begins—from within. It is what drives us to satisfy our needs and wants successfully. Inside each of us, there is a voice that creates the urge and desire to succeed, to push, to exert ourselves to go on, even in the face of adversity, until we achieve our goals. A positive attitude always listens to that voice. It is the voice that "introduces you to yourself." And that is critical, because without realizing who you really are, happiness cannot come to you. A positive attitude is like a lighthouse in a storm. It shows you the way. When that beacon of light shines on you, you're automatically motivated. A positive attitude is what actually moves you toward your goal. Even if you don't accomplish everything you set out to do on a given day, you know you're going to give it your best shot.

Don't make this idea any more complicated than it needs to be. Remember what we talked about earlier. Ignoring the basics is the most common cause of failure. *Having a positive attitude* is at the top of that list of basics.

The Power of Positive People

Never leave your home for work without taking a positive attitude with you each and every day. Arriving with a bad attitude is the surest way to ruin all the hard work you put into your preparation. It'll be an uphill battle all day. Your biggest enemy will be YOU because you brought the "wrong" person to work with you. I knew that if I decided ahead of time to have a positive attitude, that would automatically motivate me to reach my goal before I even got to work. I was determined to turn obstacles into opportunities. My mindset was focused on winning. That approach has always been a key part of my daily preparation from the moment I get up in the morning.

This might surprise you, but as much as I like to work, one of my favorite things to do is sleep. In fact, I like sleeping so much that I have often told audiences that in another life, I must have been a bear. I love to sleep. I love sleeping so much that when that alarm bell rang in the morning and I had to get ready for work, I used to get out of bed, get in front of the mirror, and tell myself, "Someone is going to pay for this today." That's all it took to put the fire in my belly to get going. The adverse effect of being awakened from the joy of sleep had now been transformed into a positive tool for success. In a word—attitude.

A positive attitude is most important when you're faced with things you just can't control. And let me tell you, there were many obstacles in the auto business when I was selling.

>> Domestic manufacturers were constantly plagued with poor-quality issues.
>> Recalls in the millions were commonplace every year in the auto industry.
>> I witnessed the rise of Japanese manufacturers like Toyota and Honda as they invaded our markets.
>> Frustrated and angry customers began to defect in droves to these imports.

Unfortunately, if you let them take over, these obstacles can become real problems. They can have a serious impact on the morale where you work as well as a direct effect on how well YOU perform. This is not an environment that lends itself to a positive attitude for the average salesperson. Is yours a positive environment or a negative one? Are you surrounded by people who feel good about their careers, or are you swimming in a pool of losers?

There's no doubt that many of the conditions in the workplace are impacted by the products or services your company provides. If they're no good and people aren't buying, then a negative atmosphere is bound to creep into the workplace. But if you have no control over the product, what can you do?

Here's What Joe Girard Recommends

This is the time to kick your positive attitude into high gear. If you don't, you'll sink into the quicksand with all the others. This is a real moment of truth that many potential success stories drown in. They feel they have to join the ranks of complainers and whiners. They just can't say no to peer pressure. If you're in that group, the reality is you're not saying "no" to anything at all. You're really saying, "Oh *yes*! Sign me up! I want to be a lifetime member of the Losers Club. Please, please let me in!" Is that what you want? Then just sink to the bottom with all the others. Our time together will be brief.

I must tell you that most of the people I worked with didn't look at attitude the same way I did. Everything was an obstacle. It seemed as though they could only see what was wrong with life. All they ever did was complain and waste time doing it. I remember a guy who came into work one morning "mad at the world" because his wife and kids just couldn't understand why he didn't want to spend time with them after having a rough day at the office. He obviously didn't see what they were seeing. It was people like that that I competed against— advantage *Joe Girard*!

I wanted to get as far away from complainers and crybabies as I possibly could. I didn't want to get *infected* with their disease and be brought down to their level. It's easy to fall into that trap, especially if you're having a bad day too.

If you're in retail selling and bad weather has an impact on foot traffic, then treat the day as an opportunity to double up on your phone contacts or send out a dozen more direct mail introductions. Make use of the time. It's a gift! Grab it with both hands. Don't be like everyone else who sees only rain on a cloudy day.

Stay clear of negative people. They're losers. Only spend time with positive people who can give you a boost up the mountain, not drag you down into the pits where the losers live. I know I wasn't the most popular guy in my dealership. I was just the most successful. You decide who you want to be.

By the way, the idea of having a positive attitude is important in your home too. You have the opportunity to shape the way others see you. Whether it's your spouse or your kids, they all see you as a model to follow. When I got home after work, I always made time for family before anything else, even when I was tired after a long day. I spent time with the kids and my wife. It wasn't always as much as I wanted, but it was always good quality time, and thankfully, they knew that.

What kind of example are you setting? What happens to the atmosphere in your home the minute you walk through the front door? Make it a positive one that can help build a healthy and loving atmosphere for your family so that they will respond with the same positive pride in having you as a special part of their lives. Unfortunately I wasn't able to enjoy that kind of experience in my home growing up. That's probably why I am so aware of its importance and what it can do to a family both positively and negatively. The good news here is that YOUR ATTITUDE PLAYS THE KEY ROLE IN MAKING THAT DECISION. You control that every step of the way.

Focus on YOU

I hope you get the picture now about why a positive attitude is so important and how motivation will flow naturally from it. If you still don't get it or are stuck on the false security of being motivated *only* by what you can get someone else to give you in this world, then you've led a sheltered and uninspired life. Failure will come hard for you. In fact, rebounding might be practically impossible.

Focus first on YOU, then on what someone says they will *give* you. That will determine whether or not you can accomplish something. You have to make yourself right for the task by first getting into the proper frame of mind—a positive frame of mind. Unless you're doing something improper or illegal to gain an advantage (in other words, cheating), without a positive mindset, you will almost certainly fail.

Here's the good news: being positive and confident that you're going to fulfill the needs of every person you come in contact with generates enthusiasm—and it's contagious! I can recall on several occasions receiving cards and phone calls from buyers who thanked me not just for the new car or truck they bought (I should have been thanking them, and I did!) but also for the experience that lifted their spirits when they were in the dealership.

One of my customers was a teacher who once told me that after our time together, she approached her class with renewed enthusiasm going into work the next day, and she could sense the positive feedback from the students. I made a carpet layer feel just as important as a doctor. After he bought his new truck from me, his attitude was so positive on his next job that the customer gave him two new referrals.

I went out of my way to make every prospect feel like a million bucks. When they sat down in my office, I wanted them to tell me all about the things that were important to them—their jobs or careers, their hobbies, and, most of all, their families. If you follow this advice, you will actually see the positive vibes begin to form in the person sitting across from you. You'll begin to see it in their smile and how relaxed and happy they seem. *Here's the lesson*: the moment is all about them.

The people you come in contact with feed off your enthusiasm. Turn them into "millionaires" without spending a dime! Your positive attitude is giving them a great gift, and that reward is priceless. As I said earlier, success also means becoming a better person.

As hard as it may be to believe, many people remain stubborn disbelievers about putting the power of a positive attitude first. They continue to rely on the shortsighted *charity* of someone else as their sole source of motivation to satisfy their needs and wants. Of course, they too finally join the ranks of other nameless victims who failed to look out for themselves. Worst of all, by not adopting a real positive attitude about the direction of their lives, they never realize the full potential of what they could have accomplished. They exist purely and totally on the uncertainties of someone else. That's what motivates them. That's what motivates a lot of people.

I remember two salespeople in particular we had in the dealership who had all the talent and potential in the world. Jack and Bob were both younger than most of the other sales reps. They were filled with energy and seemed to have a lot on the ball. You could see two bright careers emerging on the horizon as long as they kept focused. Surprisingly, they both turned out to be losers.

Jack thought he could set the world on fire in a few weeks. Predictably, his initial progress was slow (like all people starting out). He became impatient and developed a serious attitude problem. He began to blame management for his lack of success: they weren't doing enough for him, he didn't like the training materials, he felt the products weren't as good as the competition. He wasn't willing to put in the necessary time to hone his skills. He thought he could do it all on pure instincts.

In his mind, everything was wrong with everything around him except him. He was wrong.

Bob, on the other hand, seemed to spend his time and energy on all the wrong things. He appeared to be easily distracted. When I would walk by the water cooler on my way to the service area to check on a customer, I often saw him hanging around there with some of the other salespeople wasting time. He also seemed more interested in the ladies that worked in the dealership than he was in trying to get new customers in to sell them a new car or truck. He thought he could "charm" his way to success. Both of these guys had their attitudes and priorities screwed up. They were both essentially waiting for success to come by and tap them on the shoulder. Bad choice. They were both tapped on the shoulder all right—fired for lack of productivity. Too bad. Two potentially bright lights snuffed out because of bad choices they made. The root cause—*attitude*. Is that you?

If you're waiting for someone to make the world just right for you so you can succeed, you're on the road to nowhere. Before you go down that path, remember this: *No one ever got any recognition for climbing up half a mountain.* Either aim for the top beginning with a positive attitude, or get the hell out of the way and let someone else through who does have his or her sights set on conquest.

The most famous mountain climber who ever lived was Edmund Hillary. Although his conquest of Mount Everest came nearly 60 years ago, the *message of his story is as relevant today as it was back then.*

Edmund Hillary didn't say, "This mountain is too high. It's too cold up here. These rocks are too uncooperative. There's no trail to follow. My equipment doesn't feel right. It's all the manufacturer's fault. Mount Everest can't be conquered." He probably did have moments of doubt because he was human. But he never let them take control. He was always in charge. He knew what he was up against.

This was going to be the most dangerous and greatest challenge of his life. Everyone else had failed before him. He knew it was going to be tough. But he also BELIEVED *he was the man* for the job. Hillary had more guts and determination than just about anyone you'd ever want to meet. There were no large crowds cheering him on with encouragement. He looked inside the jaws of adversity and clawed his way to the top, step by step, in remote isolation with his small team as he struggled in silence to over 29,000 feet in unimaginable conditions. But he never lost sight of his goal.

On May 29, 1953, Sir Edmund Hillary conquered Mount Everest. That's courage. That's inspiration. That's *having a positive attitude.* That's probably about as close to perfection as you can get for human endurance.

A Positive Attitude—the Weapon of Winners

Life is not perfect by any means. If it were, there'd be no challenge to it. We all have our moments of personal joy and tragedy. Whether it's family, money, or job-related issues, we all have our problems, big and small. One thing I never did was share my personal problems with others at the office. I think some people made this a hobby.

Not me. Two reasons: first, it was none of their business, and second, the office was a place to work, not waste time gossiping. Keep your problems to yourself. We all have them. It's part of life. Nobody wants to hear about your problems. When it came to the workplace, I was all business. You should be too. Don't let anything distract your positive outlook. Unfortunately, I knew of a few people in the dealership who were easily distracted from what they should have been focused on. One case in particular comes to mind.

Although I always hit the bricks running from the moment I got to work, I was always willing to take a moment to offer advice to other salespeople if they were sincere about asking for help. Since most of them resented me because of my success, it didn't happen that often. On one occasion, a salesman asked me what he could do to close more sales. Ernie actually sounded almost desperate. He had a habit of bringing up all the negative things that were happening to him, whether it was on the job, his finances, or something in his personal life. He was always focused on the dark side of everything. I could see he had a very negative attitude about things before his day at work even started. It was almost as though if something could go wrong, he was going to make sure it did. All he did was dwell on why he couldn't accomplish something. He was making no progress and was also chewing up valuable time when he could have been developing more leads and closing more sales. I finally told him, "Ernie, you have a problem, and it's YOU. Everything will fall into place, but first you've got to change your attitude and focus on the task at hand. You're here to work, so leave all that other stuff at home. The people you come in contact with can SEE exactly who you are, and they won't like it." He thanked me for the advice, but pretty soon he found himself slipping right back into the rut again, telling the whole world about his personal problems. Some habits are hard to break.

The most important reason for having a positive attitude is not to get you through smooth sailing, when everything seems to be falling in place for you. Nobody needs any coaching on how to enjoy things. We're all experts at that. It's to get you through the tough times; the stormy seas, when you really need to hunker down; the times when attitude can make the difference, especially when difficult decisions have to be made. Make no mistake about it—even the most inspired person has good days and bad days at work and home.

One of the most memorable recent examples is actually one of tragedy, courage, and hope in the face of a terrible event. Congresswoman Gabrielle Giffords of Arizona survived an assassin's bullet to her head that left her paralyzed and facing what will probably amount to years of rehabilitation and adjustment. Her survival was nothing short of miraculous. Her husband, astronaut Mark Kelly, by her bedside every day for weeks following the tragedy, was faced with the difficult decision of whether to continue his role as commander of NASA's last shuttle mission to the International Space Station, which coincided with her recovery. In his own words, "I ultimately made the decision that I would return and command . . . I absolutely think this was the right thing for me to do. I know my wife very well, and she would be very comfortable with the decision that I made." Mark Kelly's decision was decisive optimism. Clearly, this story goes beyond just having a positive attitude. It profiles the healing power found in deeply shared love and courage—something this couple knows a lot about.

You will question decisions you made that you believed were carefully thought through. You will have doubts. You can't control that. It's called being human. You can, however, control *how you respond* to those kinds of situations. The key is *attitude*. That's where the difference lies between winning and losing.

Living a successful life is about coping with and continuously perfecting how you go about dealing with adversity. If you want to know the best way I know of to go about handling life's shortcomings, then a positive attitude gets you a front-row box seat on how to do it. When I felt that things just weren't going my way some days, I would always rely on my attitude to see me through. I didn't have to do any searching on what to do. I "programmed" myself to behave this way every morning as part of my preparation until it became second nature to me. *I was instinctively positive every day, no matter how the day ended.* I knew if I missed my target or goal for that day, I'd make up for it on the next day.

One thing I always did was present a positive and confident image to everyone I came in contact with. I never looked like a troubled person. Never. It was that confident image, above all things, that really made me the success I became. I not only believed I was going to be successful, I convinced customers I *already* was. They were being sold *Joe Girard* from the moment our eyes met—and getting the best deal they could find at the same time.

It's true I had a very successful career, but I don't want to mislead anyone into thinking it came easy. It was actually pretty rough in the beginning. I can remember practically begging a dealer to let me sell cars for him. I had absolutely no experience or knowledge about selling automobiles, no helpful tools, not even a demo car to use for personal transportation—and not much direction or management support either. All I had was a phone book for leads, a desk, and a phone. It can't get any more basic and depressing than that.

Whenever I asked for help or had a question, I felt I was treated more as a nuisance than as a sales representative. Turnover was always high in the auto business (often over 60 percent a year). Management felt we were a dime a dozen, and they treated us accordingly. Respect for the frontline salesman was at the very bottom of their list. On top of it all, the other salesmen (there were no women selling in our dealership back then) viewed me as a leech—someone who was there to try and steal something from them. I was rarely spoken to, just sneered at. They despised me. I remember one guy, Al, who came up to me one day and said flat out, "What the hell are you here for? Stay the hell away from me and my prospects and customers. You got that?" I took him at his word. From that moment on, I was always careful to keep my personal and prospecting lists with me at all times. I didn't trust any of them. That's exactly where I started. Try putting on a positive mindset under those conditions.

Not everyone you see who displays an air of confidence is necessarily a positive-minded person. Some may simply be born rich and so have never really been tested on the battlefield of life. There's a lot to smile about in their world. There are a few of those types in the neighborhood where I live. They are the exceptions though. Most people are like us—you and me. Nobody gave us anything, or at least not very much. We have to get our piece of the pie on our own. That's certainly my case and probably yours too if you're reading this book.

"So how do I get a positive attitude, Joe?" you ask. "I've got nothing to be happy about or proud of and certainly nowhere to go. Even my family has doubts about me." The most difficult thing you will have to do in order to adopt a new positive attitude is to *break the shackles of the past* that are holding you back. Forget who you were. That's not where your future is. You don't have to *be* where you started from for the rest of your life. You are not bound to follow in the footsteps of all the losers you ever hung around with or abide by all the bad decisions you ever made. If that were the case, I would be sleeping in some dark alley somewhere.

Take control of your fate. Get angry (not at the world, but at yourself) and forge ahead. Once you do that and your anger is vented, make peace with yourself and move forward. Transform yourself into a positive-minded person who will stop at nothing to become a more complete person both on the job and at home.

Don't confuse this with putting on false airs about who you are. I'm not asking you to put on a mask. I'm asking you to reach deep within yourself to free the person who's been locked inside all your life—release the REAL YOU!

I must warn you, making this transformation will undoubtedly be the most difficult thing you must do. That's why I'm talking about this right off the bat in this second of *My 13 Rules*. It's far more natural to continue being who and what you have always been. It's also much easier. No real effort involved. Most people never do make the switch. It requires more effort than their desire to succeed can tolerate. This is the main reason why there are more people who either fail or live ordinary lives than succeed in this world. They're just not moved to do anything about it. They might as well be trapped by the devil. *Only a person who has walked in those shoes can author this kind of advice truthfully and with credibility.* You're reading the words of one who has been there. I escaped from this trap! YOU CAN TOO! YOU MUST DO THIS! The rest of this book will not benefit you without this crucial commitment.

I know this sounds so simple, yet so few people seem to be able to do it. When people experience failure day after day, eventually one of two things is certain to happen to them. They're either coming closer to succeeding or coming closer to switching to try something else (in other words, failing). They won't stay where they are. Where are you headed?

A Positive Attitude "Under Fire"

I'm sure, like me, you had your heroes growing up, people you looked up to and admired as you matured. People about whom you said, "I want to be just like him or her."

I was always impressed with two heavyweight champion prizefighters, Muhammad Ali and Joe Louis, but for different reasons. Even though their peak years were decades ago, I'm telling you about these two in particular because their differing styles were important influences on me personally and *demonstrate an important point you should understand.*

Ali was great. If you asked him, he would say, "I am the greatest." He had everything. He could hit. He could dance the "Ali shuffle" and put his opponents down almost at will. He also liked to tease his opponents and make fun of them by telling them how "pretty" his face was. His poetry would "float like a butterfly and sting like a bee" as he predicted his opponent would "go down in three." To many, his swagger seemed so smug and arrogant that almost everyone, the press and public alike, wanted to see him hit the mat from a swift uppercut.

The reality is, Muhammad Ali's goal wasn't to taunt anyone. He was smart. *What he was really doing was psyching himself up to such a high positive attitude level that he believed there was no possible way he could lose a fight.* He was so psyched up that once he stepped into the ring, his mind and body became one as the adrenaline flow in him obeyed his every command. Nobody ever reached that level of motivation in the ring. That's really why he was so successful as a world heavyweight champion. His attitude about himself was so positive that he was unstoppable.

Joe Louis, on the other hand, was the most courageous boxer I ever saw. He was a far more modest man and fought at a time when prize money was a lot smaller. He was also a smart fighter. *What I like most of all about the "Brown Bomber" from Detroit, as he was known, was his spirit and determination to get up off the mat and continue the fight.* He demonstrated this several times in his career on his way to many come-from-behind victories. He is my hero. *He is the guy you should use as a model when things appear to be at their worst for you.* Think of Joe Louis lying face down on the mat, groggy and in pain, bleeding from the nose and eyes, listening to the referee count down the numbers to his defeat. Relief is a moment away. I can box again another day. Not for Joe! He finds the resolve, the desire, the anger, and the will to get up from the mat for more. He not only continues the fight but goes on to knock out his opponent. His will to win and positive attitude brought many of his opponents to their knees as he ripped the glory of conquest from their grasp!

Having a Positive Attitude—the Big Picture

Let's take a look at the big picture of what we've been talking about and why a positive attitude is so important. A positive attitude is the driving force that keeps everything we do in our daily lives on the right track. We begin our day with our needs and wants. These are the important personal and business things we believe we must have for our families and ourselves. We prioritize them according to their importance. My needs list might be different from yours, but both would certainly include things like food, shelter, and clothing, for starters. Our wants might be different too. Yours might include a tropical vacation home, a big flat-screen TV, a luxury car, or a fancy boat. We could also call our needs and wants our goals. How important or desperate we are to reach these goals determines our level of motivation. Anything that is a life-threatening crisis or medical emergency involving any of our loved ones will obviously create the highest level of motivation you can imagine, especially if all of a sudden more money is needed to cope with expenses. I'm using this drastic example on purpose to make the point about what it really takes to get you through life's toughest challenges—*having a positive attitude.*

There is no better way I know of to cope with life's roadblocks than with a positive attitude. The worse the situation is, the more you need it. Without it, your strength and ability to endure will suffer greatly. This is especially difficult when others are counting on you to take the lead. I've shared several examples in this chapter of the power of a positive attitude in my own life as well as in others'. We've also seen what can happen when attitude takes a wrong turn in people who had the raw talent to succeed.

Remember what I said earlier in this chapter. The real test of a positive attitude is when you're "under fire," not when things are sailing smoothly (e.g., Congresswoman Gabrielle Giffords and astronaut Mark Kelly). The best way to attack that is with a positive attitude. It will eventually outlast and conquer anything thrown in its path. You must believe this. You must believe in yourself. If you do, you will be successful.

There were many times I could have just said, "I quit. I've had enough," and just walked away from it all like so many people do. Like the time they cut out Saturday selling days in the metro Detroit area. That was a killer blow. I honestly had some doubts about how I was going to fill that gap. BUT I DID! I hung in there, stayed positive, and put in a little more effort. And it made all the difference in the world. The reward that follows effort will almost always be equal to the *amount of effort* you put into maintaining a *positive attitude* along the way. It won't be long before you'll figure out that the *smarter* you work at something, the greater the reward. If you're just aimlessly "putting in time," then don't expect much in return.

Sometimes the reward may be of a different or unexpected nature, especially when the desired outcome or goal may not be reached. For example, a loved one may not survive medical treatment. In this case, as hard as the loss may be, the reward may be a newfound way to cope with tragedy or a deeper appreciation and love for existing relationships. Even in sorrow there are priceless rewards that might otherwise never have been experienced or understood fully without a strong positive attitude at a time of one of life's most difficult moments. Sadly, I know this experience firsthand only too well.

My first wife, June, at only 46, died too young from complications during brain surgery. Yes, it was a tragic time in my life. I had to dig deep down inside myself to find the resolve for me and my family to go on. *I credit my experience weathering and surviving adversity in my life as the main reasons for overcoming this great loss.* I was no stranger to being dealt lousy cards from the time I was a kid. I decided that this hollow time in my life would be conquered too. Years later, that void was eventually filled with the arrival into my life of my lovely wife, Kitty.

As I said in the Introduction, *My 13 Rules* are meant to influence your personal life as well as your professional one.

You may find some of what you have read in this chapter repetitious. It is that way by design. I can't emphasize enough the importance of a positive attitude. It is what everything hinges on. It determines whether you will go forward with a plan or be stopped dead in your tracks. It will take you beyond the crucial point where success and failure cross paths.

In a way, I wish I were writing a book about my "secrets" to success. I would simply publish my secret formula and charge a fortune for sharing it (and I mean a helluva lot more than the price of this book). Everyone would then say, "Oh yeah, Joe Girard. I've heard of him. He's the guy who invented the 'secrets to success.' He's like the explorer Ponce de Leon, who spent his life searching for the fountain of youth." Do you see the problem? None of that exists—*no fountain of youth and no Joe Girard secrets!*

What I'm trying to drill into you over and over in this second of our 13 rules are simple, fundamental basics about the importance of *having a positive attitude* and why they work. This is exactly how I did it, folks. The only secret or mystery here is knowing whether or not you have what it takes to unlock your desire to be a positive person or not. That answer is not in this book. It's inside YOU. Only you have the "secret" combination to that answer. The best part about all of this is that you don't have to go on some mystery hunt searching for a map or something that doesn't exist. What you need is right here! Right in front of your face—in this book! Read this chapter again! Do what it says to do! How much simpler could it be?

If you go back and reread any chapter in this book, let it be this one, the second of Joe Girard's *13 Rules: Have a positive attitude.* There is nothing more basic you need than that to get you started on your climb to success.

RULE THREE

ORGANIZE YOUR LIFE

A person who dares waste one hour of time has not
discovered the value of life.

—Charles Darwin, scientist and naturalist

*When I arrived in my office I was primed,
pumped, and ready to go.*

n the previous chapter, we emphasized the second of *My 13 Rules*—the importance of *having a positive attitude* and why it is so fundamental to success. Without it, you will almost certainly fail, if for no other reason than for lack of determination and the will to succeed. The key to capitalizing on the energy of a positive attitude is to have a plan in place that maximizes that energy. That plan will be discussed in this chapter, Girard's third rule: *Organize your life.* As the title says, I'm not just talking about your workday here. The principles of this third rule apply to everything you do in life, both on and off the job. They have everything to do with how you prioritize your time and goals. They can be family-related objectives as well as career goals. So don't think this is restricted to just work because it isn't. Remember, I am trying to emphasize the importance of being a *complete* person. By that, I mean prioritizing the things that are meaningful in your *total* life.

Organized Planning—the Critical Link from Chaos to Success

You have to begin by first deciding what's important to you. Organize a list that prioritizes those things according to their significance in your life. Even if you've never taken the time to make one up before, do it now. You can update it over and over as often as your circumstances change. Recognize that everyone's list is going to be a little bit different. Maybe your list contains things like:

1. Earning a good income to be able to afford your needs and wants
2. Providing a safe, secure, and comfortable home for your family
3. Providing proper health care for your family's well-being
4. Making time for family activities, such as religious services and vacations

5. Supporting your children's education and other interests, such as sports or music

6. Setting aside special time for you and your spouse

7. Scheduling time for your personal interests and hobbies

Many things on this list mirror my own goals. I was determined to show the world what a shoeshine boy could become. I swore I would never let my family live in poverty the way I had. One day I'd have a beautiful home in a fine suburb. I wanted my family to have the best I could afford and never have to worry about a roof over their heads or the opportunity to have a good education. To this day, my wife Kitty and I always set aside quality time for vacations away from other interruptions.

If you don't make up a list like this, you're going to find yourself wandering aimlessly through life without any real reason for existing. To me, living life with purpose is what makes it special. Give your life meaning—organize a list of priorities! Don't just do it for you—do it for your family! I did!

I didn't have to write anything down on my first list since it was a bag of groceries for my family to get us through the next few days. Even before I started selling cars and trucks, I had developed a planned set of goals that I constantly updated. As my success grew, my goals evolved to suit my means. BUT I HAD A PLAN! Start one now. Plan on updating it often, but get one started!

By the way, if the number-one priority on your list is to earn a good living, there's nothing wrong with that as long as you don't do it for money's sake alone. In fact, it'll go a long way to helping you experience a lot of life's really important things for you and your family. And always remember to share some of your good fortune with the less fortunate in this world.

I hope it's starting to sink in why Rule #3, *Organize your life*, is so important. Without organization, you have chaos. This will become painfully obvious at work. Could you imagine anyone trying to run a company or anything of any importance by just showing up? That's essentially what you're doing without an organized plan of action.

No matter how positive you are, if you don't have some kind of organization to your day, time will become your enemy the minute you set foot in the place where you work. You'll wind up spending the day trying to figure out what you should be doing and where you should be directing your efforts. As a result, you will have basically wasted the day away and accomplished little or nothing. All that kind of stuff should be done *before* you begin your workday.

The minute you arrive in your office, and after you've said your greetings, you should be ready to "hit the bricks running." You're primed, pumped, and ready to go. You're organized. You've got a plan. NOW WORK THAT PLAN! There's no stopping by the coffee machine first to "shoot the breeze" with the "dope ring," as I used to call them. I was not a member of that club. Believe me, because of that, I wasn't liked by any of them. But I knew better. I didn't have time for that nonsense, nor should you. I once read that prosperity makes few friends. It's true.

When a football team arrives on the field to the cheers of the stadium fans just prior to the opening kickoff, the coaches don't gather on the sidelines and say, "What strategy or plan of action should we use against the opponent?" That's already done. They've analyzed the opponent. They've determined where their opportunities are. They've looked to see where their strengths can make a difference. The time for analyzing and organizing is over. They've got a game plan. It's time to play the game! They're ready to go!

This approach is even more evident in business today. Whether a company provides a product or service doesn't make any difference. The successful ones always do their homework and planning way "upstream" in the process by bringing in experts who are involved in every aspect of the timeline early on. No surprises.

In the auto industry, the competition is so keen today and the communication technology so fast that companies like Ford Motor Company, General Motors, and Toyota all have to commit to research and development, design, engineering, testing, manufacturing, and marketing and sales planning with "the pedal to the floor." There was a time when the planning process for models used to start as much as five or six years out before the first one ever rolled off the assembly line. That timeline is now shrinking to 30 months (and narrowing). The major players are discovering more reliable, faster, and more profitable ways of accomplishing things in a fraction of the time it used to take just a couple of decades ago. *Speed is the name of the game* today. (Innovation, quality, and profitability are assumed.) **The premium here is on sound planning, organization, and execution!** But you don't have to be a Boeing, a General Electric, or an AT&T to adopt this approach. **THIS APPLIES TO YOU TOO!**

When you leave your car in the parking lot on your way to your office or place of work, think of it as though you're leaving the locker room to enter the playing field. You should be focused on getting yourself psyched and emotionally "up" for the day. This is not the time to be trying to figure out what you're going to be doing. At this point, it's all about *execution*, not planning. You should be completely immersed in YOU. If you're not, then you're not organized for success. You've already fumbled away the day before you even enter the front door of wherever you work. The worst part of it is you might not even know it if you don't appreciate or understand the importance of organizing your life.

I don't know of any successful planner who doesn't first start by writing things down. A to-do list is a great place to begin. If you're one of those people who doesn't write things down or never kept a diary or planner, you're not alone. It's true there are some jobs that don't require detailed diaries. However, there are lots of people out there who don't use planners who should. Those people are usually easy to find. Many of them are in the unemployment lines.

Whenever I'm on tour giving a motivational presentation, I always emphasize the importance of organized planning. I recently got back from a series of lectures in China, and I could see several people in the audience taking feverish notes when I got on that topic. Everyone is looking for an edge—anything that can give them a slight advantage on the competition. I often get letters or see people in audiences a year later who thank me for the advice as they tell me how it has helped them.

Having an organized plan is a must for efficient use of time. And that's one of the major keys to success—how you use your time.

If you don't understand the importance of organized planning, you'll never be able to appreciate or gain a deeper awareness of the real key to effective organizing—*time management.*

Let me give you an example of how I went about managing my time. In the evening when I got home, and after spending some quality time with my family, instead of watching endless hours of brain-dead TV programs, I would set aside some quiet time to analyze what I did earlier that day. I would meditate on everything I did from the moment I came in until I turned off the light in my office to go home. I was looking for anything that could improve my productivity and better utilize my time. I would ask myself:

"What did I do that really helped today?"

"What did I do that got in the way?"

"Could I save time by doing *this* instead of *that*?"

Here are a couple of examples of changes I made in the life of Joe Girard on the front lines that came directly from my *end-of-the-day analysis* of how I was managing my time:

» I found that by simply closing the door to my office, I was able to stay more focused on what I was doing. I noticed I was using my time more productively. I was actually able to make six additional calls in a day without any distractions or interruptions simply by CLOSING MY DOOR.

» My customers were like gold to me. I would often walk over to the service department myself to check on my customers to make sure they were getting the proper treatment. This was especially the case if I had been recently getting customer complaints about how they were being treated. Unfortunately, this was chewing up a lot of my time when I could have been prospecting or closing the next sale. While I felt it was important to stay connected to my customers, I decided to forge a stronger partnership with and trust in the service department staff. It paid off. I took good care of them, and they treated me with the utmost respect. That bond of trust grew to the point that I was able to spend more time selling rather than checking up on them. The results were happy customers, a happy service department, and a happy Joe Girard—a win-win-win proposition.

Once I got into the habit of reviewing my day in detail as in these examples, my awareness and productivity soared to new heights. I was perfecting my approach, getting better and better, stronger and stronger, each and every day. Finally, I ended the session by charting my course for the next day just like the captain of a ship. I knew where and how I was going before I ever "set sail" in the morning. No surprises. That was my routine—I planned my work and worked my plan. If I had a good day, then I would pat myself on the back. "I'm proud of you, Joey," I would say to myself. Then I'd thank the Lord, kiss my lovely wife good night, and call it a day.

Time—That Precious Gift

The hardest thing to recapture in life is lost time. It's virtually impossible. When it comes to guarding this precious gift, beware of public enemies one and two: LAZINESS and PROCRASTINATION. Yes, you know *procrastination*. That's the one where you keep postponing and putting off decisions. Your progress is always in "delay" mode. Don't let those two thieves, *laziness* and *procrastination*, anywhere near your life.

I can tell you that, like me, most of the salespeople had routines they followed the minute they arrived at the dealership for work. That's where the similarity ended. Although some of them did work hard, many of them would come in, hang up their coats, and then head for the "dope ring." They'd go get coffee, talk about last night's game, and joke around with the other salespeople.

One guy in particular spent almost an hour practically every morning babbling on and on about the Detroit Red Wings' game the previous night. Ice hockey's a big deal in Detroit, so George never seemed to have problems getting an audience. By the time he was done (I could hear them all chatting on their way back to their offices), I usually had already closed my first sale and had at least a couple of hot prospect appointments lined up for the afternoon. I remember the wall behind George's desk. It had a colorful poster of the Red Wings National Hockey League team photo. I always thought it was odd that a guy who was surrounded by one of most successful NHL franchises all day long would have so much difficulty closing sales. Sadly, George never made the connection. He was gone before the end of the hockey season.

For many of these guys, this was the kind of routine they followed practically every day. Before you knew it, they'd shot half the morning. Nobody in that group was organized or had a plan to do a damn thing except *fail*. And most of them did.

When I talk about organizing, I'm talking about organizing for success. When it comes to the office, there is only so much time in the day. You've heard that "time is money." In my game plan, TIME IS KING. It is PRIORITY ONE. I understood time management better than anyone else. I was organized. I had a plan. And nothing—nothing—got in the way of my working that plan every day I was there! I was in control. In my plan, time was my *friend*, not my enemy. I'll go into more detail on time management in the next chapter. For now, remember that the effective use of time is critical to organizing a plan to achieve your goals.

One of the most common reasons people fail to accomplish what they've set out to do in a day is that they're just not organized for success. Too much time is wasted trying to find things that are needed right at that moment and are nowhere in sight. They find themselves fumbling around for information.

As I said earlier, I rarely interfered with or made suggestions to other salesmen unless they asked for my help or advice on something. One time, though, I did happen to ask one of them how he could find things quickly. Whenever I passed by his office in the showroom, I was absolutely amazed at what I would see on his desk. It was a mixed bag of training manuals, data books, and invoices piled so high on either side of the salesman that it had to be a challenge just to be able to *see* his prospect, let alone find the paperwork he needed. How could he survive in this jungle of clutter? His response was that when customers came into his office, he believed they would be so impressed with how much stuff he had around him that they would think he must be the busiest and most successful guy in the place—*the man to deal with*. That's not the picture I would have had as a potential customer. What I saw was chaos. I just nodded my head and walked away.

THINK AHEAD! What are you going to need? Have it ready. Get rid of the piles of paperwork on your desk and transform them into efficient files that are readily available. Remember, we're talking about organizing time here.

If you looked at the desk in my office, it was always organized. I used an appointment book diary, or planner as some call it, to organize my entire day. I didn't fill it out or plan things for the day when I arrived at work either. I never did that. That was all done the day before. Once in a while, I would have to rearrange some appointments on the spot. That stuff happens. Because I was so well organized, I was always able to deal with it and stay on top of things like that. The last thing I did before calling it a day was to organize the next day's agenda. That's how my day ended—planning tomorrow's day. If I worked late at the dealership, since we were open in the evenings on certain days, then I did my pre-planning and organizing for the next day at home later that night. But I never came to work without having an organized plan for the day. This was a routine I developed very early on in my career.

My actions all had two things in common:

I did more of the things that paid me money:
> prospecting
> making appointments
> staying in touch with existing customers by phone and direct mail

and less of the things that didn't:
> spending time chasing endless paperwork (I had secretaries help do that)
> chumming around with other salespeople (when I went out to lunch, it was with bankers and customers—people who could help me)

I did all my research ahead of time and cultivated work habits and routines that maximized my productivity and efficiency for the upcoming day:

>> I had prepared lists of all the prospects I was going to contact by name.

>> I had all my appointments locked and identified.

>> I had background information on everyone I would see at my fingertips (their jobs, income, credit, family info, hobbies).

>> I was continuously improving my filing systems to make sure getting the information I needed was readily available when I needed it. I was never fumbling around trying to find things.

Like life, it wasn't perfect, but it was damn close. *I had a grip on time.* I operated like a well-oiled machine. And my results proved I was doing it the right way.

Believe it or not, some of the people in the office actually wondered how I became so successful since we all were given the same car and truck catalogs, the same color and trim books, the same product facts books and data guides, the same product and training videos, and the same competitive comparison information and pricing. The truth was, I had no edge on them at all when it came to information. Yet they would wonder what *inside track* I had that enabled me to become so successful. They were spending far too much time trying to figure out ME instead of THEMSELVES.

I just laughed to myself and shook my head whenever I heard that kind of stuff. For many of them, training was a complete waste of time. We had no training videos on how to overcome laziness. All they really needed was a giant mirror so they could see how they operated all day long, wasting precious time. That picture alone would have been worth several training sessions. The funny thing about all this is that I wasn't hiding some secret method or approach. I just followed the same basic common sense ideas that formed the foundation for the things that are right here in my book—*My 13 Rules*. Pure and simple—that's exactly what I did. Yes, I was persistent in my desire to succeed, but I was also well organized. I made sure that my enthusiasm to succeed wasn't cheated by not having a solid organized plan of action every day I came to work. I wanted every hour of my time to count for something.

I didn't think I was a genius or a specially gifted organizer for doing this. It just made perfect sense to me. In fact, most of us are not organized by nature. As I said in the introduction of this book, "If I can do it, anyone can." Organization is a learned skill that we all develop in life as we mature. How well we organize is usually matched to the priorities and goals we set for ourselves. If they're important enough to us, we'll definitely find the time and a way to organize to get them done. Call it "forced" organizing if you like, but it will happen. It's a helluva lot easier, though, if you don't wait for a crisis to realize you should have had an organized plan to deal with life. What kind of crisis are we talking about here?

>> If your boss suddenly came into your office without warning and said this was going to be your last day of work, where would you go and what would you do? How would you deal with your finances and responsibilities in the meantime?

>> What's your plan as a parent for making sure your kids have the opportunity to pursue a higher education, assuming they aren't going to get an academic or athletic scholarship? How does that get paid? What advice will you give your child?

>> What would you do if a member of your family got seriously ill and needed expensive medical treatment your health plan wouldn't cover completely? What's your plan for that circumstance?

Okay, I agree, these are tough examples. Unfortunately, they are real-world examples. This is what actually happens in life. One (or all) of these three things is likely to happen to each of us at some time or another. I know firsthand. Take this opportunity to add your very own examples (and how you'd respond).

Organizing a plan forces you to look ahead—to plan for and anticipate the unexpected. With the turnover as high as it is in several retail sales businesses (not just the auto industry), there must be tens of thousands of people experiencing life's shortcomings every day. How do they cope without having some kind of organized plan for the rainy days in their lives? With an organized plan, you will not be spending endless amounts of time spinning your wheels and panicking over your next step.

IMPORTANT: *Even though having an organized plan doesn't solve your problems, it does give you the tools and the best shot at knowing how to deal with them effectively.* And that's the critical first step many never take. They jump into the deep end of the pool without even having a clue on how to swim.

Sometimes there are more pressing things that will get your attention in a hurry and will decide how you'll prioritize your time for you. Let me give you a couple of examples.

>> If your doctor calls and says he wants you to come in to discuss some test results that aren't quite right, you won't forget to make that appointment!

>> If a guy is out on parole and has to check in with his probation officer every Friday at 11 a.m., you'll be amazed at how well organized he can become to make that appointment when motivated with the threat of returning to jail.

By comparison, trying to find a spare hour or two to increase productivity suddenly seems like a small matter. Have I got your attention yet? Do you get the picture on the importance of time?

Don't be one of those people who looks back on his or her life saying, "If only I had made better use of my time." That's the sob story of almost every loser. In the end, losers usually have plenty of time to think about what could have been. Old age is filled with emptiness and regrets. DON'T BE THAT PERSON. Be the one who says, "I'm thankful I had the opportunity to change my life for the better. Even with all of life's shortcomings, I wouldn't change a single thing about how I did it." Thankfully, that is what I tell myself every day. Once I was organized for success, I never looked back.

I think the most gratifying feeling I get today is when I hear from someone either by mail or in person whose life has been changed after reading one of my books or attending one of my seminars. I remember vividly when I closed a motivational presentation at Oral Roberts University. I asked anyone who wanted to be "number one" to come up and join me on the stage. Several came up, but one young man in particular charged up to the stage with his hands raised and proclaimed to his classmates "I'm number one!" The applause was deafening. I promptly pinned a gold "number one" pin on his shirt.

After being blessed with a very successful career, whenever I sense positive vibes from the letters I receive or the gleam I see in a person's face, being able to pass along some inspiration to help make someone a better person is priceless. For me, it doesn't get any better than that.

Organize Your Mind by Prioritizing on Paper

I think many people are either intimidated by or just can't get excited about keeping appointment books, diaries, planners, or whatever you'd like to call them. They see them as extra paperwork, needless detail. They feel they can keep everything in their heads and don't need to micromanage themselves to that extent. An occasional note here and there on scrap paper or a desk pad is all they think they need. Maybe even a corkboard with stick-pinned notes will do. If you're thinking along these lines, you need to step back and understand what I said earlier in this chapter. You don't plan your day when you get to work; you do it at the end of the day or the night before for the *next day*! How the hell are you going to plan tomorrow's day with everything pinned to your office wall or scribbled in haphazard notes on a desk pad? What happens if you have to go home a little later because you're working that night? Are you going to just scoop up all this stuff and drop it in a bag and hope it makes sense later? You'll spend more time just sorting everything out before you can really begin to move forward with an organized plan of action for the next day. By that time, it will be late into the evening. And who pays for that?

No, I don't care if you're tired! The people who get cheated are your family! You missed dinner with them. Your kids wanted to spend some quality time with you except you're not available now. And your spouse spends an evening alone again because you're up working on something that should (and could) have been done hours ago. You know, I get really angry whenever I hear about or think about people doing things like that. In fact it's hard to even *want* to help someone who is that selfish and shortsighted.

Hey listen, I know there are times when you can't control things that happen at work. Maybe your boss told you he or she wanted something prepared at the last minute that must be completed by first thing the next morning. Or maybe a client called with an urgent overnight request that cannot be ignored. I know how that goes. Sometimes I worked late. Dealerships stayed open late a couple of nights during the week, and that represented an important opportunity for me to make some extra money. But my family always knew they were uppermost in my life. Be sensitive to the ones you love. They're the reason you're doing this anyway. Make those instances when you have to compromise family time the exception, not the normal plan of how you go about organizing things.

When you do organize, do it the right way. Organize smart by making efficient use of your time, and whatever you do, make sure you *put it down on paper.* It will help you do a couple of things:

» track your progress
» make sure you don't miss anything

Fortunately, *remembering* to do something was rarely, if ever, one of the things I neglected to do. Probably the most important thing about writing things down in my appointment book diary was that it forced me to NEVER FORGET. To me "forgetting" is unforgivable, especially if it involves your family or a customer. *I never missed an appointment because I forgot.* That's the cardinal sin in selling—missing a customer appointment. That's money out the door you'll never see again. By relying on my appointment book instead of my memory or a bunch of sticky notes tacked up all over my office, I was able to not only remember all my appointments but also to be well prepared when they arrived. I was then able to focus my attention on how I was going to handle my prospects and customers. Everything else that was of any importance was written down in my planner. I can't say enough about this.

The most effective way I know to manage time is by using an appointment book or daily planner for *all* your activities each day—business and personal. You will immediately know how much time you have set aside to accomplish your goals for the day. The rest of the time will be for you and your family. Force yourself to put everything in this one spot, your appointment diary, to organize how your day will go. It's also portable and can be taken home with you to reflect on how the day went, which, as you know, is what I did every night before calling it a day.

My approach worked like a charm. I sold new cars and trucks for 15 years. My system worked so well that, after the third year, if you wanted to buy a vehicle from Joe Girard, you had to have an appointment. You heard me correctly. You had to have an appointment to see me. Eventually I was able to hire additional help (at my expense, not the dealer's) to give me a hand with the tremendous growth in business I was experiencing. But for many years, I was strictly dependent on myself to make things happen, like most of you probably are. That's why you have to be well organized in everything you do. It's really all about maximizing time, of which there is only a limited amount. Getting things prioritized on paper is the key to efficient and organized planning.

In my business, things happened at a pretty fast pace all day. It was partly because of the nature of my business but mostly because that's the way I designed my day. I loved what I did. I loved being busy. I thrived on it. I liked the pace. I felt like I was in a Vegas casino. I liked the action. I was making money! The great Chinese philosopher, Confucius, had it right when he said, "Find a job you love and you'll never have to work a day in your life." *Bull's eye, Joe Girard!*

I felt like I was on top of the world (and I was). I was either with a customer in person, on the phone with a customer, or meeting with someone in service about a customer. It was always about the customer. For all these reasons, it was important to write things down. I couldn't depend on myself to remember everything. That would be unrealistic. Too much was happening too fast. That's where my appointment diary became critical. And with today's digital technology, there's no excuse at all for not being connected and having whatever you need instantly at your fingertips.

Listen. To be perfectly frank, I don't really care if you use sticky notes, a planner, or your memory to map out your day. All I'm telling you is that if you're not enjoying the success you want right now because you're not getting the most out of your time, then there is obviously something wrong with whatever tool or approach you're using. I'm giving you the advice of someone who has been more successful than anyone else in history selling big-ticket retail items. Additionally, I'm telling you exactly how I did it and the tools I used. Now if that doesn't work for you, then fine. But here it is in this book for you to follow. Plain and simple. DO IT!

Select Your Target and Organize to Hit It

So how do you know when your plan is as well organized as it can be? That's a good question. Sometimes you think you've got it right, but you're still falling short of the mark. There are a couple of ways you can tell if you're planning and organizing as smart as you could to reach your goals. Just ask yourself these two questions:

1. Are you able to find precisely what you need when you need it?
2. Are you able to accomplish what you have set out to do in the time frame you've set aside to complete it by?

If you can say "yes" to both of these questions, then you've probably got a pretty good method or approach already in place that works for you. If you don't feel you're reaching the goals you've set for yourself, then most likely organization is not your main problem. Either your goals aren't realistic or you're not properly following one or more of my other 13 rules. Don't worry, we'll find out what's slowing you down as you go through the book examining the rest of *My 13 Rules* so you can take corrective action to redirect your efforts.

If, on the other hand, you're not able to answer "yes" to both of these questions, then we know it's probably a lack of organization that's the culprit. Take a closer look at what's getting in the way of how you're organized and make a change. I think that, growing up, my fear of failing was so great that I must have developed a natural instinct for preparing things ahead of time. Through trial and error, I finally arrived at an approach that I divided into two categories: WHAT I NEEDED and THE TIME I NEEDED TO DO IT.

Are things where they should be for convenient access?

> Is all the background information on the project gathered neatly on your desk or credenza in a logical flow (by date or by topic)?
> If your process requires several documents needing signatures, for example, are they in proper sequence?
> Have you double-checked to make sure you're not missing any key documents or steps?

Did you realistically think through the amount of time it takes to do something?

> Have you scheduled the appropriate amount of time to complete your task or to meet objectives? Go through each step and determine the amount of time needed and see if the total adds up to a realistic amount of time.
> Have you advised your client or colleague as to what the expectations are for this event in terms of time and outcome? Are they expecting an hour when in reality it's going to take two or three? Get this on the table up front. Remember, no surprises.
> Are people you may need to contact during your meeting (in finance or service, for example) easily or readily accessible for input without delay? Get them on board before they're needed so they're ready when you call.

If you learn to "look around the corner" like this, you'll never be surprised at what you see when you get there. I found that this approach enabled me to always be prepared for the unexpected and allow for some flexibility, like a customer arriving a little bit late, while at the same time enabling me to do things very efficiently. The bottom line was, I was using my time most effectively. That allowed me to make the most money in the least amount of time. Now that's what I call effective TIME MANAGEMENT.

Obviously, if you work in an office environment or a place where many employees function together as a unit, and you discover that something is wrong with a procedure and needs management's attention, by all means take it up to the next level.

However, before you start complaining to someone, make sure you first look at what YOU can do to create efficiencies that can get the job done better. Believe it or not, most people immediately go to someone else, like an immediate supervisor, with a complaint that could easily have been fixed right in their own office or department by thinking a little bit smarter than the next person. Don't think that will go unnoticed by a supervisor, because it won't. Until you've made an honest effort to figure out how to fix it, it's still your problem. You own it. Be proactive. Take the initiative and self-manage yourself. Don't wait for someone else to decide what happens to you.

You decide!

Don't hesitate!

Take action!

Life isn't about waiting for the storm to pass; it's about learning to dance in the rain.

There were more than just a few times I took the initiative and did things that the dealer wasn't crazy about, like letting prospects take home cars before actually purchasing them, or paying for minor repairs out of my own pocket to keep customers happy and coming back for more. I knew what I was doing, though. I was building trust and long-term relationships. I'll go into more detail on that in Chapter 11, *Lock up every opportunity.*

I didn't wait for someone to tell me if I could do something. If it felt right and helped me close a sale, I was not afraid to take the hit for making an on-the-spot decision.

Don't misunderstand what I'm telling you here. I'm not asking you to make some drastic changes that affect how your company operates without going through the proper channels first. I'm talking about YOU and YOUR WORLD. If you let someone else direct the next step (in YOUR WORLD), it becomes their plan and their approach instead of yours—and you may not like their solution. On top of that, *you've lost the opportunity to control the action in YOUR WORLD.* You've let an outside force in when you may not have had to. You've also let them know they had to show you how to do something because you didn't have the know-how or planning skills to solve the matter yourself. And don't think *that* will go unnoticed.

Never stop refining your organization plan. Your goals and circumstances are continuously changing. What worked last year won't necessarily get it this year. In the beginning of my sales career, I relied most heavily on cold calling using the phone. Before long I began to notice that direct mail was a very effective way to reach more people just from the stuff I would get at home in the mail. I recognized how effective this could be.

I started small, but eventually this led to thousands of people hearing from me every month by direct mail. It turned out to be one of my best weapons. I changed my tactics. More on that in Chapter 9, *Stay in touch.*

Targets change and move. Yours will too. Keep your eye on them at all times. You should continuously be refocusing and organizing your plan to hit those targets when they do change. For example, your financial objectives will change dramatically if you want to buy a new and larger home, or when your kids reach college age and want to attend a top university, or when they need you to foot the bill for a memorable wedding. As long as you plan where you're going ahead of time, you'll get there. If you don't, then you're LOST!

When I first started setting my *personal goals*, I found it easier to figure out what I could do in a week to save money or add income rather than trying to project two to three years out. I didn't think in terms of months or years. I was thinking in terms of "the here and now." For me, a bag of groceries for the next two or three days was once a goal. Think near term at first. You'll get a good and realistic picture of what you can do. Multiplying what you can do in a week by months and years becomes more attainable if you start with short steps. Pretty soon you'll know how long it will take to achieve those larger goals like, for example, buying a new home.

Match Your Tools to Your Goals

There are many organizing techniques and tools out there to help you reach your goals. The trick is to match the right ones to your particular goals. Why is this so important? It's not as simple as it sounds. It's possible to organize the wrong plan by mistake. In fact, you might even "overmanage" what you're doing without even knowing it at first. Let's say you've fallen in love with an elaborately organized and detailed plan you created that manages practically everything you do throughout the day. At first glance, it looks great. When you review what you've done at the end of the day, you realize you don't seem to be making any headway or progress toward achieving your goals in spite of checking every single detail in your plan.

Now you're puzzled and maybe even depressed. You believe you had the right plan, and you tried hard to do all the right things. You feel lost. I'll give you an *A* for effort because of your attitude. That's about it, though. What's really happening is you've probably organized such a detailed plan that, instead of helping your productivity, it actually gets in the way of it. Let me explain.

You find yourself practically handcuffed by your plan because you won't make a move without noting every little thing you do in your diary. The result is you're actually "stealing" the very time you need to get ahead. The reality is you're *tracking your failure.*

What you've done is design a fancy noose to fit around your neck. If you organize something too complicated, you will surely hang from it. That's not planning for success; that's DOCUMENTING YOUR DOOM. There's a happy middle ground between perfection and thinking smart—keep things practical and simple. You don't work for your organization plan. *It works for YOU.*

There's really only one important purpose behind a well-organized plan, and that is to keep you on track to achieve your objectives. That's really all you want it to do. Don't fall into the trap of using it as a crutch. Use it as a pole vault! Start with the main things you want to achieve, like the number of customers you want to contact or the number of products you want to sell or service. Perhaps it's the number of patients you will see, or the number of students you will counsel. You decide what that is.

I always planned to contact a minimum of at least 20 people every day about buying a new vehicle. There were many days when that number was two or even three times that depending on the weather or what else I had scheduled. And it paid off. In my best year, *I was closing a record average of six sales a day!*

Once you've determined your goal, go into laying the groundwork for how you're going to achieve it and the amount of time it will require.

Here's how I did it:

>> From experience, I knew how much time I needed to make an effective phone call.

> I could easily get what I needed to know about a prospect in 10 minutes because I had a list in front of me of the top six things that were important.

> › I knew how to politely take control of the conversation and keep things on track, including overcoming the typical objections.

> › If the call took longer, it was usually a good sign that the prospect was more engaged and wanted more information.

> ›› I also knew that once a customer came in to actually purchase a vehicle, I could accomplish this in less than an hour.

> ›› I had everything lined up: the paperwork, the accounting department, and of course, the vehicle—checked out, polished, and ready to go.

Knowing this information about time management enabled me to project how much money I could average in a given week. My financial goals were organized and set using this model. While I didn't have precisely the same results every week, overall it was pretty accurate. If you can't make your goal align with what you have to do to reach it, then you'll either have to find a way to increase your productivity by adding more time or by lowering the goal you've set.

Don't be disappointed if at first you don't hit every target. Over time, you'll become more experienced and *smarter* as you begin to organize more accurate and realistic plans. There's an ancient Chinese proverb worth remembering: "The person who moves mountains begins by carrying small stones." Another one I like is from a twelfth-century monk, Francis of Assisi, who said, "Start doing what's necessary; then do what's possible; and suddenly you are doing the impossible." He was gradually easing his way into the fast lane. He had a plan. Success comes faster to those who plan for it. Whatever techniques you use, like planners and appointment diaries, remember that they are tools. YOU control how they're used. Make them work for you.

Raising the Bar on Expectations—Organizing a Plan of Action

I admire people who like to "raise the bar" a little when it comes to setting goals. Those are my kind of people. You'd be smart to get into the habit of always setting a target that makes you "reach" a little bit higher. That way you won't be disappointed if you fall a little bit short. That's the way to stay centered on your personal growth and development. Organize a plan of action that keeps you focused on winning. Anyone can achieve modest goals. That's why modest goals always yield modest rewards. Will you be satisfied with that? I was never happy with that.

I never set a modest goal *for my life* in my life! I always wanted to be the very best I could be, and I organized my efforts to achieve that. And it worked! I hope you share this view too!

Yes, I started out with more attainable short-term goals, but they all added up to what I really had my sights set on— becoming the very best I could be in my chosen field! Once I became the world's number-one salesperson, the only person left for me to challenge was, well, myself. And I did that too. Most of the records I ever broke were my own. I was never content with staying in the same place. I would reorganize my efforts using every tool I could get my hands on to achieve new goals.

One of the most important aspects of your organizing plan is how you prioritize the to-do list in your planner. Your priorities may differ from mine because of the business you're in. Even so, make sure you get the priorities straight. What does the company expect of you? Where does what you do fit in?

As you know, I was in the business of selling cars and trucks. My approach was actually quite simple. If a task had anything to do with losing or gaining a customer, it was a priority—plain and simple. Nothing got in the way of that. We're not talking about internal dealership operations, marketing, or training here. Now we're talking about *money*—MY MONEY. It doesn't get any closer to home than that for me. A customer-centered focus—that's how I would prioritize my day and everything in my planner.

If there were other meetings or things I had to do, they were slotted around those customer priorities. Sometimes there were conflicts I couldn't do anything about. But my customer-priority mindset made everything else take a backseat whenever possible. That's the way I operated. I didn't have to be told what was important. I already knew that. And *my customers knew I knew they were numero uno*! That's what counted.

The higher you "raise the bar" on your expectations, the more you must be tuned in to an effective plan of action. Once the bar is raised, not having an organized plan is a little bit like running out of gas before you even start the race. It is critical that you keep your train of thought focused on the task at hand and not drift into unnecessary distractions because you're not ready to go. If you are properly organized, you'll stay the course and get the job done. Train your mind on what you have to do and nothing else. You'll hear more on that in our next chapter on Rule #4, *Work when you work*.

Follow the Patterns of Successful People

By now it should be plain as day that an organized mindset is the perfect partner for your planners and appointment books to get you organized for success. In the Introduction to the book, I mentioned one of the things I did was to compare my approaches with those of other successful people in a variety of industries.

I always admired what Rich DeVos and Jay Van Andel accomplished when they cofounded the Amway corporation. I was captivated by the grit, determination, and hunger for success they both had. I wanted to know: What are they doing that nobody else is doing that makes them so successful? I studied their approaches and methods. I spent a lot of time in libraries and bookstores reading and researching as much as I could about how successful people like them did things. It took a lot of work, but it was well worth the time. I learned a lot. In his book *Believe!*, DeVos emphasized the importance of believing in yourself as the ticket to success. That became my story in a nutshell.

Another success story that always captured my attention was one of the most successful and dynamic businesswomen in history, Mary Kay Ash, founder of Mary Kay Cosmetics. This gal had smarts and guts—"Diamonds, trips, and pink Cadillacs" for her top sales performers. She was a beacon of hope for women struggling to make their mark in a male-dominated business world. Ordinary people became millionaires under her strong leadership and motivation. That connected with me greatly since it was very much my own track to success.

Another person whose words always inspired me early on in my career was Dr. Norman Vincent Peale, author of *The Power of Positive Thinking*. I had the privilege of meeting him later on. He became a personal friend whom I greatly respected. It must have been mutual because I had the honor of receiving his nomination for the Horatio Alger Award, which recognizes American success stories in the face of difficult circumstances.

Whenever I was drawn to individuals as models for how I would approach achieving success, it was always because two things stood out:

1. They all had *positive attitudes*.
2. They all respected the *value and importance of time*.

Today you have two big advantages over me. First, I didn't have the Internet to help me. You do. It's a great way to maximize your time and link you to valuable resources and contacts. Use it. Secondly, you have *Joe Girard*. He is the voice of experience and your champion who would like nothing better than to see you come out on top a winner. Listen to him. *Organize your life* for success.

RULE FOUR

WORK WHEN YOU WORK

A dictionary is the only place that success
comes before work. Hard work is the price we
must pay for success.

—Vince Lombardi, pro football coach

My mother's love and encouragement produced
the gasoline in my engine when I worked.

think by now you know how I feel about the importance of time from our discussion in Chapter 3. Let me expand on that since it's so critical to success. Time wasted cannot be regained. It's a cancelled check—worth nothing. I guard my time like it is gold. In fact, to me, it's worth even more than gold, because you can't buy a sack of time with a sack of gold. That's why I don't like distractions in my life. I know they happen. But I don't like them. The time of my life is divided into four areas, and I don't let anything get in the way when I'm doing any one of the four.

1. *When I work, I work.* Nothing interferes with my workday. That's where I make my living. I want to be focused and left alone.

2. *When I sleep, I sleep.* You know I like to sleep as much as a bear. I don't want someone interrupting my sleep at three o'clock in the morning because they have a problem. Unless it's an emergency, that's my time.

3. *When I eat, I eat.* I don't like being bothered when I'm eating. I don't want to concentrate on anything else. Talk to me later, not when I'm eating.

4. *When I play, I play.* I don't want someone trying to get ahold of me when I'm on vacation. That time is for me and my family. Don't call me. I'm not listening.

Those are my four policies about how I regulate my time. If you follow this approach, you'll be amazed at how much time you'll have for everything in your life. And that's important to understand because life is not about one thing. Your life is about more than just your job. To live a balanced life, you must pay attention to everything that's important to you. That's how I do it. My approach is neat, orderly, and it works. I know exactly what I expect of myself and when—and so does everyone else. Here's the kicker, though: when it's time to work, I go into action mode. I get off my butt and get moving. You won't make any footprints in the *sands of time* while sitting down.

Making the Most of Your Day

You'll never go wrong if you simply follow Girard's Rule #4: *Work when you work.* And I mean no cheating. Put in an honest 8–10 hour day. If I had a nickel for every hour people waste away on the job in just *one* day because of poor habits or lack of discipline, I'll bet I could fill the Empire State Building from the basement to the top. In fact, coins would be flowing out of the windows like a stack of Vegas slot machines. I'd be a rich man. It's sad, but we know it's true because we've both seen people doing just that at work—*nothing.*

I was once told about a University of Michigan survey that revealed a disturbing statistic about time. According to their findings, in a week's time, the average person *really* works only about $1^1/_2$ days. That means in a month, they work a week. If you extend that out to a year, it amounts to about three months that they actually work. Three months! That means for nine months out of the year, the average person does nothing—NOTHING. Many of them actually feel they're getting a "free" ride when in fact they're only cheating themselves. They think the people who toe the line for everyone else are suckers. Have I got a news flash for them.

The actor W. C. Fields used to say, "There's a sucker born every minute." Let me tell you something: people who just "show up" for work but do nothing all day are the *real* suckers. Their lives amount to nothing and prove the point that there are bums indoors as well as out on the street. Tell me you're not in that crowd. If you are, your career just received a life sentence without parole. Get used to your jail cell. You're going nowhere. You're a BUM! Take it from Joe Girard:

People who do nothing know nothing.

If you know nothing you get nothing.

Without knowledge you will surely fail.

I'm not the only one who thinks this way. The great ancient Greek philosopher Socrates had a thing or two to say about that too. One of his young devoted followers pleaded with him to share the secret of acquired knowledge. Socrates willingly consented and led the young man to a nearby river. "This is how," Socrates stated, as he pushed the young man into the river. And then, jumping in himself, he held the young man's head underneath the water. The young man struggled frantically to free himself, but Socrates held him tight and kept his head submerged. Finally, the young man scratched and clawed and fought with every ounce of his being. He was able to break loose and emerge from the water. Socrates then asked him, "When you were drowning, what one thing did you want most of all?" Still gasping for breath, the young man exclaimed, "I wanted air." Socrates smiled and then wisely said, "When you want knowledge as much as you want air, then you will get it." Truer words were never spoken.

Faking, Falling, and Failing

Even the most detailed time management planner won't save you if you find yourself slacking off at work and not giving 100 percent. It isn't just the losers who fall into this trap either. I've seen some decent salespeople get caught here. Danny, one of our young rookie salesmen, tallied up 84 prospects who promised to buy a new car or truck from him by mid-December. "I'm gonna sell more cars than Girard," he boasted. He was so sure he was going to rewrite the record book, he took his eye off the ball and went out and spent a small fortune on Christmas gifts for his wife and three young kids in anticipation of his earnings. Sadly, he was able to close only three of the 84 prospects. He "put the cart before the horse." Had he spent his time being more thorough and persistent with his prospects, he might have been able to close an additional 60 to 70 percent of them. Danny's story is similar to the fate of so many other sales reps I've run into over the years.

They start off by working hard and making good use of their time. They have a few weeks of good results. All of a sudden they begin to believe they're so good that things will happen automatically, that success is some kind of ticket to the easy life—an entitlement to slack off. They begin to believe that things can't possibly go wrong now that they've enjoyed a taste of success.

Now watch what happens here. They ease up on their effort. They get cocky, and then they get lazy. They're on the way down—FALLING down to the reality that they're not for real after all. They're FAKES. And all fakes have something waiting around the corner for them—FAILURE. Failure is always lurking in the "alleys of life," watching and waiting for the right moment when it's least expected to spring out of nowhere and mug people like that.

Let me tell you something: people who enjoy success too quickly can often be doomed to failure if they forget what got them there and where they came from. That's why I always keep that picture of me shining shoes as a nine-year-old kid on the wall in my office. I never want to forget where I came from. It kept me in line and prevented me from thinking I was a hotshot.

How many professional athletes and Hollywood actors and actresses and singers do we know who have fallen victim to "stardom" in their careers? There's too many to count. The media gets to them and props them up as "larger than life" figures. Worst of all, they begin to believe it. Suddenly they're "special." They think they don't have to live by everybody else's rules.

Here's what's really happening. The imposters of success—*glitz and glamour*—have them by the throat, and they don't even know it. They have no clue as to what to do or how to handle the spotlight. Suddenly they forget where they came from. All that hard work to get launched and climb the mountain goes down the drain with inflated egos, drugs, alcohol, bad marriages, and eventually financial ruin. The dream becomes their worst nightmare. Many a professional athlete's career or image has been spoiled or tarnished by activities off the playing field: O. J. Simpson, John Daly, Tiger Woods, Mike Tyson, Pete Rose, Mickey Mantle, and Barry Bonds, just to name a few. Sadly, some lives are even tragically cut short on their meteoric rise to fame and fortune: Whitney Houston, Kurt Cobain, Amy Winehouse, Hank Williams, Janis Joplin, Michael Jackson, Elvis Presley, John Belushi, and tragedy's poster child, Marilyn Monroe. Incomplete lives lost in time.

Why does this happen so often? In most cases, it's because they took their eye off the ball. They fell into the *celebrity* trap. They let distractions lure them away from success and suck them into the quicksand of failure. They left who they were to become someone even they couldn't recognize. What a pathetic waste. It's no coincidence. We've seen it happen over and over. What does this mean to you? Let me give you some pointers to make sure none of this ever happens to you:

1. Never forget where you came from. Keep a picture of yourself as a kid nearby.

2. Remember your success is NEVER ALL ABOUT YOU. If you're in sales, you represent a product or service backed by lots of other people without whom you'd fail.

3. You will have your ups and downs. Be thankful for the UPS and humble during the DOWNS.

4. Winning isn't about being arrogant. It's about being appreciative.

5. Always put yourself second. Put your family first. That's why you do what you do.

If you keep those five things in mind, you will never have to look back on your career with regrets about the empty trail you left behind.

Stay Focused

Keep your eye on your goals at all times. Don't get ahead of yourself. And don't get bigheaded about yourself. When you arrive at your place of work, never forget that you haven't accomplished a damn thing yet. At this point, you're no different than anyone else until you prove it. There's only one mindset to bring as you go through that front door—*the most valuable thing you have is your time.* Never forget this. Make the most of every hour in your day. Make every moment count for something. If you have a good day, don't fall into the trap of "rewarding" yourself the very next day by slacking off. Do it again! Whatever you did worked! You're doing something right! Be thankful. Learn from that experience. There'll be plenty of time for rewards later.

As I said right up front in this chapter, when I arrive at work, I am there to work. When I go home or take a vacation or trip, I'm there to play. Don't mix the two. Trust me. It doesn't work. Business and pleasure are not good companions.

Only you know for sure when you've put in a solid day of work. If you shave an hour off here and there by taking an extra long lunch, phoning a buddy or friend instead of a customer, or by calling in "sick," only *you* know for sure what's *really* going on. Since most people can't be supervised that closely, this kind of work ethic can go undetected for months or even years. But you know what? Even though you're cheating the company you work for, the one who's really being cheated is YOU! You've stolen away precious time that could have been productive. Instead, you chose to "work the system" and do the bare minimum. Eventually that approach becomes your model for how you work. Pretty soon you don't know any other way to work.

And who suffers? Besides the company, YOUR FAMILY! That's right. Every day you slack off, you're cheating your kids out of a better education that costs a little more. You're cheating your spouse out of a better home or vacation he or she richly deserves. How proud of yourself are you now? If that describes your approach to work, you're a LOSER and a cheat. If you're around people like that in your place of work, avoid them like poison because they will change you forever for the worse. Take a "bite out of that apple" and you'll never get out of jail.

Listen, I'm not telling you to avoid being friends with people at work. You don't have to become a hermit to be successful. What I am telling you is *hang around with people who can help you.* Depending on where you work, those people are not necessarily in your department. In my line of work, I never had lunch with other salespeople. Why? It didn't matter if I liked them or not. THEY COULDN'T HELP ME. I spent more time with people in the service department where I knew my customers would spend the majority of their time once I sold them a car. I wanted those customers to be taken care of so I knew they were having a first-class ownership experience.

If you're in the business of insurance sales, you might want to spend some time getting to know underwriters or people in claims to better understand what they do that can help you. Maybe you're in real estate sales. Spend some time getting to know who's who in the title companies you deal with. They're the key to processing your paperwork when you close on a sale. Get to know the bankers and their key people your company does business with. After all, that's where the loans are approved and processed for YOUR customers. These are the types of people you should be having lunch with, not the guy in the office next to yours who wants to talk about last night's game.

Picture a rotating Ferris wheel as it comes around again with those same customers back in the market for a new car or truck. You want to be there to greet them with a smile and take their hand as they step off to see you about their next purchase. I didn't want my sales to be lost in some other part of the dealership because I wasn't paying attention. I took good care of my service reps and showed them my appreciation. You should always invest some of your hard-earned money to advance your career where it counts.

In fact, every third Wednesday of the month, I took the entire service department out to dinner, on me (and Uncle Sam). I'm talking about 36 people here. I made a deal with a very popular Italian restaurant in Detroit, Schiavi's, to take good care of my service team. I wanted to *service them* for a job well done the same way I wanted them to service my customers, the way Joe Girard did it, with TLC—Tender Loving Care. They were *reminded and rewarded* every month. As a sidebar, I sold more than just a few cars to the people who worked at the restaurant too!

The owner of the dealership thought I was nuts for doing this. Once again, I knew exactly what I was doing. I wanted the service department to know that I trusted them with my customers. I respected their expertise. And most of all, I appreciated what they were doing for my customers and me. I considered all these people important parts of the Girard "sales machine." I wanted them as primed and focused on success as I was to get the job done right every time for my customers.

And they responded. There were many times that the service reps and techs would stay a little bit longer to take care of one of my customers. They were only too happy to put in a little bit of extra time for me. They were appreciative that I respected them and took good care of them. They were all on my team. Yes, it cost me more than $500 a month to treat these special guys (tax deductible, of course). But in the long run, it was well worth it. If you want a motivated team behind you, be thoughtful and treat them with kindness, not harshness. As the saying goes, "A teaspoon of honey goes a long way."

The driving force behind why I did this was pretty straight-forward thinking. You see, I never for a moment believed that these customers belonged to the dealership or Chevrolet. These customers belonged to *Joe Girard*. And I wanted them to know that I was better than anyone else at taking care of them. How I did that would determine if they'd come back to me to buy a new car or truck. Like I said—straightforward thinking. The name of the game is *service, service, service*. And in case you don't know how to spell it, it's L-O-V-E. Love.

Jealousy and Envy

We talked about how precious time is in the previous chapter. Many of the sales guys hung out together and would sometimes take extra-long lunches. They were only hurting themselves by doing this. They were stealing their own time. I never went out for lunch. I brought a brown bag from home that my wife made for me. I made sure my time was spent in the dealer-ship where I made my money. My long, leisurely meals were taken on my time. Besides, that's when and where I enjoyed them the most, with family or close friends away from the job. I knew the value of time better than anyone in the showroom. Distractions were something I avoided like the plague, and my colleagues all knew that too. I was never one for small talk. If it had something to do with work, and specifically something that was important at that moment, I listened. If not, I would politely excuse myself. Do you think they would learn some-thing from that? Unfortunately, most of them didn't, and many of them disliked me because of that.

As bad as it may sound, I often tell people that once you're not liked at work, *you've arrived*. It never occurred to them that maybe there's something to Girard's idea of using your time well to succeed. I was probably the best example of how to do that in the entire industry, and yet many seemed completely unaware of it. I know it may sound like I was surrounded by a lot of idiots. That was certainly not the case. Some did work hard and wanted to improve. But they were the few. Most couldn't cut it. Selling cars and trucks isn't for everyone. I guarantee you, it's one of the most difficult jobs to do well. It's a tough racket filled with competition, cutthroat dealing, and a lot of disappointment. That's one of the reasons you often see such high turnover in retail auto sales departments. Some years, many dealerships would lose more than two-thirds of their sales force. That's huge! As hard as it is to be successful selling cars and trucks, not knowing how to focus your time properly is like pounding nails into your own coffin. "So why weren't they focused?" you ask. They were lazy. That's why.

And their paychecks told the story. I'll tell you one thing they all knew for sure—my paycheck was higher than all of theirs combined. It became pretty obvious that I was the only one in the dealership that really understood how to make time work effectively. Every two weeks, the manager would get us all together to hand out our paychecks (before he took off to play golf). I recall one instance in particular when I was having a pretty good run of sales. He would go through the names and publicly announce the amount of everybody's commission checks as he passed them out: $300 for this guy, $450 for that guy, $175 for so-and-so, and so on. I was the last name he would call: "Joe Girard—$11,650." You could feel the resentful undertone from the other salespeople in the room. It was okay for him to leave now and go play golf, leaving me behind with this ugly atmosphere he just created. They hated me. I went straight to the owner and told him to *never* have my paycheck given to me in front of the other salespeople again.

By the way, if you think I'm stretching the truth about the difference in what I made compared to the other salesmen, you're dead wrong! Actually, this should come as no surprise. I was selling more cars and trucks in a day than some of these guys were selling in a month! I can remember very vividly when I actually sold 18 cars in a single day! Many of my competing salesmen would have loved to have sold 170 cars in a year. I set the record with 174 in a single month!

You're forgetting I was the number one retail salesman in the world! In fact, get this: *my sales totals were consistently ranked ahead of 94 percent of all fully staffed auto dealerships' new vehicle sales totals in the country—as a one-man show!* Still questioning the numbers?

The simple truth of why the other salesmen's checks were so different from mine was not some deep secret or complicated analysis I was doing or anything like that. It was mostly about time. *I worked when I worked.* They didn't.

Here's a typical Joe Girard day:

>> **7:45 a.m.** Arrive at work (before any other salesmen).

>> **8 a.m.** Align all paperwork (purchasing agreements, insurance and loan information, etc.) and notes listed in my daily planner for customer calls and appointments that day (making sure secretaries hold all my calls during customer appointments).

>> **9–11:45 a.m.** Make customer/prospect and follow-up calls and conduct any customer appointments to purchase new vehicles in my office (I was very good at keeping customer meetings to under an hour).

>> **Take 15 minutes each day** to head over to the service area to greet and check up on any of my customers in for service and *remind them Joe Girard* is always there for them (the service reps always let me know when my customers were coming in ahead of time).

>> **12:15 p.m.** Review all notes made from morning calls, contacts, and appointments to organize and outline "next step follow-ups."

>> **12:30 p.m.** Take a half-hour lunch break in my office.

» **1–6 p.m.** Continue customer/prospect and follow-up contacts and conduct any customer appointments to purchase vehicles in my office.

» **6:15 p.m.** Review all notes made from all afternoon calls, contacts, and appointments to organize and outline "next step follow-ups."

» **6:30 p.m.** Review planner to make sure all actions and appointments are correct for the next day.

» **6:45 p.m.** Call it a day and head home to be with my family.

> › Note: If the dealership was open late till 9 p.m. (as on Mondays and Thursdays), I would take a short break for a snack before getting right back in the trenches to make more calls, contacts, and conduct customer appointments.

You'll see later on in Chapter 9, "Stay in Touch," that eventually my sales began to grow faster than I could cope with. *I was beginning to sink in my own success.* I had to get help; otherwise, I was going to lose a lot of business. I hired two people (at my expense) who worked exclusively for me to do a lot of the preliminary work. It was very important to me that they would be focused, motivated, and loyal, so I paid them well (including their car and health insurance). It worked like a charm. They both made more money than most of the salesmen in the department. (I'll share more detail on how this worked in Chapter 9.) I could now concentrate on my specialty—the important parts of the *customer interface.*

Many times I did put in some long days, and I was often quite exhausted by the end of it. *But my desire to succeed kept my energy level on fire.* It's amazing what you can do when you're winning! Here's Girard's shorthand advice on how to do it:

» If you want to stay on top of your bills, give it 100 percent.

» *If you want to be number one in what you do, give it 150 percent!*

If only the other salesmen would have caught on. Most of them never did, though. They were their own worst enemies. They were losers. The sad part is that instead of being inspired to do better by a guy in their own dealership, they became possessed by *jealousy*, the green-eyed monster, and *envy*, one of the seven deadly sins. I could see it in their eyes. Whenever they would see me, especially closing a deal, I think my success reminded them of their own failures and shortcomings. I represented everything they were not. They began to focus on *my* success instead of *their* failure. I became a roadblock instead of an inspiration to them.

I remember when I was first recognized as the national leader in sales. I had actually been selling for only three years! That's what I said—three years! That's what persistence, attitude, and hard work will get you. When I received the award, everybody cheered. It was a great achievement for me. However, no salesperson had ever done it two years in a row. That was about to change.

The next year, I received the award again to cheers, except this time I heard someone booing me from the back of the hotel ballroom we were in. I told him he ought to go outside and throw up if he was having trouble clearing his throat, to which everyone laughed.

The third year I received the sales leadership award again. This time, I was greeted by boos from the entire room. In fact, I was booed every year after that for the next nine years. Each year, they thought they were going to break me. They thought they could destroy my *attitude machine*.

What they didn't know is that's the kind of stuff I thrive on. They were actually feeding my passion to succeed. I loved it. They were making me stronger and stronger and more determined than ever. Even two of GM's top executives, John DeLorean, vice president and general manager of Chevrolet, and Ed Cole, president of General Motors—both of whom I admired and respected greatly (and it was mutual)—witnessed the booing when they presented the sales leadership awards to me. They understood the drill. They were at the top of their game too, and they had their enemies.

In that final year, following 12 consecutive years of sales leadership, I took great pleasure in telling all the salespeople there, "I want to thank all of you. You made me what I am. All these years, you've challenged me with your boos. This year, I have a very special Christmas present for all of you. Nine months ago, I told the owner that on Christmas Eve of this year, I was going to give Joe Girard a Christmas present. My present is I'm giving *Joe Girard* to Joe Girard. I am quitting at the end of the year. Thank you each and every one of you. I couldn't have done it without you. Merry Christmas and good night." For that I got a standing ovation like you've never seen before. But the joke was on them, and they knew it. I wasn't "one of the boys." I wasn't in the "dope ring." I was Joe Girard.

The odd thing is that *I* wasn't their problem. *They* were their problem. The most obvious difference in our approaches was simple. I *worked when I worked* and they didn't. Many of them left early. I never snuck out early or made up an excuse so I didn't have to be there. I realized I would only be cheating myself, and I didn't like that at all. When you're having a bad day, you too can be subjected to moments of jealousy and envy, especially if someone else is having a good one. Part of that is human nature. It means you care and won't settle for poor results. That's fine. But if you let it take control, it will get in the way of your productivity because your focus will begin to shift onto finding ways to take the other guy down instead of boosting yourself up. If you let that kind of thing fester, hatred can set in. And that's not good. That's like jumping into jail. Stay focused on you and your goals.

Working Hard or Working Smart?

If you're looking for ways to improve your work output and performance, then think beyond just the *quantity* of work you're doing (meaning the number of hours you're working in a day) and think about the *quality* of the work you're doing. Just because you're working long hours doesn't mean they're always productive. You could be working hard but really *hardly working.* You can't just work; you have to work SMART to be successful. There's a huge difference. In almost all cases, working smart means using your time effectively. If you have a job that requires lots of interaction with others like I did (and still do), then think smart. Focus on repeating successful approaches you have used in the past. If you build on your past experiences, emphasizing the good things you've done while avoiding the bad things, you'll undoubtedly begin to see a positive pattern. But you have to *work* at it. If you study the approaches of other successful people in your business (or any other, for that matter), one thing you'll find they all have in common is that when they get to work, they work. Period. Distractions are just not allowed in their workday. There are no slackers in any hall of fame that I know of.

You might think working too hard doesn't "taste" so good after a while, especially if you aren't getting the results you want right away. Remember the road to success takes time, and you have to work at it. It will come, though. Be patient and stay the course. We're not talking about an overnight success formula here. We're talking about a commitment to transforming your outlook on how you live and how you work from now on into the future. We're talking about your life. If you've been in a rut for 20 years, then you already understand the virtue of patience. That's one of the reasons why I'm emphasizing the idea of staying so focused, hour after hour and day after day, when you work. The minute you lose that focus, you start to falter. Distractions take over. Bad thoughts might even enter your mind. You begin second-guessing and doubting yourself. Did that ever happen to me? Of course it did! I'm human too and subject to the same challenges of providing for a family as everybody else. But I had a trump card to play that few had.

If I had any advantage over my sales colleagues, it was probably that I might have witnessed the darker side of life at home and in the streets growing up more than most. That was the fuel I needed to say, "THAT WILL NEVER BE JOE GIRARD AGAIN!"

I have never looked back. *That, my friends, is as powerful a motivator to succeed as you will probably ever see. You'd be hard-pressed to find that in an MBA textbook.*

Don't let any kind of negative thinking anywhere near your day. Stay positive and keep working. There is yet another reason why you should give at the very least a 100 percent effort that's equally important.

The Opportunity of a Lifetime

There's no question that working with a purpose and staying focused have the obvious benefit of creating more chances to be successful, more chances to "make a sale," more chances to refine your approach, more chances to improve, more chances to make more money. That's pretty clear. So whatever your goals or targets are in a workday, working smart improves your odds of achieving success. It's a game of numbers. Right? If you understand and believe that, then you're correct. No argument there.

For Joe Girard, it goes much further than that, though. Let me take you to a deeper level of appreciation and understanding. The reason I believe you should always *work when you work* is one word: OPPORTUNITY. No, not the opportunity to close a deal or anything like that. I'm talking about the BIG opportunity. The opportunity you only get once. Let me give it to you close up.

No matter who you are or what you are in this life, there is one gift we all share equally; that precious gift from God to all of us is *time*. On any given day, we are each given the same gift. We all get the same thing—1,440 minutes. That's how many minutes there are in a 24-hour day. How you use them, spend them, or ignore them is what separates us from each other. I think I could write an entire book on just *time* alone. I understood the value of time early on in my career. If you came into my office on any day and asked me to spell *time*, I would say to you M-O-N-E-Y. Money. That's what time meant to me, and that is what it should mean to you.

When I combined my respect for time with my approach to *working smart,* I had an unbeatable combination. None of the other salespeople in the dealership ever made the connection between time and money the way I did. They never seemed to catch on to the fact that you only have so much time in your life to create wealth and stability. The problem is you don't know *how much* time that is. How many more years are you going to be able to work? How much time do you *really* have to know and love your families? How long are you going to live? The only time you are certain of is the time you have right now: this day, this hour, this moment. That's all any of us have.

Here's something I've shared with many audiences over the years to make my point about gaining a deeper appreciation for the value of time. Get your hands on a stopwatch and an index card and try this experiment. As you will see, this is no ordinary stopwatch. It will be your conscience. It will watch over you. It will make you proud. It will make you feel guilty. It is always truthful and never lies. Any time you're doing nothing at your place of work, like shooting the breeze in the "dope ring," simply click it on. After you've had your fun for the morning, stop the clock and note the amount of time that has gone by. Write it down on the index card. When you go to lunch, turn it on. When you get back to the office, turn it off, again entering the amount of time gone by on the index card. If you take a call from a buddy or friend who calls to talk about something unrelated to work, click the stopwatch on. When the conversation is over, stop the watch and note the time on the card again. Maybe you spent some more time in the "dope ring." Click the watch on and off again. At the end of the day, add up all the time you spent screwing around instead of working. You'll be absolutely floored at the amount of time you've wasted away doing NOTHING. Even with a minimum amount of "down" time chitchatting, you could probably tally up an hour in the morning and one in the afternoon. While you're doing that, I'm either making a dozen contacts in those two hours or closing two sales! **In a month, that's 240 calls or 40 closed sales!**

Don't be surprised if on a typical day you spent more time doing nothing than being productive. If you're perfectly honest with yourself, you'll probably notice there are times when you actually shot the entire day—never to be recaptured again.

If you put off (or slack off) till "tomorrow," the clock may have stopped ticking. Listen, I'm not trying to sound like the voice of doom and gloom. I hope you live in good health for over a hundred years. But reality is reality. How you apply the hours you *do* have is what's important. Some of you may already feel you're in a catch-up mode trying to make up for earlier mistakes in your life. That's okay. You're trying to get yourself on the right track now. There's very little I won't do or say to try and get your attention NOW, while the opportunity exists. You will see a difference *if* you stay the course with *My 13 Rules*. That's the whole idea behind this book—discovering and unleashing the real you!

Concentrate on the Moment

One of the biggest distractions to putting in a full day's work is losing your power of concentration. If where you work is anything like where I worked, there's a lot going on around you.

It's noisy. People are always talking. Phones are ringing and so on—it's an auto dealership. You probably have a similar situation where you work. You have to learn to shut all that out. Sometimes people will want to come into your office. Maybe they just want to chat. The way I handled that was simple. I was never impolite, but I made it very plain to everyone who worked around me that unless it was an emergency, I didn't want to hear from anybody. If someone didn't seem to understand, I would say, "Bob, please excuse me but I've got a lot of things scheduled that can't wait. If it's important, please drop me a note and I'll take a look at it later. Thank you." My message was clear: "Not now, Bob." I rarely ever got a note or message back, which told me they just probably wanted to chew the fat. As a rule, I also kept my office door closed. I wasn't trying to be rude. *I was focused on Joe Girard's agenda for the day.*

I didn't want anybody bugging me or disturbing me for any reason when I was working. Period. They all got the message, and that's the way I operated. A lot of them disliked me for that. I probably did offend a few people with that approach along the way. But I made the choice, and it was the right one!

Listen, I'm no different from anyone else. Sure, we all want to be liked. We all want to be accepted. But that was a sacrifice I was willing to make. I wasn't there to become a member of a social club. I was there to make a living. That was my priority. I had no other reason for being there whatsoever. That was my only purpose for being in that showroom every day. That's why I was successful.

At the end of the day when I would be driving home, I remember the good feeling I had because I knew I had given it my best shot and put in a full day's work, even if things didn't go quite my way. I never had the sense of disappointment in myself that a lot of others must have felt because they slacked off. My appreciation of time was too ingrained in me to ever have that be an issue.

If you think you can cheat time, you're dead wrong. You're cheating yourself. *Time is master over all of us.* There is nothing on Earth that can stop its irreversible march. Only God can stop it. And that happens the day you're told to "cash in." That's the day the party's over. There's no going back.

Time is like a thief in the night. It picks your pocket while you're not watching. You finally realize what it has robbed your life of when it gives you a full open view to stare at in your old age when you have little of it left.

Thankfully, that will never be a regret of mine because I don't believe one should retire from life at *any* age. And I am living proof of that too.

All you have is this golden moment—NOW! Right now. What are you going to do with it? Make the most of the opportunity this book encourages you to take advantage of. *Work when you work.* Think of it as the very last race you will ever run. For the *time of your life,* give it *all* the gas you have in you! See you at the finish line!

OBSERVE GIRARD'S NO-NO'S

The chains of habit are too weak to be felt until they are too strong to be broken.

—Samuel Johnson, author, poet, and literary critic

I never let my appearance or habits get in the way of selling someone a car.

How you communicate and the impression you give others weigh heavily on how you are received and understood. The habits you cultivate are especially important and critical to success in your business dealings. And they are noticed.

It all begins with the first impression you give. The first time someone sees you, before you've even said a single word, they already know something about you—your appearance. They see how you look to them, how you carry yourself. The first communication has already taken place.

If that first general impression is that you look good, then you've made it past the initial stage of contact to the next level—actually talking. If you don't look good to the other person, then you're stopped dead in your tracks. There is usually no next step. You're all done with this person. You've been dismissed before you've even introduced yourself. You might as well go on to your next appointment now because you're wasting your time chasing this one. The appointment is over before it even begins. As far as *that* person is concerned, your looks killed the deal or opportunity.

Looks That Could Kill

Just so you know, when I talk about looks, I'm not talking about clothes (that's the next chapter), whether you're handsome or cute, tall or thin, or what color you are. I'm talking only about what *statement* your appearance makes to another person. When I chose "Looks That Could Kill" for the title of this section, I was referring specifically to *looks or impressions that could "kill" a deal* or an important moment or opportunity before a single word is uttered.

» Do you look smug or overbearing?

» Do you seem to have a chip on your shoulder?

>> Do you look down on your luck or depressed?

>> Or do you look confident, welcoming, and caring?

In other words, **do you look like a winner or a loser?** That's what I'm talking about when I refer to how you look.

I think most people with common sense can appreciate that saying something out of place can create a negative atmosphere. However, they don't always think this applies to their appearance. Many feel it's their right to look however they please and that other people just have to deal with it—that's who they are, and they have a right to look and behave any way they want. And that's certainly true. Is that what you say? Does that description fit you?

But your image might be hurting you. It might be a tattoo. Ladies, maybe it's extra heavy makeup or painting your hair a strange color. Guys, it might be an earring or two or a much needed haircut. Perhaps it's just smoking on the job outside where others can see you (that's a nice welcoming odor to greet a customer with). Worse yet, maybe it's alcohol on your breath from a long lunch break at the local tavern.

I realize that in this day and age, individuality is very important, especially to our younger generations. You may not like what I have to say, but understand that any comments I make on appearance or habits are made only to indicate *how they impact the opportunity to close a deal or make a positive impression on someone.* They don't necessarily represent how I personally feel about any of this. That's my business and not the subject of this book. Do you understand the difference? *I'm talking about IMPACT,* how your looks and habits impact the people you come in contact with.

What Statement Does Your Image Make?

I want to be very clear on this. I wrote this book to help you become successful, not to champion any cause for change or personal freedom.

So here's Joe Girard's take on all this: unless you have a job in a hippie community, to most rational-minded people in today's business world, if you look like a bum, you are a bum. Why? Because the vast majority of people won't take the time to find out that you're really an intelligent, nice, hard-working person after all. Instead, they pass instant judgment on you based on what they see. If you look shabby, you are shabby. Period. Like it or not, that's how it is. *We live in a judgmental world and the bottom line is, YOU LOSE.*

Even in the face of this logic, there are people who still won't change or conform to any moderation in their appearance. They just refuse to clean up their act. If you belong to that group, and interacting with people is key to success in your profession, I have one thing to say to you. HEY PAL, why did you come to work today? Why are you there? To make a living. Right? In other words, M-O-N-E-Y. If your appearance or bad habits are getting in the way of your success, you need to make a change—either into some new clothes or to a new job. This is not rocket science. Let me put it to you simply—YOU *need them.* THEY *don't need you. SHARPEN UP YOUR IMAGE!*

Wear your politics or social reform views somewhere else. If you've got a political statement to make, then go to a rally on your own time. When you come to work, you have to decide whether you're there to change the world or to satisfy a single individual's needs. If you're on a crusade for individuality, then you probably need to head off in a different direction. You're wasting your time and everyone else's by parading yourself in a place where you're taking up valuable space someone else could be using to make a living.

In my world of automotive retail selling, I always believed that the time in the showroom belonged to the customer, not me. It's not about me. It's always about them because they can walk out any time they want without leaving a nickel behind! When I was selling, I knew I was there for one reason—to create a professional and welcoming atmosphere that would make my prospects feel comfortable so they would enjoy the experience of doing business with me. That's how I made a living. Listen to me now. I MUST HAVE KNOWN SOMETHING BECAUSE I WAS THE VERY BEST AT DOING WHAT I DID. I always eliminated or minimized anything that got in the way of closing a sale. That meant any distractions—anything that could take them off the track of buying from me. I wanted to be in control at all times. The last thing I wanted to have happen was to lose a sale because I looked too flashy or wasn't considerate. I *never* let my appearance, my behavior, or my habits get in the way of selling someone a car or truck. If I lost a sale, I wanted it to be because I just couldn't beat their price (which was almost never) or I didn't have what they wanted (also very rare)—not because I looked bad. How stupid can you get?

As far as my personal, political, or religious views go, those are *my beliefs*. It's none of anyone's business what I think or how I feel about those things. Those are personal matters that don't belong in the workplace—ever. Besides, if you bring those things up, the chances that your prospect is going to believe and see things exactly the way you do are slim to none. That gap can easily be enough to tip the scales away from closing a deal. Now how smart are you? You'd have to be pretty naive not to understand this.

For example, I had one customer who I knew was a hunter because I noticed a bumper sticker on the car he was trading in. But I was careful not to get into controversial discussions about hunting, regardless of my personal views. So one day, when he came in to look at a new model truck and bragged about a 12-point buck he had just snagged, I simply congratulated him with a smile and a handshake. Why? This was important to *him*. I sensed an appreciative feeling from him that I noticed and cared about the things that were special to him. He warmed up to me and before long was signing the purchase order to buy. Repeat after me: IT'S ALL ABOUT THE CUSTOMER. I needed him more than he needed me. I was always on guard and careful about not making dumb mistakes like saying the wrong thing to someone whose views differed from mine.

Don't make the clumsy mistake of turning your customer off before you even begin. YOU'RE THERE TO MAKE MONEY AND INFLUENCE THE OUTCOME OF YOUR CONTACT WITH OTHERS. You should come across as the sharpest, best groomed, most positive, most *neutral* person they ever met. If you're not prepared to make these changes, then find another line of work. Interacting with all types of people is not your calling. Trust me—you will fail.

This chapter is a very important one in your preparation for success because it focuses on the very specifics of what NOT to do, especially when it comes to your habits and behavior with a customer or contact. By the way, this chapter also applies to the home front too. As a role model for good habits and appearance, think of how your family sees YOU, especially your kids. What statement are you making? What are you teaching them?

Understanding and recognizing the pitfalls of what NOT to do will go a long way toward helping you avoid making the kind of mistakes that can knock you out of the box before you even get a chance to bat. Let me lead you through a critical list of things that can kill your day (and possibly your career) if you do them. I call them *Girard's List of NO-NO's*.

The smart way to look at this list of *NO-NO's* is to embrace these three points:

1. Don't try to figure out which on the list are worse than others so you can see which ones you can get away with doing.

2. It's the CUMULATIVE IMPACT of doing any of them, even just two or three, that's the problem.

3. You don't know what could turn off a customer. You don't know their hot buttons. WHY TAKE A CHANCE ON BLOWING THE SALE?

If you pay attention to these three suggestions, you'll stand a much better chance of making a positive impression on others and getting ahead in your profession. Here it is then, *Girard's List of NO-NO's.*

What Not to Do

1. Don't Smoke or Chew Tobacco

First of all, they're bad for your health. It's a complete turn-off in an age where very few people engage in either of these habits anymore. It's also an indication of your bad judgment, lack of common sense, weak willpower, discourteousness, and thoughtlessness to others. All the wrong signals and red flags go up here. IN THIS DAY AND AGE, many people won't even step into a salesperson's office if they smell cigarette smoke, let alone buy anything. They're concerned about passive or "secondhand" smoke being cancerous. They may have allergies that would kick in immediately. Or maybe they just don't want the odor finding a new home in their clothing. In fact, in most states now, office buildings and public places are declared "smoke-free" environments. Chewing tobacco may seem harmless in comparison to smoking, but serious cancer health risks exist there too, and the same stigma will follow you. *Sharpen up—this isn't the 1970s!*

Let me run the math on these filthy habits for you. Let's assume that 80 percent of the *potential* customers or people you come in contact with don't smoke or chew tobacco. By doing either of these in front of them (or smelling like you do), you've basically turned off about 80 percent of all the prospects and people you come in contact with. All that hard work of planning, putting together lists, making contacts, setting up appointments—down the toilet. How smart is that? Now you're stuck with the remaining 20 percent to fight over with the rest of the competition. You're a loser. If you're having trouble quitting, then GET HELP! It's out there. There are many places you can go to help you clean up. Your health is more important than anything else. DO IT!

2. Don't Chew Gum

Although many people think it's not as bad as smoking or chewing tobacco, chewing gum can also be very distracting. Suddenly your customer or contact is focused on your mouth instead of your eyes and your brain. It can even be noisy. It's as though you're in your own world and they're not part of it. That's not the signal you want to send. Maybe you chew gum because it helps freshen your breath. Forget it. Take a breath mint instead. It smells better, it's better for you, and it's not distracting at all. If you think this all sounds trivial, I've got news for you. These are the little things that kill deals.

Until you become a little bit paranoid about losing a deal or making a bad impression because of the small things that you think go unnoticed, you're likely to go through life scratching your head, never quite knowing why you failed to achieve your goals or become successful. For all your hard work, how would you like a stick of gum to have been the reason for your failure in life? It's almost laughable. But you and I both know how painful that realization would be if it were true. C'mon— not for a piece of chewing gum!

3. Don't Use Heavy Cologne

This one can turn an atmosphere sour as fast as anything. And ladies, it's not just you I'm talking about here. Some of you guys smell like you're "working the streets" for a brothel. This is not the distraction you want a customer or person to be greeted with the moment they see you. All sorts of red flags go up here—you're inconsiderate, you smell cheap, you're focused only on yourself, you have low-class taste and, worst of all, you've just given your prospect a migraine headache. Some prospects might even have a touch of asthma like I have. And that's no laughing matter. Congratulations—you couldn't have scripted a more complete disaster for yourself if you tried.

Understand that Joe Girard never leaves the room before closing a deal with a customer. But it has happened. I am a very fit kind of guy, but I do have a little bit of asthma. I remember having to excuse myself from my office (they're not that big in a dealership) because a lady I was selling a car to had on such strong perfume that I just had to get some fresh air. I didn't want to offend her, but I just had to get out of the room. I returned in a few minutes to complete the deal. It didn't come soon enough.

If you want to put on fancy colognes and perfumes, then do it on your own time. Save it for your date AFTER WORK, not DURING. Use common sense. This one is so obvious, it boggles my mind that anyone, especially someone in sales, would do this. I mean, how ignorant can you get? Even though the offensive odor that comes from heavy colognes is literally right "under your nose," you can't even begin to smell it. Pay attention to what's going on around you and what others see and sense about you!

4. Don't Use Profanity

This one really takes the cake. If you want to find out something about a person's character or their upbringing, just listen to the language they use in a normal conversation. From a person who grew up on the streets of Detroit, believe me, I've heard it all. And it ain't very pretty. Perhaps that's why I'm so tuned in to the impression the language you use can make on another person.

If you use profanity in your discussions with a customer or another person you've just met, they instantly learn several things about you. First of all, you're telling them that you're a low life with no class and were brought up without any regard for what others may think of you. Second, you're telling the person you're talking to that, regardless of how uncomfortable they may feel listening to your filthy mouth, you will require them to stoop down to your level in this conversation. Third, you are communicating the fact that they too must be a low life like you since you have chosen that level of language for your conversation. And last of all, you're broadcasting the fact that you're really too stupid to see that this path might cost you a sale or a positive next step with that person.

I never saw it happen in the dealership with a customer because (1) that wasn't my approach, and (2) I didn't eavesdrop on what other salesmen were saying to their customers. However, I do recall having it happen to me when I was buying furniture some years back. The salesman was trying to explain the difference in quality between two credenzas my wife and I were looking at. He used some unnecessary expletives (let's just say) to downplay the lower-priced piece. Not only were his comments unnecessary, they took me quite by surprise since this was an upscale place. I was very offended, especially in the presence of my wife, and I immediately asked for an apology, which he gave. Needless to say, he was embarrassed, but I think he learned a valuable lesson—presenting a bad image can cost you a sale. Which, in his case, it did.

I won't even get into the morality of profanity since that is a very personal matter. Clearly, though, your decision to choose profanity as a main way to communicate would indicate you have little regard for anything really sacred in life. And that is probably more telling than anything else. Is this the person you want to do business with? Is that you? Clean up your act and your mouth!

5. Don't Tell Dirty Jokes

Dirty jokes are almost in the same league as profanity as far as I'm concerned. They tell a lot about a person and what they think of others. They're an indication that you like to travel low with the scum and slime of the earth—the losers. Nice company, eh? I remember that dirty jokes were the main attraction of the "dope ring" at the dealership where I worked. Those guys spent more time exchanging dirty jokes than chasing leads. Anyone who has time for this has no time for success. It's a great way to dull the active cells in your brain with dirt. What customer would want to be around that? I do remember hearing about a customer who complained to the management that she went to get a drink of water from the fountain (which was near the coffee pot the "dope ring" used) when she heard a bunch of salesmen chuckling after one of them delivered a sexist punch line to a joke.

I certainly had no time for that (or them). They were losers and it showed. If you hang with that kind of crowd, sooner or later you become those jokes. The dirt begins to shape who you are. Eventually, you can't even hide who the "real" you is from your own family. Your children will be so proud of you when they discover who YOU REALLY ARE. Grow up!

6. Don't Have Alcohol Breath

You've got a real problem if this is you. You may not be an alcoholic (yet), but no one else who can smell you coming back to your office after an extra long lunch knows that. At the very least, you have a serious image problem. Just to make sure I cover the bases: it's bad for your health; you can be a safety hazard to others as well as yourself if you're driving; you cast a dark shadow on your value system and just who's in control of your life; and you send a negative impression of a failed life to all who come in contact with you, including prospects, work associates, family, and friends (soon to be former friends). Yours will soon be a solitary life. But you will always have one friend you can count on—the bottle. And that, my friend, is the devil. For all practical purposes, YOU'RE DEAD. Get help while you still can!

This was a real problem for a couple of guys I knew in our sales department. They both had drinking problems that eventually impacted their performance. They would take longer lunch hours and come back looking visibly tired. Then they would stay out late after work hitting the hot spots before finally making their way home. Then, of course, they had to sleep it off, and that meant coming into work late the next day. Since their sales were poor, they were both given an ultimatum—clean up or get out. To his credit, one of them did clean up. It was a struggle, but he did manage to turn things around. The other one was fired within two weeks, never to be heard from again.

By the way, this same advice about alcohol applies to what some people call "recreational" drugs. First of all, don't let anyone kid you: there's no such thing as a recreational drug. There are only DRUGS. The only thing you're "re-creating" is yourself. You've become a monster. It WILL kill you eventually. If it's not prescribed by a doctor, it shouldn't be in your body. PERIOD.

7. Don't Wear Earrings, Men

This may be the touchiest one of all. I know earrings are becoming trendy for both sexes today. We see male athletes and movie stars sporting them all the time. Some of these rings are starting to appear in more places than just ears now (lips, noses, and even tongues). Still, very few people actually like them. Your decision here is really very simple. DO THE MATH. Most men don't wear them at all (less than 10 percent, depending on what survey you look at). This means most men you come in contact with won't be wearing them either. Many find them in poor taste. So whatever you think, why risk turning off a potential contact or sale because you feel you must "express" yourself and who you are to the world? The reality is that most men who do wear earrings don't do it because it's an original idea that fits their personality. They do it because other guys they know are doing it, and they'd rather "fit in" with the crowd than "stand out." Not what I call smart thinking.

Me? I wanted to stand out. I wanted to distance myself so far from that type of person I couldn't run fast enough to get away from them. I wanted to have *my own* personal image, *my own* approach to life, *my own* success story, and *my own* set of values. I didn't want to have some cheap "what's hot now" image nailed to my face for everyone to look at and say, "Hey, there goes Joe Girard. He looks and acts just like everyone else." How special is that? Be who YOU want to be, not who others want you to be. Believe me when I tell you this. Losers will never want you to be anything more than what they will ever be. They will go out of their way to hold you down forever with them. That's why they're losers.

If you're already wearing an earring or are considering one (or two), the next time you see an earring on any part of a man's face, I want you to do something. Picture that earring around your neck choking the very life out of you until you can hardly breathe. As you fall to your knees with your arms outstretched begging for another gasp of air—another chance in life—get up, pull the ring from around your neck, and promise yourself right on the spot that, if you are ever going to be anyone from that moment on, you will only be who YOU are for the rest of your life. That transformation will be shocking to you. You will have discovered WHO YOU CAN BE—THE REAL YOU.

8. Don't Leave Cell Phones On

There are all sorts of technologies out there today that were just getting started when I was actively selling. One of them is the cell phone. They're everywhere. Everybody has one. Some of them stick out of people's ears as they walk through malls looking like they're talking to themselves. Others are fancy "text-messaging" devices that seem to preoccupy practically everyone's lives. I'm all for technology. However, there's a point when it can get in the way of productivity.

You read that right. Let me explain Joe Girard's definition of *productivity*. To me, productivity is not just a measurement of how efficient you are when you work. It's not about computer technology, communication systems (like cell phones), and the Internet coming to the rescue of a salesperson so that that he or she can get information faster and more efficiently. It's much simpler than that. *Productivity* is how much M-O-N-E-Y did I make at the end of the day. If answering a cell phone in front of customers or even having one ring while they're in my office becomes a distraction or turnoff, I want to throw that thing into a bucket of water. If they get up and leave because I appear to be so in love with all my electronic "stuff," I've just lost a sale. What the hell good are all those *techno* gadgets now?

Technology, cell phones especially, will never—REPEAT, NEVER—replace the power of the positive interaction that takes place, the bond that is formed, and the goodwill that's exchanged for life between a good salesperson and a customer. That relationship is better than gold. In fact, it's priceless. That's how I became the world's best, bringing those customers back to me over and over. A cell phone will never do that for you. Don't even bother calling 9-1-1 with your cell phone because no one's coming to the rescue at the other end. YOU'VE LOST. When you're on the job, use the cell phone for what it was intended—emergencies. I realize that some of your jobs are very dependent on actively using cell phones on the job. But for heaven's sake, don't use it when you're with someone, especially someone you're trying to impress that they're the most important person at that very moment. That's just plain rude. And for goodness's sake, if you do have one clipped to your belt or in your purse, put it on "vibrate" mode so that only you know when it rings instead of playing a ridiculous song that everyone within fifty feet of you can hear. Don't be a fool. THINK! THINK! THINK!

9. Don't Be Late

This one can really be a deal buster. The cardinal sin of selling is missing an appointment. To me, missing an appointment doesn't mean being a few minutes late. Missing an appointment to me always meant not being there *ahead of time* so I could get myself properly focused on that specific customer's needs and wants. That's how seriously I took being on time. I needed a few minutes to review my strategy and approach before they got there. Once my sales really began to take off, I saw that my new customer appointments were really starting to stack up. That's when I realized I needed help and hired a couple of people to assist me. To not be there when the customer actually arrived was unthinkable to me. I was so motivated to succeed, I never let that happen.

Being on time means never having to apologize. Regardless of whatever else happens, missing an appointment is a little bit like forgetting to cash in a lottery ticket by the expiration date. All that anticipation—the opportunity, the chance to make some money—gone forever. You might think it's only one sale, but it's an indication that you're either not focused or you're not properly organized. If so, you're doomed to repeat that mistake again and again. You may not realize it, but you are basically shaping your reputation. And word gets around. This will haunt other opportunities if you don't wake up and correct this immediately. You need to go back and reread Chapter 3, "Organize Your Life."

There you have it: *Girard's List of NO-NO's*, **nine things you should never do**. Avoid these traps like the plague and you're on the right track to focusing on the things that will help you become successful.

Sharpen Up for Success

During my many years of retail selling, I've observed several potentially promising salespeople fall into the bad habit ruts we've just reviewed in *Girard's No-No's*. Trust me. They will have a negative influence on your paycheck if you ignore them. Be smart about this.

I want to remind you of what I said earlier that I think bears repeating. I'm not trying to tell you what to think or feel about anything. That's your business. What I am telling you is that, no matter what line of work you're in, you're going to run into

all kinds of people who can make a difference in how successful you become. Some of these people you will genuinely like.
But quite frankly, you're not going to like a lot of them. Some
of them may even turn you off. You can't control that. You don't
know who's coming through the door on any given day. You
have to be ready to play the cards that are dealt to you. Be
open to everyone. That's critical to your mindset because they
all have one thing in common to you—M-O-N-E-Y.

That's right. Remember, we're not picking personal friends
here. We're trying to make a living. WE NEED THEM MORE
THAN THEY NEED US. Sharpen up! I'm telling you how to
maximize your opportunities in life with people, whether you
like them or not, so that you can enjoy the success your hard
work deserves. That's all this chapter is about. Plain and simple. The focus here has intentionally been on what NOT to do
when it comes to habits and behavior. In the next chapter, we'll
be focusing more on appearance and what TO DO to make the
right impression.

RULE SIX
DRESS THE PART

Eat to please yourself, but dress to please others.

—Benjamin Franklin, statesman and inventor

Looking sharp with the best—John DeLorean,
VP and GM of Chevrolet.

n the previous chapter, I made several comments about your appearance and the influence it could have on the impression you make with others. The main emphasis was on cultivating good habits and behavior by paying attention to my list of *DON'Ts*. In this chapter, I'm going to focus on the most noticeable aspects of your appearance—how you dress and how well groomed you are. Nothing will make you feel better and more confident about yourself than knowing that you look sharp and are ready to take on the world. Give your image a boost by dressing with style and class. This doesn't mean being flashy. It means dressing with good taste.

Dress for Success

Unfortunately, over the years many retail businesses (auto and furniture, in particular) have been tagged with bad reputations for how their salespeople dress, especially the men. They've often been pictured as dressing with "loud" colored jackets and slacks with print patterns that could give you an instant migraine. When you add cheap glittering jewelry to the picture, you've got what amounts to a greeter at a disco bar right out of the '70s. And then when they start *fast-talking* the customer, the picture is complete. Yes, it's true we had some of those back then but, to be fair, so did every other business and industry at that time. We had one guy, Larry, who always wore white shoes, paisley print slacks, and psychedelic-patterned ties. He thought he was making a really "cool" impression on his prospects. I thought he might be auditioning for John Travolta's role in *Saturday Night Fever*.

While you might be able to spot one of these flashy dudes a mile away, you couldn't find a decent paycheck in any of their pockets if you had them frisked at a police station. These *were not* the success stories. Whether you're a guy or a gal, this is *not* who you want to be.

So who should you be? How should you look? Right behind the front door of my home is a mirror with a sign above it that says, "Would I buy *me* today?" This is the last thing I see before I leave for work. I see my hair. I see my clothes. I notice if I'm well groomed or not. I see the complete picture of what prospects are going to see when they come in to see me. That's where it all begins for me.

William Shakespeare probably said it best years ago: "All the world's a stage, and all the men and women merely players. They have their exits and their entrances, and one man in his time plays many parts." Before you leave your home for work, look in the mirror and ask yourself, "Am I dressed right for the part I'm going to play today? What kind of a package am I about to present?" Specifically, "Do I have *eye* appeal and *buy* appeal?" If you see something that isn't quite right, don't leave. Maybe the tie is wrong or the pantyhose just isn't the right shade. FIX IT! You're not ready to go yet!

If you don't correct your appearance before you get to work, especially if you're in sales, be prepared to get a lot of what I used to call "be back" talk from potential customers. "Well, Joe, I'll be back" or "I'll get back to you. I need to talk this over with my wife (or husband)." The real message here is that they saw or heard something they didn't like. Quite often they just didn't like the "package" on the other side of the desk—YOU. What's frustrating is that this is something you CAN do something about. Get in touch with your customers. Know who they are. Learn to fit in with them. Be who they want you to be.

Many of my customers were blue-collar workers. So I was careful not to overdress and make them feel uncomfortable or, worse yet, envious. If that's your buyer, keep the alligator shoes and silk suits in the closet. If anything, dress down slightly. They might even feel a little sorry for you, and that can't hurt. When I say dress down a little, I'm not telling you to wear socks or shoes with holes. I am telling you to not look like you've got the most expensive designer casual wear money can buy. You might as well be in a tux or evening gown if you're going to do that. Be smart about your dress. Remember, you're there to make them feel comfortable so you can close the deal.

We've all heard this term used many times before: *dress for success*. It was the title of a book written by John Molloy and published back in 1975. The book examined the effect of clothing on a person's success in both business and personal life. He provided many great insights that remain true today. Two years later, he launched a second book, *The Women's Dress for Success Book*. Both books popularized the idea of "power dressing." And that's what your appearance really means—putting the power of how you look and come across to others in your hands. You're in control. The image you present to others must always reflect the positive qualities of the person you want others to come to know as WHO YOU ARE. Don't let your appearance get in the way of your success. Separate yourself from the crowd and *dress the part*. I was always drawn to the best groomed and most tastefully dressed person whenever I shopped in a retail environment. I just felt really good when the person who walked over to me had a nice suit (and smile) on to greet me. They appeared confident and successful, and that's who I wanted taking care of me. In contrast, a scruffy looking person with scuffed up shoes sent all the wrong signals to me. I started "filling in the blanks" about them immediately. They *appeared* unaware, uniformed, and uncaring. That's not who I wanted to do business with. Understand, this is not about being judgmental or not giving someone a chance. It's about making decisions based on what you see that could impact your business dealings positively or negatively. *It's all about business*. The shabby look loses.

If you wanted to see a confident and smartly dressed business executive at his best, John DeLorean, vice president and general manager of Chevrolet, took first prize every time. He was sharp and smart. His image and presence were tailor-cut with class that drew admiration the minute he walked into a room. He not only looked the part, he *was* the part. James Bond had nothing on this man.

Groomed for Success

There are other equally important aspects of your appearance
that influence both how you look and how you come across to
others. And, yes, some of them are personal. If they weren't
important, they wouldn't be in this book. Some of them may
sound like very small or petty suggestions, but remember why
you're doing this—*nothing* should be allowed to get in the
way of influencing the people you meet to do what you want
them to do. I call these *Girard's Eight Rules of Body Care
and Good Grooming*:

1. **Shower or bathe daily.** You'll not only look better and feel
   better, but others will not be turned off by your presence.
   We once had a sales rep who didn't seem to be very aware of
   this until one day someone (thoughtfully) put a private note
   on his desk anonymously. Things changed for the better
   from that moment on. It was the only time I was ever in his
   office. Enough said on that. As I mentioned in the last chapter, if you use a cologne, make sure it's not overpowering.

2. **Take care of your hair.** First of all, shampoo regularly.
   Dandruff is a big turnoff. Make sure your haircut or hairdo
   is in current fashion too. I don't mean spiking it or painting it purple, either. How do you know what style to wear?
   Simple. Unless you're Lady Gaga, if your hair calls attention
   to itself and upstages YOU, it's the wrong look. *Observe how
   successful people in business wear their hair* and always
   keep it well combed and brushed. Resist the temptation to
   "make a statement" by turning a done deal into a lost sale
   just because your hair turned a potential customer off. Use
   your head here and make sure what's "on top" of it matches
   the smarts beneath it (for the better, that is).

3. **Use makeup sparingly.** Ladies, start by applying it carefully to emphasize your best features. "War paint" is out.
   Your goal is to positively influence someone, not conquer

them. The traditional Japanese geisha look is beautiful and elegant—just not on a sales call.

4. **Shave as often as necessary.** Guys, this one's for you. Shave twice a day if necessary. "Five o'clock shadows" are no excuse. The appealing unshaven look of an NFL quarterback may work in a beer commercial, but it doesn't get it in the real world of business. It's simple enough to keep an electric shaver or small razor at work. Use a good aftershave that's not overwhelming.

5. **Manicure your nails regularly.** This one applies to the ladies. A color that complements your hands is best. Extra-long dagger-like nails painted in black or flaming red send all the wrong signals.

6. **Keep nails clean and trimmed.** If you're a man, manicuring your nails is a matter of personal preference. However, keeping them trimmed and clean is a must for everyone. Stains from cigarettes or a garage project you worked on at home the night before can be a major distraction, especially when your hands become more visible when seated around a table and documents are being reviewed. Remember—NO DISTRACTIONS.

7. **Keep physically trim.** I talked about the importance of this in the book's first chapter, "Make a Healthy Choice." You want to look your best. If you're not on an exercise program, then get on one now. Al Roker (of NBC TV and the Weather Channel) has done a remarkable job of controlling his weight over the years with proper exercise and diet. Talk to your doctor and ask how you can safely get those extra pounds off. Believe me, you'll feel more confident than ever, and, most importantly, it's great for your health. People will see this as an indication of how you take care of important things (like their business dealings with you).

8. **Check your posture.** Here's a quick way to remember what proper posture should be: WINNERS never slouch, whether

they're standing or sitting. Period. You should always stand tall and walk tall with your shoulders back and your belly in. That's not arrogance—that's *confidence*.

If you remember to follow these simple suggestions about your appearance, you'll always look like someone who cares, is confident, and is successful. That's the image you want. Now all you need to do is drop that image into a smart outfit and you're good to go. "But exactly what should I wear?" you ask.

The most important thing to remember about clothing is to first dress appropriately. You don't wear a tuxedo or evening gown to sell pots and pans to someone. By the same token, you don't wear jeans, a T-shirt, and sneakers if you're presenting to a group of board executives at a Fortune 500 company. It's not about your personal preferences. It's about using common sense and remembering *why* you're there. We talked a lot about this in the previous chapter. Believe it or not, people dress inappropriately quite often.

We've all seen people who seem to be totally underdressed or overdressed for an occasion. In some cases, it's almost ridiculously funny. But the joke is on the person wearing the clothes. I get a kick out of seeing what some of the stars wear to the Oscar and Emmy award TV shows. Sometimes it's hard to find a guy in a tux. In their world, blue jeans rule if they so choose.

That isn't how it is in our world, though—the real world—where making a living isn't filled with glamour. Like it or not, in our world most people will make *appearances* of success or failure decisive factors in determining a person's capacity to provide good service. It may seem unfair, but that's the real world. Get over it and get in step. Sadly, many would-be success stories don't have a clue as to why they can't get ahead in this world. In my opinion, all they need to solve their problem is a sober mind and a mirror. The next step would be to FedEx them a copy of this book.

Not everyone looks the same in certain types of clothing. If you're a man, and depending on your size, height, and shape, a certain cut to a suit doesn't look as well on one person as it does on another. That's also true of certain fashions. Most fashions are moving targets that change with the wind. So don't get too attached to a certain lapel shape or tie because they'll be out of style before you know it. You'll be better off picking out something that's a little less trendy but will stay in style longer. It's easier on the pocketbook too.

That Million-Dollar Look

The best advice I can give (and this applies to both men and women alike) is to keep these guidelines in mind when deciding *what to wear* and how to look. Let's call these *Girard's Eight Rules Concerning Clothing*:

1. **Buy the best clothing you can afford.** Yes, it's true that quality clothing costs a little more, but it will look better and last longer than a cheap outfit. When you're looking at different clothes, think of them as investments in your career. Ask yourself, "Will this help my image?" When you decide what's right for you, make sure it fits you well. Nothing baggy or so tight that buttons are ready to pop off. You know the rule by now—NO DISTRACTIONS.

2. **Build a complete wardrobe.** You should always be careful to select clothing that's appropriate for work, for dressing up, and for more casual and leisure activities. If you go about it smartly, you can select good-quality clothes that can often be mixed and matched into other outfits. That'll help stretch your buck a little further as well as give you a little more variety.

3. **Dress for the occasion.** This one I commented on just a little earlier in this chapter. Be smart here and use common

sense. If you're not sure what to wear, especially if it's a more formal occasion, ask. Find out if it's a "black tie" event *before* you show up in your corduroy jacket and loafers. If you're going to a football game, leave the tux at home. For everyday business attire, go with a smart, neutral look that doesn't overpower the color wheel.

By the way, neutral means smart and classy, not boring. YOU want to overpower the suit, not the other way around. If you're wearing bright orange, you better be damn good at what you do; otherwise, you won't stand a chance by blinding your customers.

4. **Hang your clothing properly.** Even the finest-quality clothing will not help you *dress the part* if it starts to lose its shape. Treat your investment in good-quality clothing with respect by hanging your clothes neatly on hangers. This goes for suits, sweaters, dresses, slacks, or anything for which maintaining shape is important.

5. **Have your clothing cleaned and pressed regularly.** Nothing will get in the way of selling yourself any faster than stains, spots, and wrinkles on your clothes. Why broadcast what you had for lunch with a mustard stain on your tie? As a practical matter, keeping your clothes clean and neat will also help them wear better and last longer.

6. **Choose accessories that complement, not distract.** I mentioned a few things about distractions earlier in this chapter. This is especially true about accessories. For example, a "loud" tie on a man is a distraction. This also applies to oversized belt buckles, shirts with wide stripes, or a suit with, for example, a high-contrasting color plaid pattern. If it's instantly attention-getting, *don't put it on for work*. These are not the things you want the person across from you concentrating on when you're trying to close a deal or get a point across to them. This is also true for large dangling earrings on a woman. Save them for Saturday night. And ladies, the charm bracelets are, well, not so charming for the office.

Notice how people dress on TV talk shows, especially news and business programs; they're almost always wearing clothing that lets you focus on them and what they're saying. They know *their message is the most important thing* on their agenda, not what they're wearing. Look smart and sharp. That's what successful people do, and that's exactly what you should be doing.

By the way, accessories aren't just fancy cufflinks, oversized Rolex watches, or earrings and necklaces. Accessories, in my book, are more than just the obvious things that are on the outside—they're what are *inside* as well. "What do you mean by that, Joe?" you ask. If you've got a nice, neat appearance with shined shoes, why not add something that will shine right through your eyes? Give your look some *personality*. Show off your *positive attitude* and unmistakable *enthusiasm*. And while you're at it, why not dress your face with a *smile*? These are the *real* accessories that give you that "million-dollar" winning look. Now you're the complete package. That's what you want your customers or people you do business with to see.

7. **Match your shoes to your wardrobe.** For men, keep your shoes to basic browns and blacks for work. Don't fall into the trap of putting on some loud patent leather shoe that looks like you're going to a Caribbean pool party. Yes, you'll be noticed, but for all the wrong reasons. Make sure you have separate footwear for business, dress-up, and casual occasions, and for heaven's sake, don't get your events confused. Ladies, tastefully matched shoes to wardrobe always make a good impression and tell people you're one who cares about appearance.

8. **Take care of your footwear.** If you've invested good money in a quality pair of shoes, by all means use shoetrees to help them keep their shape. Watch for scuffmarks and replace worn heels. For everybody, please, please, remember

to keep your shoes shined every day, not once a month. It takes only 30 seconds on the way out the door to work. (You heard it from a shoeshine veteran.)

If you pay attention to these eight guidelines for clothing, they'll go a long way toward helping persuade others that you're the person they should be doing business with.

Investing in YOU

I know I've been harping on a lot of detail. But that's the critical factor here. The picture of WHO you are is not about any one thing. It's the *sum of all the little things* that come together to tell the world who you are. So when I say don't wear a loud tie or a charm bracelet, what I'm telling you is, "Why drop the ball on an opportunity that was 99 percent there except for that one little thing?" I wasn't perfect, but I didn't make those kinds of mistakes. My success was based on a lot of things coming together to make a complete winning package. And that's what you should be doing. Do everything you can to make yourself the most *buyable package* from top to bottom—no mistakes in between.

Can all this happen overnight? Can someone transform herself on a Thursday so that on Friday she is a totally different-looking and feeling person? Realistically speaking, probably not, but *dressing the part* can probably be done a lot faster than most other things that have an impact on your success. In fact, as we've just reviewed, a lot of what you may need to do doesn't involve buying anything. It involves taking a close look in the mirror and making some instant changes.

I know, for me, appearance was always a thing I was very aware of from the time I was a youngster. Maybe it was because we didn't have much back then that I was so tuned in to what others had and how they looked. As a result, one thing I learned to do many years ago is observe people. I studied their appearance and habits. I could tell by just looking and listening to people if they were the "real thing." In almost all cases, appearance was a tipoff.

I mentioned John DeLorean of General Motors earlier and what a positive image he carried in part because of his appearance. The other side was also true. In my business, flashy clothing (not always, but usually) was a dead giveaway that the person was "all sizzle and no steak." Once I got to know some of them, it was very clear that they also had inferiority complexes they tried to hide with cheap jewelry. It was the same predictable performance—they talked too much and too loud. They were fakes. To me it was so obvious that I knew their prospects couldn't help but notice it too. It was as though these guys all took a crash course from the "school of bling" out of desperation to succeed.

As I grew up, I believed there was a distinct connection between success and appearance that created the winning image. That was a big driver for me personally. Although I wasn't able to afford the best-quality clothing when I first got started, I always looked better the next month than I did the one before. Appearance became a continuous growth process that matched my success pattern. For me, wearing nice-quality clothing wasn't something I rewarded myself with for doing something well or achieving some goal. I believed a sharp appearance and image were *necessary tools* to getting into the winner's circle.

As such, quality clothing and good grooming were investments. Investments in me—Joe Girard. What could be more important than the impression you give someone the moment you meet? If you want to score runs, the first place you have to get to is first base. I must have known a thing or two because I hit a lot of "grand slams" in my career. Listen to what I'm telling you here!

Separating Yourself from the Pack

Dressing the part may seem like something people who want to get ahead in this world would do instinctively. You would think so. But that's not the case, especially today. When it comes to appearance, we live in a very freethinking and individualistic "anything goes" society. Even though some of you may think I cling to old ideas about appearance, *NOTHING COULD BE FURTHER FROM THE TRUTH!*

Some workplaces encourage a more "creative" casual atmosphere to promote innovation. A lot of the hi-tech companies like Apple would certainly fit that bill. Their founder and CEO, Steve Jobs, who many regard as a genius, was almost always seen dressed very casually, usually in jeans.

However, when you're talking about people who *represent* a company in a sales, marketing, or executive leadership position, people who are *making a pitch for new business*, you will be hard-pressed to see them dressed in anything other than smart business attire—Apple included.

If you take the time to study today's successful men and women, you will note, almost without exception, that regardless of whether they're in the medical field, law, education, retail sales, service, or construction industries, they all look a little bit more businesslike in their appearance. They always stand out, looking well groomed and confident. You always know who's in charge. For example, the successful manager running a machine shop always looks smarter in casual attire than the guy in coveralls on the line. The doctor will always be more distinctive in her lab coat than the nurse. It's more than just the stethoscope she has around her neck. It's mostly about embracing and projecting the image of leadership and looking the part that separates successful people from the pack. Why? They're winners! That's why. That's what I'm trying to pound into your head here.

Separate yourself from the pack. In my business, I always believed I was a one-of-a-kind person. My sales records attest to that. Appearance was a significant part of it. I believe that's one of the reasons I was so successful. I distanced myself from anything that felt wrong, looked wrong, or that would slow me down. Yes, I was different. I was SUCCESSFUL! And I loved that distinction most of all!

If you can't break with your "look" or the people you hang with because it's "who" you are, then fine. It's never too late to pass this book on to someone else who really wants to get ahead in life. Not everyone is cut from the same cloth. Life will have other things in store for you. If, on the other hand, you're really looking to make a change to your image for the better, even though you're not quite sure how to go about it, then your appearance and grooming should be the place to begin. As I said earlier, think of this as an investment—an investment in YOU. You're the most valuable stock you will ever own, so why sell yourself short when it comes to how you look to others?

I think one of the most disappointing wastes is to know someone who has extraordinary gifts and talent but will never get the opportunity to develop them to their fullest potential or capitalize on them in their lifetime. Why? For some unknown reason, they seem to be completely unaware of how poorly they appear or come across to others they're trying to persuade. It's like going to the plate with half a bat in your hand.

A friend of mine in the neighborhood where I live had a son in his early twenties. This kid really had something on the ball. He was a straight-A academic both in high school and college. He could have nailed practically any job he wanted after he graduated. He had one problem, though—his appearance. For someone who came from such a good and well-off family, he had a pretty scruffy appearance. You'd never know he graduated *cum laude* from one of the top universities in the state. His hair was long, he needed a shave, and his clothes looked as though he slept in them. He couldn't get past the interview stage anywhere he applied. Even in the face of lots of parental advice, he resented the intrusion into his life of having to "conform" to standards he thought were for a different generation. Somewhere along the way in college, he got involved in a rebellious group of students who preached the virtues of self-expression. He was going to be himself. And he was—jobless. He wasted away at least two years after he graduated doing odd jobs because he refused to see the light. Now he sulks at the world. It is so very sad because we knew this kid was so promising growing up.

As the great Renaissance inventor and artist Leonardo da Vinci used to say, "Wretched mortals. Open your eyes!" Look in the mirror.

Could you appeal to MOST PEOPLE, or just to a handful of weirdos you know who couldn't put a single loaf of bread on your kitchen table? Is that your target audience? GET SMART!

The perfect situation will occur when you make a complete transformation. That is, when you make a positive change to your appearance that coincides with a similar change in how you feel about things in life. *I am living proof of that transformation.* If you're only prepared to make a change to your outward appearance where you work for practical reasons because it has an impact on your career and how much you may earn, then at the very least do that part. *You're there to be what others need you to be.* You can live your double life on weekends on your own time. Who knows? One day you might see the light and make a complete transformation into a complete person with the positive outlook on life that is to be respected at work, admired by friends, and, most importantly, loved and looked up to by family.

Dressing the Part Gets You on the Fast Track FAST

Becoming successful is undoubtedly a challenge no matter what field you're in. Whether you sell, service, or counsel people, your success will be dependent on many things coming together. This book—*My 13 Essential Rules of Selling*—embraces this idea to the fullest by bringing together all the critical areas you need to focus on to help you reach your potential and create the complete winning package for success in business as well as in life. It's all here in one volume—this book. I want to remind you that the threat of failure is always present to take you off the path to success and down the alley where the losers live. And there will most certainly be times when you will be tempted to give up and settle for an ordinary kind of life. But *failure is never final. Giving up is.* That's an outcome YOU determine.

I know some of you believe that everything that happens in life is a matter of luck—some have it and some don't. I'm not going to debate that with you. I will tell you this, though. **The smarter you are, the luckier you become.** You can take that to the bank. Be smart. Give your confidence level a boost. *Dressing the part* is the quickest path to getting your image back on track on the path to success. Pay attention to all the small details of how you look to the rest of the world. Look in the mirror and see what others see. Are you satisfied with what they will see? That is your appearance. To them, your appearance is your image. And your image is who you are to them. That's the only YOU there is to them. There is no other. Make sure they see YOU. *Dress the part.*

PART II
INTERACT

RULE SEVEN

LISTEN

It is the province of knowledge to speak.
It is the privilege of wisdom to listen.

—Oliver Wendell Holmes, physician and author

I'd whisper to them, "You can make a lot of money with your ears."

Up to this point in the book (Chapters 1–6), we have concentrated on the first six of *My 13 Rules*—what you do in *preparation* to get ready to interact with potential customers and other people you come in contact with who are important to you, including family and friends. This next set of rules, Chapters 7–10, will focus on *interaction*. Now we'll be putting those preparation skills you've been learning into action. I'll show you how to apply some very dynamic traits that will change you dramatically. They will make the difference between success and failure. This chapter will center on perhaps the most critical aspect of interaction—*listening*.

Ears Open, Lips Sealed

When you first meet someone, the natural thing is to think of something to say once you've exchanged greetings and introductions. Wrong! Don't do that. Say nothing. Think about listening. If you train yourself not to speak first, you stand a much better chance of minimizing your mistakes. A good rule of thumb to follow in life is, "Your ears will never get you in trouble. Your mouth is a different matter." You will find that the top people in all professions are as skilled in listening as they are in talking. This is a hard concept for some people to grasp. They can't imagine making a positive impression without talking. The truth is more often just the opposite.

The best way to sell yourself is to let the other person do most of the talking. Unless they begin with direct questions about a vehicle, I rarely ever begin by talking about what type of vehicle they're looking for. *I focus first on their favorite topic: themselves*. That's something they know a lot about. I want to know what makes them tick.

» Where are they from?

» Do they have a family of their own?

» What's their profession?

» Do they like to travel?

» What hobbies interest them?

Get them comfortable by making them feel like a full participant in the conversation instead of just a spectator. That works even better if they have big egos because people with big egos love having a good audience. The more the prospect talks, the more they reveal about themselves to you. *Just listen.* The more you understand about their needs and wants, the better equipped you'll be to provide them with the right solution. *They're offering you money, pal. Listen to them.* The only thing you should be doing right now is "stalking your prey." Pick up their signals and cues. Think of yourself as playing a high stakes poker game. You want the other guy to tip his hand first. Only then can you play the winning card, not before.

Listen with *All* Your Senses

Whether you realize it or not, how people feel about the conversation they're having with you is not always communicated with the spoken word. Quite often the most important message they will send doesn't include a single sound from their lips. Their main message to you can come simply in the form of *body language*. Let me say it again—*body language*. That's right. It is crucial that you understand this. If you don't, you will miss one opportunity after another without knowing why. You must learn to "listen" with *all* your senses, not just your ears. What are they telling you?

Start by using your eyes. Notice how your prospects are dressed.

» Do they appear successful, or just getting by?

» Are they giving off signs of nervousness, impatience, or disinterest in what you're saying?

» Does your sense of smell tell you anything important? Maybe they're not that well groomed.

» Are they wearing too much perfume?

» Can you smell liquor or cigarette smoke odors?

» What does your sense of touch reveal?

> When you shook hands, was it a confident or a timid handshake?

> Was it a cold or warm hand?

> Was it a smooth hand or a workman's hand you touched?

You may think this is overanalyzing or more information than you need. If you do, you're dead wrong again! When you add up all the things you observe in others, using *all* your senses, you get a much more complete picture of the person you're dealing with and what they're really "saying" to you. The complete image becomes much clearer. What you visualize becomes reality. *But don't make the mistake of checking just one or two things out and jumping to conclusions.*

A customer came in to see me one Saturday morning (when we worked on Saturdays). She was an attractive young lady in her late twenties wearing a pair of nice-fitting jeans, a jacket, and an over-the-shoulder purse. I didn't see a wedding band, so I thought she was probably single (or maybe divorced). She seemed rather shy and not very talkative. I thought she might not have a very good job, and that led me to believe she might even be a credit risk. I figured at best I'd be putting her into one of our economy cars, where the commission wasn't as good as on a midsized car. All sorts of yellow flags started to go up, and she hadn't even said very much.

I could have *cut to the chase* and asked her if she had a line of credit from her bank to buy a car or if she was "just looking." That might have seemed rude, but it sure would have saved me a lot of time if my hunch was right. *I knew better, though.* Don't ever gamble on the things you make a living at. That is sacred. And it was a good thing I didn't. For the next 10 minutes, *I did a lot of listening.*

It turned out that Wendy was a brilliant graphic arts designer who had just recently moved from New York. She had just accepted an offer from a recruitment firm to become a corporate vice president heading up the creative department of one of the top ad agencies in town! Today was her day off. When she finally came around to the discussion of the type of vehicle she wanted, her mind was already made up.

Although I didn't have the exact color she wanted, I did have her second choice right there on the lot (that I packaged with a very attractive price if she'd take it that day).

We cut a deal, and Wendy opened up her purse (a beautiful Gucci leather bag upon closer inspection) to get her check-book out. She put an 80 percent down payment on the car right on the spot! She came back later that afternoon when the car was fully prepped and ready to go. Wendy happily drove away in a new white Corvette with all the bells and whistles! It turned out to be my biggest single vehicle commission of the month. By the way, those jeans she was wearing were top-of-the-line designer-marked slacks costing at least $250. **The lesson here is clear: Be observant. Be thorough. Don't jump to conclusions.**

Remember what I said in Chapter 6 about how I learned to be a very observant person from the time I was a kid shining shoes. That childhood discipline followed me into my professional life and had a lot to do with my success as I learned to size up people with precision.

Don't misunderstand how I did this. I didn't stare at people or make them feel uncomfortable as though they were being strip-searched by an airport body scanning detector. *I always observed by glancing with discretion.*

By choice I was a very busy person, but to sharpen my own skills, I would occasionally take a moment and just observe the other 41 salesmen on the showroom floor as they interacted with prospects. (Just a reminder, we didn't have any women selling back then.) In my office, I had a one-way glass window. Even though I couldn't hear them, because my office door was always closed, I would "listen" to them by observation. I could tell what was right or wrong about practically everything they were doing. I felt I had developed a sixth sense that became especially useful with *my* prospects.

Very few of the salespeople I worked with had any idea about using all their senses of observation for "listening." Most of them would make generalizations about people and would then charge off blindfolded to blow another golden opportunity. All they ever did was talk, talk, talk—talk themselves right out of a sale while the prospect just sat there helplessly trying to get a word in. The prospect was never able to tell the salesperson what they wanted because he was too busy telling them what *he thought* they should have. If only they could have seen what I saw from behind my one-way glass window. It was another picture worth a thousand words.

I remember observing a conversation going on between a salesman and a customer. Twenty minutes had gone by, and it occurred to me that none of the paperwork on the desk had moved at all—no catalogs, no pricing sheets, no pens or pencils. Nothing seemed to be happening. Then I noticed the customer start to slump back in his chair a bit. The salesman was doing all the talking, along with a lot of hand gesturing. The customer started to appear a bit anxious. He looked like he wanted to leave. And he did. He got up and excused himself rather abruptly, leaving the salesman sitting there with a look of disbelief on his face. What I saw was a salesman controlling the conversation to the point where the customer couldn't get a word in. If he saw what I saw, he would never do that again.

I told myself, "Joe, don't you ever do that. Let the customers take the lead. They'll let you in when the time is right."

My attentiveness to the smallest details about what I saw in other people helped me to understand who I was dealing with. Once I knew that, my instincts went into action to evaluate the situation accurately and very quickly. Over time I got better and better at this until reading people became second nature to me. I was able to capitalize on this skill and direct my efforts correctly so as to avoid making any stupid mistakes before it was too late. It was like being in the other team's huddle. I was reading the enemy's playbook. I wasn't listening with just my ears. I was paying attention with all my senses. My experience with Wendy was a good example of why I never made assumptions about any of my prospects until I first evaluated them thoroughly through personal observation.

My first experience becoming a good listener happened when I was a kid. Oddly enough, it wasn't because I had a real problem. It was because I didn't talk well. I stuttered badly from the time I was about eight years old. It all started about the same time my father began beating me. I can still remember the embarrassment it caused me. It got to the point that, rather than call attention to my stuttering, I went out of my way not to talk too much when I was with a group of kids.

As far as work went back then, what I was doing didn't require me to speak well. I was doing a lot of odd jobs growing up. After my shoeshine days were over, I was a newspaper carrier, dishwasher, dock loader, stove pipe assembler, and fruit and vegetable vendor. You name it and I probably did it.

Anyway, speaking well didn't really matter to me except, of course, for the social embarrassment it caused. About the only advice I got was to try and learn to talk slower. I suppose it helped some, but I didn't have that much pressure or motivation to do it—that is, until I became a retail salesperson. By that time I was 35 years old. Now I had to do something about it.

I taught myself to concentrate on what I was trying to say so that I would speak slowly and carefully. The more I concentrated and practiced, the more improvement I noticed until I overcame that handicap. Learning to overcome stuttering was one of the most important things that ever happened to me for two reasons:

1. *It forced me to* think *more thoroughly about what I was going to say. I began choosing my words more carefully.*
2. In the process of curing my stuttering, I also learned some solid fundamentals about communication and something very special that would prove itself to be invaluable to me in my career: I LEARNED TO LISTEN. And listening is the greatest tool you can have.

I'm not the only one that thinks that either. I believe when God gave us two ears and one mouth, He was trying to tell us something.

Did you know that practically everyone you ever come in contact with in life is trying to tell you something? They're continuously sending you signals and information about how they feel about their interaction with you. In a crowded airport when perfect strangers passing by each other make eye contact, here's what they may be "saying" to one another:

» "I'm not really paying much attention to you."
» "My, you're good looking. Too bad these three seconds are going to be our entire communication in life."
» "That wife of yours sure is a knockout."
» "Why are you looking at me like that?"
» "I like your suit."
» "Do you always wear that much makeup?"

Remember, not a single word was spoken in any of these examples.

Now in an actual one-on-one interaction, the signals will be more personalized:

>> When your bank teller smiles at you just before you leave, she's telling you, "Thanks for being a valuable customer (even if you have the smallest account in the bank)." When you smile back at her, you're telling her, "Thanks. You're a really nice person, and I hope you have a great day."

>> When someone pulls out in front of you in a parking lot with a smug glance, they're saying to you, "I'm not waiting any longer. I'm going now whether you like it or not."

>> When you sink a putt to win a golf match against another golfer, even a sporting smile can't hide their real message: "I'll get you next time."

>> When you know you've *hit a home run* with a competitive bid presentation you just made in front of key buyers, their eyes often reveal the truth about how they feel. They may say, "Thank you." But the real message is, "That was a great presentation, and we really appreciate how much time you put into it." You respond with, "It was my privilege to be considered for the project." But your returning eye contact and smile says, "When can I start?"

If you want to know what people are *really* telling you, then get *all* of your senses into the *listening game* and put the pieces of the puzzle together.

Very few people do this well. To me, listening has always been something I do with *all* my senses, not just my ears. It was one of the most important methods I used when doing home-work on my prospects and customers. I made it my business to know and understand who they were long before they came into my office. I knew if they were married, had kids, where they worked, what they were currently driving, their hobbies and interests, and even where they would take their vacations. How did I know all this? Yes, by research and pre-qualifying, but mostly by observation—*listening with* all *my senses.*

For example, if a prospect had a trade-in, I made sure I knew if that vehicle had any bumper sticker messages I should be aware of, like vacation destinations or clubs they might belong to, or if the back seat had baby seats in it—anything that would tell me something about that person. One customer had a sticker that identified him as a member of an antique car club. I asked him what type of car he had. It turned out to be a mint condition 1957 Chevy. I told him that was one of my favorites, and if he'd let me know the next time he was entering it in a show, I'd like to come down and see it. Before long, he was looking up dates and our conversation was already moving in the right direction.

Having that kind of knowledge enabled me to steer conversations to the things prospects liked to talk about. It relaxed them and made them feel comfortable. Before long, we were on common ground. It was the first step in getting them to exchange their money for my product, and that was the name of the game and the bottom line. I *knew* exactly who they were.

Don't let anyone tell you that you have to be a psychologist to know and understand people. Use your God-given senses and instincts, especially that other important sense—common sense. Believe me, you'll know more about people than you ever thought possible, and you'll come out a winner the way I did. Begin by listening.

I must tell you, in all modesty, when it came to being an observant detective, I learned to do this as thoroughly and as well as anyone I ever met. Even Sherlock Holmes would have a hard time measuring up to "Girard's magnifying glass."

Look Like a Listener

Perhaps the most important thing about listening you should remember is, *silence is golden.* Ask for the order, then remain quiet until your prospect speaks first. The more you sell at the wrong time, the smaller your chances are of closing the deal at the right time. We'll be discussing this in a lot more detail in Chapter 11, "Lock Up Every Opportunity." For now, the thing to remember is that no matter where you are in your career— whether you're a seasoned veteran or just starting out—you must first learn to listen if you're going to be successful.

This advice doesn't apply only to people in sales, either. I don't care if you're a teacher, a doctor, a lawyer, a plumber, an electrician, or someone who works on the assembly line. Your ability to listen will become evident in the way you understand and follow instructions as well as solve problems. Before long, that skill and ability (or lack of) will quickly identify WHO YOU ARE to those who work with you. If you're not listening or paying attention, you'll quickly find yourself on the path to nowhere.

I remember a meeting I had with a remodeling designer who came over to our house to discuss some custom work I wanted done on my home to enlarge and enhance a particular area. My wife and I were very specific about what we wanted, right down to the materials for the walls and floors. After he heard what we told him we wanted, he immediately started to *tell us what he thought we should have.* He just kept talking and talking. It was as though he hadn't heard a single word we said. I thought maybe he was going to tell us there was a structural problem in our idea or that we would get some great savings by picking a special package he was offering. Nothing like that happened at all.

Although he had a good reputation in the area, I honestly didn't know what to make of his comments. It turned out what he was proposing was not only going to cost more but also wasn't anything like what we were looking for—*two strikes if Girard is umpiring this.*

I explained to him *again* that's not what we just told him we wanted. He grew impatient and said that we'd be better off if we followed his idea since he'd done this particular design many times. That comment irritated me quite a bit. I didn't want to pay extra for what was easy for him. I wanted a unique custom look for our home. Period. Girard called him out—*that was strike three!*

Three things happened because he didn't *listen*:

1. He lost the sale.
2. I couldn't give him a recommendation to any of my friends and family.
3. We were back to square one looking for a new supplier (which we eventually found and are very happy with the results).

If you're one of those people who doesn't listen or pay attention because you can't keep your mouth shut, sooner or later you'll have all the time in the world to talk and tell others why you lost your job. The only problem is they won't be listening. To the rest of the world, YOU'RE AS GOOD AS DEAD.

If you want to learn a lot about yourself and who you are, then try listening, not to yourself but to others. You'll be amazed at what you will learn. You'll start to picture yourself as others see you, and that's a significant development. When you're in a fact-finding session with someone, let them see you taking notes (even if you don't need them). Demonstrate your interest in truly understanding what the prospect needs. Remember, you don't communicate just verbally. Let them see this caring side of you. When they smile, you smile. When they feel down, be supportive and understanding. Get on their side of the table. The more people notice you intently listening to them, the more likely they're going to be doing business with you or be persuaded by your point of view.

To put it simply, listening shows that you care more about them than about yourself. *Give your customers your complete and undivided attention.* Win them over with this technique. They will begin to see you in a totally different light. You will be thought of as more than someone who sold them a product or service. To some, you will become a sounding board for their challenges. To others, you may become a trusted counselor or someone who went the extra mile to help them. To another group, you may be looked upon as a role model they should try to be like. When you reach this point in your relationship with a customer, you are planting the seeds of trust and longevity that will pay dividends again and again and again in the future.

A young lady came into my office one day to discuss purchasing a small family car for herself. She was a single mom with two small, well-dressed daughters. Although she had a decent job as a nurse, her divorce was fairly recent, so she hadn't had the opportunity to establish much of a credit rating for herself. Unfortunately, this is one of the things single women had to deal with back then more than they do now. I decided to make every effort I could to try to get her a credit break with one of the banks I did a lot of business with. It took a few calls, but it worked and she got the loan approved.

I could tell by her smile when she came in the next day to pick up the car that I had brought a little sunshine into her life that might have otherwise been missing for a while. Sometimes *listening* is best done with the heart.

A Lesson in Listening

I don't have to tell you how important repeat business is in any industry. That's how I made as much as I did during my career. I knew how important getting those customers back was, so I worked at sharpening my listening skills my entire career. But I too had to learn that lesson the hard way. I can remember a very specific instance early in my career when I took my eye off the ball for a moment and it cost me a sale. But it was a valuable lesson. A well-known contractor came in to see me one day to buy a loaded, top-of-the-line model. After going through all the steps with this prospect, including a demo ride, I handed him the pen to sign the purchase agreement.

He balked, politely excused himself, and left. I couldn't figure out what happened. "How did I blow this sale?" I asked myself. Later that evening, when I was going through my meditation process as I reviewed the day, I could only think about that failure. I kept pressing myself for an answer to the question, "What went wrong?" Finally, as the evening wore on, I couldn't stand it any longer. I picked up the phone and called Dominic. I told him that if I wanted to become a better salesman than I was that afternoon, I needed to know what I did or said that made him leave without buying.

"Dominic, would you tell me what I did wrong?" I asked.

He said, "You're serious, aren't you?"

"You bet I am."

"Alright. ARE YOU LISTENING NOW?" he said bluntly.

"I'm all ears."

"Well, you weren't this afternoon."

He then proceeded to tell me that he had just made up his mind to buy from me when, in a moment of final hesitation (after all, he was plunking down a lot of dough for this model) and to ease his mind, he started to tell me how proud he was of his son, Jimmy, who was studying to be a doctor. He talked about his son's academic and athletic achievements as well as his ambitions. As he recalled these comments from our meeting, I must confess I couldn't remember him saying any of it. I was obviously not focused and not listening to him. He went on to say that he had noticed (the customer has keen senses too) I didn't seem to care much. It was as though now that I had this sale clinched, I didn't need to show any interest in anything he had to say anymore, not even something that was dear to his heart. And that's when he began to lose interest in me and the product I was selling him. In his mind, he went from being a customer to a guy with a checkbook. I only listened to him when I was qualifying him because that's all that was IMPORTANT TO ME. The truth of the matter was that he had far greater needs than transportation; he needed to be complimented on something that was more important to him, a son who was his pride and joy—something I rapidly dismissed. In other words, I BLEW IT!

You might say, "Why was it that important whether you listened to the story about his kid or not? You had the product he needed at the right price. That's all that really mattered. After all, that's what he came in for. Right?" Wrong again. I have said repeatedly in this book that the product or service a customer buys from you is YOU before it is anything else. What he was really buying that afternoon, along with the car, was me. And quite frankly, on that particular day, I didn't measure up. At the end of the conversation, I apologized to him for not paying attention and thanked him for being so straightforward with me. I also told him that no wonder his son was doing so well because he had a very special dad who cared so very much about him. My parting comment to him was, "Perhaps the next time you'll give me a second chance and buy from me."

I learned two lessons from that experience. First, failing to recognize the importance of listening carefully can cost you a sale. Second, if I took that lesson to heart, maybe, just maybe, I could one day recapture that lost sale. Those were the lessons I never forgot from that day forward. I never made that mistake again. And yes, there was a next time. Dominic did buy from me. I did recapture that sale.

Stop Talking!

We all know people who just love to talk, talk, and talk. It gets to the point that listening to their silence becomes a very gratifying experience because it's so rare.

Why don't they just shut up?

Don't they realize this is hurting their business and personal relationships?

Don't they have a clue how annoying this is to others around them?

How can they possibly not know this when it's so obvious to everyone else?

That's just it. In most cases, they are not aware. They've been this way for so long, they don't see things from the other person's perspective. There are undoubtedly many medical reasons as to why some people behave or act in ways that others do not. Fortunately, talking constantly is a trait that's easy to fix if you follow this simple advice. I call it *Girard's Success Pattern*: LISTEN. THINK. SPEAK.

First you listen to what's being said. Pay careful attention to the details of the message. Then you digest the message. Take a moment to THINK about what it means and how it impacts the outcome you're looking for. After you've thought about and analyzed its meaning, you're then in a position to evaluate it and reply with the correct response. When you reply, be precise and make sure you respond to what's being said. Don't rush your words. Relax and SPEAK clearly. Select your words carefully, using as few as needed to make your point, but be warm in your delivery. Remember, you're trying to engage the prospect with trust and, yes, a little TLC—Tender Loving Care. A smile wouldn't hurt either.

There's an old saying: "The less you say, the more you say." On the other hand, if you talk too much, you stand a very good chance of making the wrong statement about yourself and talking yourself right out of an opportunity. I'll always remember what my friend, the great preacher and author Dr. Norman Vincent Peale, who wrote the bestseller *The Power of Positive Thinking*, said: "The less you say, the more you *heard*." What he said is so true. In other words, if you're not talking, then you must be listening. When the person you're with notices you listening to them intently, their positive impression of you grows. Your silence "speaks" loudly to them. You're actually saying, "The less I say to you, the *more* I say to you." They know you respect them. You're the kind of person they want to be with or do business with. And that's *the power of positive listening*. I wish I had a dollar for every time I've watched salespeople make a sale and "buy it back" in five minutes because they couldn't keep their mouths shut. I can't even begin to tell you how many times I've watched some of our salesmen shoot themselves in the foot just when they had "the bride at the altar."

I remember getting a drink of water at the fountain and overhearing a customer tell a salesman about the size of a fish he had recently caught and how proud he was of the catch. Instead of complimenting the man, the salesman responded with, "That ain't nothin'. You should have seen the one I caught!"

When coming back from a demo ride, I noticed another customer pulling out a photo of her three-year-old girl as her eyes lit up with pride. The salesperson said, "Wanna see a picture of my kids?"

The lesson couldn't be more simple: Nobody gives a damn about *your* fish or *your* kids—NOT AT THIS MOMENT. It's all about HIS FISH and HER KID! *Stop Talking!* We all know that light travels faster than sound. *This story proves why some people appear bright until you hear them speak.*

The Need to Be Heard

We've been talking a lot about business situations in which listening is key to understanding what your client or prospect wants or needs. It's not something that pertains to just selling, either. Teachers need to be tuned in to their students to help them with their education. Priests and other clergy members listen to console those in need. (Our local parish priest certainly gave me strength during my wife June's final days.) Lawyers need to listen intently to their clients to prepare effective cases. And certainly politicians need to listen to the voice of the people they represent in order to enact effective legislation. Doctors need to listen to their patients to assist in their diagnosis. Perhaps the best example is psychiatrists. You seldom hear them talk. They're there to listen. Period. If more people would behave like psychiatrists, they'd get a lot further ahead in life. Listen!

Listening also plays a significant role on the home front in your family life. What your spouse has to say matters. If it affects you both, you need to listen because it's important to your future together. You don't dominate. You share. No one's "in charge."

You both have an equal role to play. That's how your love and respect for one another deepens and grows. *Listen. Think. Speak.* If you're a parent, listening is critically important when it comes to your kids. They have things to tell you. They have questions. They look to you to help them learn. Be a compassionate parent. Show them the love and care they deserve. Give them your undivided attention and *listen.* Many a child has made a left turn early in life because they had a parent, or parents, who never listened to them. They only told them what was wrong with them and turned a deaf ear to whatever the child said. Pretty soon they begin to believe they're not worth much. And that's when the trouble begins. I know. I was one of those kids. My father's indifference to me hurts to this very day. Thank God for my mother. There's nothing more satisfying in life than knowing that the people you care about most know that as well as you do. That message is never clearer to them than when they see you listening to them with love, respect, and with your undivided attention.

The Fine Art of Good Listening

When I was invited to speak before the student body at Harvard Business School, there were several hundred people in attendance that day. I guarantee you they didn't bring me in because they wanted to know how to sell cars and trucks! They had read about my success in several national business magazines. Word got around that I knew *how to reach people and satisfy their needs.* They thought I had a magic formula until I hit them with the *fine art of good listening.*

My message is all about people—how to reach them, and how to touch them deep down inside in their innermost secret place where all their important decisions are made. It is in that very spot that I firebrand the name Joe Girard on their hearts. From that moment on, they belong to me. I know them well because I LISTEN TO THEM! I listen to them with my entire being! That's why when people ask me: "How did you do it, Joe?" "How did you become the world's greatest retail salesperson?" I tell them I started by *listening* first. The rest is history.

So how do you go about being a good listener? Before you can become a truly good listener, you must first make an honest effort to *pay attention* to what is being said to you. This means blocking everything else out and *focusing* on the message. The biggest trap most people fall into is that when someone else is talking, they think that's the time to prepare for what they want to say next. They're so focused on what they're going to say that they completely miss the message that's being communicated right then and there. And that can have disastrous results if they're supposed to be picking up important signals. In fact, there have been studies indicating only 50 percent of what's said is actually "heard" (or registers). What a waste! HALF! HALF OF WHAT THIS PLANET SAYS TO ITSELF FALLS ON DEAF EARS! No wonder we have so many political and social problems in the world. One of the world's greatest statesmen, Winston Churchill, had it right when he said, "Speech is silver and silence is golden." Is anybody listening?

I know I'm not as well-spoken as Churchill. In fact, I have a much more plain-talking approach to the subject of listening: SHUT YOUR MOUTH if you want to learn something! If you want to be "heard," keep quiet. In fact, when I'm in front of a group, I often walk toward them, and as I approach the edge of the stage, I grab hold of my ears. As I look down into their eyes, I slowly whisper so they hear me in a very personal way: "You can make a whole lot of money with these things." I don't leave that spot until I see that they "get it." We then smile back at each other, nodding in complete agreement and understanding. They "got it." When that communication takes place, we have officially listened to each other.

In many ways, the art of listening is similar to love. If you've ever noticed two people, hand in hand, strolling in a park or along the surf's edge on a beach, and you clearly recognized they were in love with one another, then you already understand the power of putting all your senses to work when you listen. The couple is communicating about their feelings with their eyes, with their touch, with their smiles. All their senses are engaged to tell each other how special they are to one another. They are in love—yet they haven't spoken a word. That is the art of effective communication. The art of good listening is the same way. Put all your senses to work to get in touch with what's around you. Be open and receptive to every detail you notice. That's how you go about being a good listener.

What are the steps to follow that will change just hearing someone's words into listening as an art form? We've been talking about several of them in this chapter, but here they are—12 of them—in a convenient list for you to review and reference:

1. **Keep your mouth shut** so your ears can stay open.
2. **Listen with all your senses.** Get the whole story.
3. **Listen with your eyes.** Maintain eye contact. Focus on each word.
4. **Listen with your body.** Use body language to communicate. Sit up straight. Lean forward. Be alert.
5. **Be a mirror.** Smile when the other person smiles. Nod when she nods. Frown (with understanding) when she frowns.

6. **Don't interrupt.** Don't break the speaker's train of thought or irritate her.

7. **Avoid outside interruptions.** Hold all phone calls when in your office with a prospect, or go somewhere where interruptions are least likely.

8. **Avoid sound distractions.** Turn off cell phones, radios, TVs, background music. Nothing should compete with your prospect for attention.

9. **Avoid sight distractions.** Don't let an outside or inside office window view compete with you for the undivided attention of your prospect.

10. **Concentrate.** Pay attention to the other person at all times. Don't yawn, look at your watch, look at your fingernails, or do anything else that could make the prospect feel uncomfortable or unimportant.

11. **Listen "between the lines."** Try to hear the "fine print." Is the person "saying" something to you, just not with words? Read her body language.

12. **Don't be an ATANA (All Talk and No Action)** as I described in the Introduction to the book. Your action should be listening carefully.

Those are 12 steps for learning to listen. If you commit to following these guidelines as part of your daily plan, good listening habits will become second nature to you. In no time you'll be well on your way to mastering the fine art of good listening—an essential ingredient of all successful people.

Listen: A Gift to Cherish

Somebody once asked the question, "If you had to lose your sense of hearing or your sense of sight, which one would you give up first?" Most people said they'd find it the least difficult if they gave up their hearing. However, research indicates that people without sight generally make the adjustment in life more effectively than their counterparts who cannot hear. There are many great stories and examples of people who cannot see who develop an "inner eye," so to speak, and learn to "see" with great vision. Many have gone on to greatness in a variety of fields including literature, sports, and music.

While there are also some very accomplished and successful people who cannot hear, the loss of all sound can often place one in a very isolated and disconnected world of silence with greater challenges than those faced by people without sight.

Although learning good listening habits is something that can be taught, having the physical ability to be able to listen in the first place is something that cannot be acquired. That, my friend, is a gift from God and yet is something most take for granted. The next time you feel like not paying attention to what someone else is telling you, be thankful you have the tools and ability to do so.

I remember being touched very deeply some years back when I came across a young man who had an excellent singing voice. I was attending a theatrical performance of a musical in which he sang several songs before a packed house. His voice rang with resonance and feeling. It was beautiful to listen to. The audience responded with energetic applause. I noticed two people in the front row, in particular, applauding with great enthusiasm. After the show, I talked to the director of the performance, who was a friend of mine. He told me that the two people in the front row were the singer's parents. I remarked how very proud they must have been of this special moment. He said, "It was special indeed. Both his parents were born totally deaf. Never once have they heard the God-given talent of their son, and they never will." The director continued, "When I first learned that, I cried on the way home from one of our rehearsals." I was quite taken aback by this. But I believe, to this day, that they were "listening" to their son. They did "hear" him because they were listening with the greatest sense of all, greater than any of our five senses—they were *listening with the heart,* and I believe their son knew it.

At the outset of this book, I said *My 13 Rules* are about more than giving you the foundation to become successful in your careers. They apply to everything you do, in your personal life as well as in your professional life. I want to help you live a more complete, healthier, happier, and successful life in every way. We've talked a lot about attitude and being positive, but you cannot put any of that into practical use without listening. If you don't listen, you are not in touch with the world. You are spinning your wheels like a bus in quicksand. The weight of your ignorance will take you down every time. Unless you truly know what's being said, you can never get on the path to success. *LISTEN UP and TUNE IN!* Get on firm footing by listening with *all* your senses—and be thankful you can.

RULE EIGHT
SMILE

The world is made up of distant lands, yet the shortest
distance between any two people is still a smile.

—Anonymous

Kitty's radiant smile and hockey's greatest,
Gordie Howe.

have a small sign in my office that reads, "I saw a man who didn't have a smile, so I gave him one." I always remembered that saying and have tried most of my life to make that the very first thing I give someone. Perhaps it's because when I was a kid growing up, smiling was not something we did in our home when my father was around. It was as though it was forbidden— especially in my case. Whenever my brother and sisters and I joked around, it was never when he was present. The emptiness and bitterness I experienced growing up are probably the main reasons I value a smile so much. Thank goodness I had the love of my mother to balance things out. The people I used to see as a kid shining shoes in the bars never smiled. They hated their jobs and went to the bars to drown in their miserable lives. But I learned how to *reach* them. I made them smile by beaming the biggest grin they ever saw until I had them all thinking I was the luckiest kid in the world, and that's exactly what I wanted them to think. Joe Girard knew what he was doing even back then—*the bigger the smile, the bigger the tip*. In fact, in that picture I have of myself shining shoes as a nine-year-old kid, the smile I'm wearing is big enough to cover my shoeshine box (well, almost). Every time I look up at that photo, I smile right back at "little Joey" when I realize how far "we've" come.

Yes, I was unhappy as a child, but nobody in those bars knew it. Little did they know how much I was hurting. As the lyrics from the song "Smile," written by the great silent movie actor Charlie Chaplin, remind us, "Smile though your heart is aching." That was me growing up—smiling on the outside but crying on the inside. As I look back on those times, I actually believe that, without even knowing it, my father actually gave me a *gift*. Because smiling was something he never shared with me, I made up my mind that it would be something *I* would give freely and often to others. Sadly, that was his loss. And *that* is nothing to smile about.

Smile and the World Smiles with You

One of the greatest gifts God gave humanity was a smile. If you think the flu is contagious, try smiling at someone and see what happens. I'll bet the odds are ten to one you'll get one back—*with interest.* They're not only smiling back, they're feeling good too—and all because of YOU. A smile makes people feel special, appreciated, respected, and recognized. You can't do any of that any better or any faster with just words. A smile is genuine because it comes from the heart. And the person receiving it knows that. No matter where you go in this world, one thing remains true: *smile and the world smiles with you.* You don't even have to speak the same language because a smile speaks them all. The next time you're having difficulty communicating with or reaching a person, remember, the best place to start is with a *smile.*

There were many times when I knew that my smile made the difference. I have had countless people tell me that they were drawn to my smile the minute they walked in the showroom. One couple even told me they felt so good about our discussions that they even decided to go for a brighter yellow color as a result of feeling so positive. Now that's what I call putting on a happy face!

Smiles never go up in price or down in value. In fact, they actually increase your "face" value. Smiling is great for your health, too. We all know it takes fewer muscles to smile than it does to frown. The reasons to smile are almost endless. But what does it *really* mean in your day-to-day affairs?

Smile Your Way to Success

No matter what we do professionally, most of us are in a competitive game to try and achieve positive outcomes with the people we do business with before someone else does. It takes a lot of prep work to get ready for the challenges we face each day. It's not any one thing either. Many things have to come together in just the right order so we can be at our very best. We have to be organized. We have to look the part. And we have to listen. But the very first thing a customer or prospect will see before anything else is your face and the expression you wear. That's where it all begins—every time. If you train yourself to have a smile every time you come in contact with the people who matter most to you in your work (and in your personal life), you'll be on the right path to *smiling your way to success*. I don't care what you call your contacts: prospects, customers, clients, patients, students. Who knows? They could even be inmates if you're a counselor. Everyone responds positively to a smile. If an initial positive impression is your goal, then this is the place to begin.

That's where I began. The impression I made on customers is what made me. And I didn't learn that in school, folks. I learned it shining shoes. Even back then, I noticed if I smiled first, I'd get one in return. I also noticed I often got an extra tip for making someone feel better even for just that moment. That became my business plan from then on. Attack with a smile and then conquer. I practice that same technique to this day.

Whenever I meet someone, I try to imagine them wearing a sign that says: "MAKE ME FEEL IMPORTANT." When you make someone feel important, they are often willing to buy or even consider purchasing their second choice. That's when you really know you've got what it takes to make a positive impression on someone. This is especially important in difficult situations. I became a master at heading off problems before they arrived. If someone was coming in to see me "loaded for bear" about something, maybe a product or service issue, I could disarm them with my genuine smile. If I tried to match their frown with mine, I'd have nowhere to go. We'd both lose. Plain and simple—I needed them more than they needed me. Do you get the point on this? Remember, you're not picking friends here. Every time you "let one of them go" by frowning at them, it's like letting coins slip through your fingers and into the hands of someone else. In other words, you've lost. The place to begin is with a smile because A SMILE NEVER DISAPPOINTS.

Sometimes life deals us some pretty lousy cards, and it's difficult to smile when things aren't going our way. *You never know what's troubling a person at any given time, so it's always best not to react until you know more about their situation.* Sometimes people want to be left alone until they sort things out on their own. Give them some space.

One customer came into my office to see me about purchasing a car. The truck he was driving was giving him trouble, and he felt he needed to get it replaced soon. He had just recently lost his wife to a terminal illness. I could tell by the sad look on his face he hadn't gotten over that and was not too focused on the discussion. I could identify with him immediately. He had a lot on his mind. He was seated across my desk from me. I placed my hand on top of his and told him how I had lost my wife earlier. When I smiled at him, he smiled back and thanked me. We understood each other completely.

I suggested he put off the purchase of the new truck for a few weeks. I offered to try and get him into a temporary lease on a demo car so he wouldn't have to worry about his truck breaking down. When he came back the following month to purchase the new vehicle, he told me he knew I was sincere in helping him by the genuine smile I gave him that day the previous month.

I could always tell when people I would meet were having troubles. They would sulk, frown, or shuffle about with their heads down. It was so obvious, I could hardly imagine anyone wanting to be around people like that. For many it wasn't a personal tragedy that was bringing this on; it was just their negative, downcast way of dealing with things that weren't going their way. They were beaten before they began.

I always tell people, "If you're not on the OBITUARY list today, you should be smiling." Even getting out of bed in the morning is something to smile about. Yes, it's the small things in life we take for granted. Like love, smiling should never be taken for granted. It should be worn as a cherished possession and given freely to others as a gift.

Look, we all have problems. The difference is, successful people know how to control and discipline themselves and *make the most* of the time and opportunities they have. To them, survival is an art form. They're never beaten. They never give up. They just keep on going but always with a ray of sunshine pasted on their faces. That's the difference.

If you're starting out your day any other way, you're creating unnecessary obstacles for yourself. You'll have plenty to frown about that evening at the end of a lousy day if you choose a path without a smile.

So how do you get rid of the blues if things aren't going your way? "I've got nothing to smile about," you say. Here's how you do it:

1. **Keep your troubles to yourself.** If you have something to vent, do it at home. Do it on your own time. It's YOUR problem, not the person's you're interacting with. They don't need to be in on what's happening in your personal life.

2. **Tell yourself, "My job is to make life enjoyable for others."** You're on "their time" now. What others need from you is a demonstration that you're genuinely interested in *them* (not preoccupied with YOU). There is no faster way to let them know this than with a smile.

I know this can be very difficult at times, but you have no other choice. You have to face life on its terms, not yours. In the end you'll be thankful you did. Trust me on that.

Smiling with the Heart

I want to be very clear about something. When I say *smile*, I don't mean some kind of slick or insincere grin. I'm talking about a genuine, honest smile that says you're glad the person you're with just entered your life. *That's* what I'm talking about. Believe me, your contacts will know the difference. You will not be able to be successful in life by putting on a fake smile. It's been said, "If the eyes are the windows to the soul, then a smile must surely be the window to the heart." Your smile must come from the inside. If yours isn't for real, don't bother giving it. They'll see right through you. One of my strengths has always been my ability to detect a *legit* smile. I know how to read lips for sincerity. If they're not on the level with me when they smile, whether *they* know it or not, I KNOW IT.

One of the most genuine smiles I ever saw came from one of the most successful business executives in the automotive industry, Ed Cole, president of General Motors. I was introduced to Ed several years ago in the presence of Phil Donahue, the top TV talk show host of the day. Ed, in turn, introduced me to Phil as the world's number-one retail auto salesperson. His smile was so warm and vibrant, it could melt a piece of steel. And, of course, he made me feel like a million bucks. Since he headed up GM, he was technically my "boss." But he never had to sell himself using that approach. He simply sold himself with a smile.

I'm sad to say with the focus on ratcheting up everything from production to communication technology nowadays, there seems to be less opportunity for personal engagement. As a result, there are not too many Ed Coles left in any industry. Yet a smile from the heart is still what everyone wants to make them feel important. Making people feel important is what smiling does better than anything else. Even if you're a shy kind of person, if you look your customer in the eye and smile, you'll instantly create an image of sincerity. And that's the foundation of *trust*.

This may sound a little bit unusual to you, but smiling with the lips is only one of the ways I would smile at people I came in contact with (similar to "listening" with more than just your ears). In my world, smiling was really a tool I used to make people feel good about *themselves*, not me. If I could get them into that frame of mind, then they would associate me with that good feeling and reward me with a sale.

I would "smile" at my prospects by always complimenting them on the things they did, personally and professionally, as well as the choices they were considering that I was showing them.

If they were picking out good options on a particular model, I made sure to compliment them for using a very intelligent approach that would help the resale value of the vehicle.

If they were telling me about their profession, I would let them know how much I admired people who could do what they did, no matter what it was. Many of my customers were middle-class working people. One of my customers was a road construction worker who worked outdoors year-round in the scorching heat as well as in the bitter cold. I told him very few people had the skill and stamina he had and how much I appreciated what he did. "Without you," I told him, "our society is at a complete standstill. We don't move without YOU." He smiled at me, nodded his head, and said, "Thanks for noticing." It's extremely important that you demonstrate a genuine heart when you smile and interact with your customers. If you appear to be a phony, they'll become uncomfortable and suspicious. You'll lose them right on the spot every time. Relax. Do it right. Be sincere.

Everything I had to say or be was positive. It was in my voice. It was in my eyes. It was in my entire body language. I made them feel intelligent, special, and important. I was there to facilitate *their decisions*, not strong-arm them into a sale.

One thing I always did was *build goodwill with a smile from the heart whenever I came in contact with people.* Before you do anything else, that's what you have to do to be successful. The reward will follow. But first the foundation has to be laid, and a genuine *smile from the heart* is where it should always begin.

Getting the Maximum "Smileage" Out of Your Smile

If you made a list comparing two competitive companies on such things as price, product, and service, and found them to be more or less equal, the difference would be, in almost all cases, how customers were treated. If you blow that, you've just met the deal breaker, even if you think your price is better than the guy's down the street. In today's world, more than ever, you've got to have it all: PRICE, PRODUCT, and SERVICE. And, above all, *service* begins and ends with a *smile.*

Let me show you how to get a little extra "smileage," as I like to call it, out of your smile with seven handy rules.

1. Smile When You Don't Feel Like It

Without a doubt, this is the most difficult rule to follow; that's why it's number one. We both know how tough this can be, especially when you're having a rough day. I remember vividly the first Monday I went to work after the Detroit metro dealers decided to shut down all dealerships on Saturdays. Not only was I at the peak of my career, but, as I mentioned in Chapter 2, Saturdays were one of my best selling days. This loss was nothing to smile about. It was really tough. I could have joined the pack and sulked and complained, as did many. I'm glad I didn't. I decided I would have to dig a little bit deeper into my *attitude machine* and **smile even bigger and brighter** to make up for the lost day. It paid off. **I had my second-best sales year in my entire career!**

No matter how down in the dumps you may feel at a given time, you have to convince yourself you will not let that interfere with the business at hand. And that's taking care of that prospect, that customer, or that contact, the one right in front of you at that very moment. **Nothing else matters.** They cannot be allowed to know what's going on in your personal life. As far as they are concerned, they should only have to ask themselves, "What has he or she got to smile about?" rather than "What is his or her problem?" Remember, NO DISTRACTIONS. Reread Chapter 2, "Have a Positive Attitude." It has a lot of the same basic success principles that apply to *smiling*. Smiling when you don't feel like it takes discipline, but discipline pays dividends. If you want to remember the power of a smile, try this on. **Think about someone who has a magnificent smile.** The world has been captivated by the smile of the stunning royal duchess Princess Kate Middleton of Great Britain. It is so radiant that she and her smile are one and the same. Or maybe it's one from what is probably the most famous painting on Earth, the *Mona Lisa*, painted by the renowned artist Leonardo da Vinci. People flock from all over the world to the Louvre Museum in Paris to marvel at this painting. They all want to get a glimpse of the magic attraction it has. When they see it, they soon realize it's not the brush strokes or striking colors that makes it so special. It's their fascination with her smile. That's right. More than five hundred years later, her timeless smile continues to touch the hearts of everyone who ever sees her. She never disappoints and neither should you.

2. Share Only Your Positive Thoughts

When you share only positive thoughts, you also create an atmosphere of goodwill. You want to be associated with and be known as a person who brings joy into people's lives. When you enter a room, your goal should be to "light it up." People should know that whatever you have to say, it's going to make *them* feel special because that's the reputation you have and because that's WHO YOU REALLY ARE. Talk only about positive things. Whether it's the news, sports, or the weather, always look for the positive angle on things. Be upbeat. Focus on the constructive things going on in the community, not the negative ones. Don't get involved in controversial discussions. If you're a positive person who talks and feels positive, then that is exactly what you pass on to the people you are with. And that, my friends, is right where you want your customers or contacts to be, feeling good about themselves and knowing *you're the reason* they feel positive. If you have nothing good to say about something, either move on to another topic or shut up.

3. Smile with Your Whole Face

If you have a genuine smile on your face, then it won't be with the lips alone. The complete smile involves practically everything a person sees on your face: the twinkle in your eyes, the wrinkle in your nose, the way your cheeks fill out. You may be better looking than Santa, but his smile is hard to top. Ear-to-ear, that's the one you want, genuine as a newborn babe's and sweeter than sugar pie. When people see you beaming from ear-to-ear, it carries an important message before a single word is spoken. The smile on your face says, "Trust me. Have confidence in me. I am your friend." What a great way to begin a relationship with anyone.

4. Turn the Frown Upside Down

When I look back on my early years growing up, by all rights I should have been a complete failure. If I hadn't made the change to become a positive-minded person, I would have wound up just like my father—angry at the world. I would have frowned on life for not dealing me a better hand. But I learned quickly that unless I learned to look on the bright side and smile about what I did have going for me, my frowning was going to spell disaster and ultimately a failed life. Is that what you want? If you keep on frowning your life away, before you know it, that frown will become an irreversible and permanent scar on your face. The whole world will read you like a book. You'll become someone to avoid.

If you don't think you have anything to smile about, I'll give you something to get you started. First of all, if you live in a country like the United States where you are free to pursue your opportunities, you are a lot better off than a great many other people on Earth who live in places where oppression, poverty, and disease rule.

Chances are you have it a lot better than you think. If you learn to appreciate your starting point, you will quickly realize you have a lot to smile about. The door is there for you to open. For a guy who had so many doors slammed in his face growing up, I know firsthand what it feels like to look back and see how far I've come. *There is no sweeter smile than the smile of success.* Once you get one on, you'll never trade it in for anything.

But if you continue to frown on life and hang around people who never smile, that door will remain shut for the rest of your life. Make the change. Get away from the losers in life who pull you down, and get going on *creating a face of happiness*. Turn that frown upside down and get your life moving in the right direction. **Turn your world around now!**

5. Exercise Your Sense of Humor

It's true there's a lot to be sad about in life. We all know that. Just look at the news headlines on TV or in your newspaper. Why dwell on it? Only a pessimist does that. An optimist never gets caught in that trap. An optimist always sees the glass "half full," not "half empty" like the pessimist. I think in my next life, I should be a news editor who lets only good news be printed or aired. If you make an honest effort to look for the good in things rather than what's wrong with something, it will go a long way to shaping your attitude about winning. Look for reasons to be cheerful. One of the best ways to do this is by *exercising your sense of humor*. Laugh a little with others—never at them, but *with* them. You don't have to be a master joke-teller to find reasons to smile about life. If the joke's on you, then take it in stride and roll with it. Lighten up! Don't take the moment too seriously. There are enough of those already in life.

6. Smile Out Loud

If you think a beaming smile is the ultimate expression of happiness, imagine what a hearty laugh must be. I always think of a good, hearty laugh as the equivalent of *smiling out loud*. There's no better feeling. Have you ever noticed how contagious laughter can be? You'll experience it in a movie theater during a comedy film. One person starts laughing and pretty soon the whole theater is rolling. Or when a standup comedian delivers a punch line to a live audience. Everybody gets in on the act. You forget your troubles. You're in a moment of pleasure and fun, and you're sharing it with others. Can you imagine stringing together an unbreakable chain of moments like that into an entire life? Now there's something to shoot for. *Smiling out loud* is one of the healthiest exercises there is. It does wonders for your mind, your body, and your soul. Brighten your day, as well as someone else's. *Smile out loud.*

7. Don't Say "Cheese," Say "I Like You"

It wouldn't surprise me one bit to learn that photographers were probably the first ones to try and get people to force a smile. They needed to figure out a way to get everyone to do that for a very practical reason—nobody wants to pay for a picture of frowning faces. If you think saying "cheese" pushes the smile to its limit, saying "I like you" does an even better job in my opinion. Why? Because the words "I like you" actually mean something that genuinely makes someone smile. The smile you get in response is not a forced response, but a natural one. Now you're getting an honest smile. And that's the photo you want.

I used to have a practice that whenever someone came in to see me in my office, I would give them an *"I Like You"* button. I would give these to everyone—kids, spouses, everybody got one. While some were a little bit surprised at first, they soon realized from our conversation that I wanted them to know they were the most important thing in the world at that moment. The smiles on their faces let me know immediately that they appreciated that. If I pinned the button on one of the kids, they would look up at me and smile. Interestingly, a customer once asked me why I never put my name on those buttons. My response was simply that I wanted them to wear them and, in turn, share *their smiles* and good wishes with others.

It wasn't important to have my name on their button. What *was* important, though, is that they all remembered it started with Joe Girard. The people who ran the dealership thought I was crazy for spending money on stuff like that. But I knew what I was doing. I was not looking to sell someone a single car or truck. I was looking to build customers for life. I wanted to capture their hearts, not their wallets. If I did that, I knew the rewards would follow.

So there are seven ideas on how to get a little extra "smile-age" out of your life. They should be easy enough to follow because they're instinctive. The most difficult thing to do will most certainly be smiling when things aren't going so well or when you have to do business with perfect strangers. But you can overcome that. There's a technique I use when I give lectures that helps "break the ice" for everyone in the audience. I don't care if they're having a bad day or not. I can take perfect strangers and instantly introduce them to a "new friend"—the person sitting right next to them. Here's how:

I tell members of the audience to turn to the person right next to them and simply say, "I like you." Their focus immediately shifts to that moment with the person right next to them. Nothing else matters. What's happened in their day up to that point comes to a screeching halt. Their shyness takes a back seat. Then I tell them to say it again to the person on the other side of them. From on stage, I can see their faces light up the entire room with the biggest smiles you ever saw. The interesting thing is that they all had that smile stashed away inside them all along. I simply gave them a reason to let it out. Can you imagine what this world would be like if we could get everyone to turn to their neighbor and say "I LIKE YOU"? In the words of the jazz singer Louis Armstrong, "What a *wonderful* world." Indeed.

Put on a Happy Face

One of the most famous smiles you'll ever see is the yellow "smiley" face that tells you to "Have a Nice Day." We all know the one. It's such a simple happy face, yet it's been cheering up people for almost half a century now. Whenever I see one on a hat, a button, a T-shirt, a bumper sticker, or even on a spare tire cover, it always has a way of brightening up my day in a snap, even if I'm having a lousy one. No matter how bad things seem, it makes me realize I can turn my frown upside down if I just let it. And that's something we can all identify with.

If you've got a chip on your shoulder about life, then "knock it off" now! If you don't, it will be the stone around your neck from which you will eventually drown in your misery. Although life may seem unfair at times, you still have more to smile about than you may think. You decide.

For the Smiles of Your Life

I've been purposely focusing on what smiling can do for you and your life. But what your smile can do for others you come in contact with can be life-changing for them. This is especially significant when it comes to the smiles that belong to the people you care most deeply about—your family. These are the people you always greet with a smile, not a frown. They are the ones you inspire and influence with love and under-standing, not intimidation and punishment. In my world, my wife Kitty's smile is the first thing I see when I come home. Behind that smile is the heart and soul of what makes me tick. She knows how to *lift my spirits* when I get down as well as how to *slow me down* when I want things to move a little quicker. It is her genuine and radiant smile that assures me she is always there for me. And for that I am eternally grateful—the love of my life.

Over the years, many people have touched me with their smiles, and I believe I have touched many people with mine, including the customers I have sold and serviced—that's 13,001 smiles to be exact, relationships and bonds all secured with a handshake and a smile. An interesting way to look back on what you have achieved in your life will be to recall all the smiles you created on the faces of people you came in contact with. It would be an interesting yardstick for measuring your success. What a perfect way to be remembered—by the smiles of your life.

RULE NINE
STAY IN TOUCH

Once you get to your highest level, then you have to be unselfish. Stay reachable. Stay in touch. Don't isolate.

—Michael Jordan, professional basketball player, MVP, and Hall of Famer

My customers and prospects knew I liked them every month of the year.

've talked about a lot of things in the book thus far. One of the most important is time—how you use it, how you manage it. Whenever you think about time, always think of it in terms of the people you do business with. It's *their* time we're talking about here, not yours. Your time starts when you go home. Their time begins the moment you arrive on the job or walk through the door of the place where you work. They're the ones spending their money with you. Right? You need them more than they need you.

It may be a wake-up call for your ego, but the truth is there's lots of "us" out there and just a few of "them." Make the most of the time you have with the people you do business with. In my business, they were customers. Depending on what you do, *staying in touch* may mean being in contact with patients, students, or other business associates. It really doesn't matter—you're providing some kind of product or service for them. As a practical matter, *they're all customers* of one type or another. The message is the same, *STAY IN TOUCH*, and that's the topic of this chapter.

It's Their Nickel and Their Time

If you have a lot of contact with people or are in a service-related business, staying in touch (especially with customers or potential ones) is critical. It's the most important thing you can do with your time. Quite frankly, if you had to do only one thing with your time all day, that should be it. It's that important. It's about survival—YOUR survival.

If you're in the desert dying of thirst, you're not going to waste time frantically digging holes in the sand looking for water until you finally die of exhaustion. If you're smart and want a better shot at survival, you'll use your energy wisely by looking for a well or an oasis that already exists and has water in it. Then you'll lower your bucket into it and quench your thirst. Good customers are a lot like that oasis. Once you find them, they're precious. They should be like water in the desert to you, a matter of life and death. You've worked hard to find them and make them yours. You never want to lose touch with them, stay out of contact with them, or, worst of all, let someone else steal *your* "bucket of water" from right under your nose. Competitors should have to cut off both your arms before you ever let a customer slip into their grasp. To make it impossible for these thieves to pick your pocket, your best weapon is staying in touch with the prize they're after—YOUR customers. **DO THESE THREE THINGS:**

1. Let them know how important and special they are to you.
2. Let them know you don't take their business for granted.
3. *Tell them often.* (This is the heart and soul of this chapter, as you will see.)

Their trust in you will grow the same way my mother inspired me to become *someone* with her love and faith in me. She *fed* me every day until I finally believed in myself.

If a customer ever does leave you because they feel neglected, it's actually a swing of TWO customers we're talking about here—the one you just lost and the replacement you have to now go out and find. When this happens, you're out in the cold again. You've just joined the pack of wolves already prowling the streets looking for a meal.

Believe me, it's a well-known fact that it's a helluva lot cheaper to keep an existing customer than it is to go out and find a new one. The cost of advertising and the amount of time involved to follow up with these prospects should make customer retention a priority in any business.

In fact, customer relationship building should be your number-one priority. If you think you're done once you've sold something to a customer, you've got it all wrong. The real selling begins *after the sale.* It's just like a marriage. The selling doesn't stop after the wedding or the honeymoon. You've got a lifelong commitment ahead of you, pal. Cherish the one you love. If you don't, you'll pay the price. Customers are the same way. Most are lost *after* the sale. In my business, that's in the service area, not the showroom. That's why you service them to death. Why do you think I took every person in the service area to dinner on the third Wednesday of every month? I'm talking about 36 people here! These guys could make me or break me. I wanted them all on "my team." I wanted my customers to be their top priority. And they were. There was nothing those guys wouldn't do for me because I took care of them.

Prospecting for new customers should be your *second* priority (we'll be talking more about that in a moment). Why? Because there will never be a greater business asset to you than *your existing customer base*—your number-one priority!

1. THEY ALREADY KNOW WHO YOU ARE.

2. THEY ALREADY KNOW WHAT YOU CAN DO FOR THEM.

3. THEY ALREADY LIKE YOU.

4. THEY CAN HELP YOU GROW YOUR BUSINESS.

As a known quantity, they represent your greatest growth potential. STAY IN TOUCH with these people! If you don't keep in touch and follow up with them regularly, like heat from the desert sun, they'll eventually dry up and disappear—the kiss of death.

I think you get the picture. The idea behind staying in touch with customers is pretty basic—*you do it to keep them*. Every time you call or come in contact with them, it adds another layer of glue to your relationship. Even if you know they're not in the market just then, let them know you're alive and thinking about them. If you stick to a disciplined plan for staying in touch with your customers, they should never find a good reason for leaving you. In this chapter, my direct mail program will outline a perfect illustration of how I did this.

I had several out-of-state customers who came back strictly to buy another new vehicle from me. Why? I made it worth their while. I had loyal customers who lived as far away as Florida, California, Arizona, and practically every place in between. These people made it a point to buy from me when they would be in the area visiting family. I was like family to them! *They were loyal to me because they knew I cared about them.* I always took a little less for myself to keep a customer. People thought I was crazy for doing that. But I knew exactly what I was doing. Sam Walton, the founder of Walmart, used to say, "Give them what they want—and a little more." I think he actually stole my idea. I was doing that long before Walmart became a household name. I always believed in the idea of "Give a little and take a little." I was looking ahead to the big picture—the next piece of business from that customer. The way I operated, I had them locked up for life on Girard's Ferris wheel. As I mentioned earlier, when their chair came around again on that wheel, I was there at the bottom waiting to greet them as they got off to buy another new car or truck—FROM ME. I looked at every customer as part of my annuity for the rest of my life. So they had to be happy. They had to believe in me. People used to say, "When you buy from Joe Girard, you have to leave the country to get away from him." I took that as a sincere compliment.

If you respect people, treat them right, and keep in touch with them, they'll become yours for as long as you want them. I embraced this concept early on in my career, and it served me well. A great part of the financial success I enjoyed later came from repeat business I worked hard and smart to retain. If I ever did lose a customer, and it did happen once in a while, it would drive me nuts. I would meditate on it. I would ponder it in great depth and detail. What did I do that I could have done better or differently to retain that customer?

Nothing irritated me more than losing an existing customer. I think it was that fire and resolve not to repeat mistakes that were major contributors to my sales success.

Bill Gates, founder of Microsoft, once said, "It's fine to celebrate success, but it's more important to heed the lessons of failure." He was right on the money. I think I remember the sales I lost more than anything else, especially if they were because I neglected a customer. There weren't many, but the lessons I learned were priceless.

There were a few occasions when I lost customers whom I never actually had a chance to meet. Once my business grew to the point where people needed an appointment to see me, some would still just show up anyway without one. My reputation for price and satisfaction was unmatched anywhere. When they found out they had to either wait or come back, they would either see someone else or just leave. One positive thing happened. I was, at least, able to help out one of the other salesmen who needed the business more than I did. However, I was not in the business of providing "overflow" services to these guys. That's when I decided it was time to get additional help to support my increasing business. I learned my lesson well.

I learned to respect time and how to use it efficiently (meaning doing things quickly and often) to *stay in touch* with my customers. I knew they weren't just sitting around waiting for me to do something. They could vanish from my list in a heartbeat and go anywhere they wanted to.

Sam Walton was right again when he said, "There is only one boss. The customer. Customers can fire everybody in the company from the chairman on down, simply by spending their money somewhere else." They call the shots.

I had to follow their golden rule: "He who has the gold makes the rules." My desire to get what they had was all the motivation I needed. They were not going to be permitted to escape the Girard hold. But I didn't squeeze them with an iron grip. I held them in my hand gently, but firmly, like a precious songbird that felt secure and loved. *They were mine and they liked it.*

What Technology Is Not

A lot of people today believe that an e-mail or *text* to a prospect or client is sufficient communication to let them know how much you care about them. What? You've got to be kidding me! That's about as sincere as picking up a bag of burgers from McDonald's drive-in window and then saying you had an elegant dining experience. You can *tweet* and *text* on your BlackBerry (or blueberry or strawberry) all day long and babble to each other at warp speed all over the planet, but is anybody *really buying*?

Listen, I understand the importance and necessity of digital and electronic communication in this day and age because I use it too. Obviously, the Internet and today's other communication technologies provide a lot of useful tools and data instantly. I know that in many businesses, both the client and the supplier are becoming more used to communicating in this way. I GET IT.

That's not the kind of communication I'm questioning or talking about here. I'm referring to something far more important than transferring data.

When you want to show a customer, for example, that you sincerely care about them and their business—to deepen your connection to *really touch them*—a "touchscreen" is not the way to go about it. Today, we are witnessing the *vanishing art of good conversation and personal dialogue* with one another and replacing it with the equivalent of what I think is "digital harassment." Instead of getting closer to people, technology actually helps to isolate them from you. They don't know who you are! You've become a "click" on a screen to them. THAT'S NOT WHAT THIS TECHNOLOGY IS FOR! I'm talking about connecting with people who make a difference in your life here.

Don't fall into the trap of thinking that effective communications is *only* about doing it fast. *Customer relationships are not built on a racetrack. They're bonded with a walk in the park.* They're not about speed—not now, not ever. Relationship building is, above all else, about QUALITY COMMUNICATIONS, NOW AND FOREVERMORE! That *mouse* next to your computer will never return the warmth of a sincere handshake, and your monitor will never smile back at you. A good customer is like a fine wine. It is meant to be savored and sipped, not guzzled down. People with smarts (you, I hope) know that *personalized contact* is how and where good relationships are cemented and renewed, preferably face to face. *That's* where the edge is, my friend.

There are only three ways you should stay in touch with the people who make a difference to you professionally. Whether you call them customers, clients, patients, students, or whatever in your business doesn't matter; this is the way to do it:

1. **In person.** Face to face. This is always preferable, but not always practical.

2. **By phone.** Let them experience the sincerity in your voice. This is an opportunity to exchange ideas and get an update on their status.

3. **In writing.** A personalized message sent to them. Make them feel special.

If you're doing it any other way, you're telling your customers that they're not that important to you—you don't have time for them, and YOU DON'T NEED THEM; they're just another "byte" in your digital world. You might as well be telling them to take a hike. Guess what? That's a two-way street, pal. You'll find out fast that they don't need you either. You're poisoning yourself to death with this approach. STAY IN TOUCH and do it the right way—with sincerity. Let me show you how.

A Letter from Joe Girard

Staying in touch with a handful of customers or prospects is one thing. But when you have to keep in contact with hundreds or thousands of people, you have to use smart methods. For me, it was direct mail. No, not e-mail, *DIRECT MAIL*. Yes, made out of paper! Why? I know the three things that everybody says the minute they walk in the door when they come home from work.

1. "Hi, honey."
2. "How are the kids (or the dog)?"
3. "Was there any mail today?"

If the spouse said, "Yes. We got another card from Joe Girard," bingo. I was in that home faster than you could lick a stamp. I was already there to greet them after a long, hard day the moment they arrived.

I was *on-time, on-target,* and *everywhere.* Every month I would send out mailers to my customers. Toward the end of my career, that had risen to about 16,000 pieces of mail a month. You heard me right: 16,000. "You're kidding me, Joe!" you say. "That's got to cost you a fortune!" I'm not kidding you. And no, it wasn't cheap. But hold on. The dealer paid half the costs, and I made sure Uncle Sam paid half of my share when I filed my tax return. So even though I had to use some of my own money, I was actually only paying a *quarter* of the cost—25 cents on the dollar. And it was well worth it.

Now some of you might say, "That's easy for you to do, Joe. You can afford to send out fancy mailings—you've got money. But what about the rest of us?" Well, the answer to that is very straightforward. When I first got started in direct mail, I didn't have any money either. In fact, it was my wife and two kids who helped me. We did all the stuffing of envelopes and mailings ourselves from home. It wasn't until later that I hired a direct mail house in Chicago to do the work.

The important thing to remember here is that I didn't come up with any excuses for not doing it or for why I was failing. *I committed to start doing it!* AND I DID IT! Yes, it was small at first, but it grew, and all because I did something about it! Will YOU? The reality of what you can do will *always* remain a mystery until you take the first critical step—*get off your butt!*

I wanted my name branded on the minds of every customer, every referral, and every qualified prospect I ever came in contact with who looked like a potential customer as often as I could. For my existing customers, I made sure they didn't forget me. From the moment they drove away from the dealership with their new vehicle, I would be in touch with them. I developed a monthly letter-writing direct mail program that made sure they heard from me year-round—every 30 days!

My mailings never looked like the typical junk mail we all get, the kind we throw away before opening it. I would always send mine out in plain envelopes and vary the color and size from time to time. Nobody knew what was in it until they opened it. *My name was never on the envelope.* You never do that. It's like playing poker. You don't want to give your hand away before you're ready to show your cards. Just an address—that's all you need on the envelope. And I always used stamps rather than machine postage.

I had custom-designed cards made with different caricature pictures and special messages to match the occasion. On the outside, they all said the same thing: "I LIKE YOU." On the inside of the card, I had an original hand-drawn caricature on the left side with the greeting on the right side. I always like my messages short and sweet. For January, it was "Happy New Year from Joe Girard." For February, it was "Happy Valentine's Day." March was "Happy St. Patrick's Day." And so on throughout the year till Thanksgiving and Christmas. In fact, my Christmas cards would go out in November before anyone else's. If it was a customer's birthday or anniversary, they got a personalized card from Joe Girard. If their kid graduated from college or they had a new baby, they got a congratulations letter from Joe Girard. If there wasn't anything special to celebrate, I would *create* a reason—"Happy spring from Joe Girard." Whatever it was, *I was in their face.*

Why did I do this? Simple—*they weren't expecting it.* I wanted them to know I LIKED THEM—past, present, and future.

I LIKED THEM WHEN I MET THEM.

I LIKE THEM NOW.

I ESPECIALLY LIKE THEM FOR TOMORROW.

I wasn't going to let my name get tossed into the heap of salespeople who, once they make the sale, forget about the customer and go on to the next one. That's not the way *Joe Girard* operates. I know for a fact that on some days, I was probably the best thing that happened to them all day. On that day, at least one person cared about them—*Joe Girard*. And all because of a little card, a card that simply said "I Like You."

I made it a point to get to know them and their families. I wanted to be a part of their lives, every day. Even the kids knew me. They would see my letters and cards arrive in the mail: "Daddy got another card from Joe Girard!" I'm surprised they didn't call me Uncle Joey. It was like being invited to a family dinner in their home. In fact, I remember a couple who came into my office with their six-year-old son to buy a car. In the little boy's hand was the colorful card I'd sent them two weeks earlier, which he offered up to me. I smiled at him, accepted his gift, and pinned one of my "I Like You" buttons on his shirt. I think it was a moment he soon would not forget. And that was the goal—to make sure people didn't forget me. And they didn't because "I Liked Them," every month of the year.

As I mentioned, all my cards had one common theme. No matter what the holiday or occasion was, when they opened the envelope, my cards all said the same thing on the cover— "I LIKE YOU." And I didn't just repeat the same thing every year. I met with my artist every August to plan the new design and content for the following year. The messages were always fresh and sincere—12 thoughtful monthly messages to let my customers know I LIKE YOU and care about you throughout the year. If you want to check out more detail on how I did this, then you should pick up a copy of my bestseller, *How to Sell Anything to Anybody.* I've got an entire chapter just crammed with everything you ever wanted to know on how to do it.

Another thing I did was to make sure my mailing list was continuously "purified" because I wanted accurate, up-to-date information on where people were. I had a couple of guys who would even check with the post office from time to time for me to make sure I had current forwarding addresses. One thing I never did was send my mail out on the first or fifteenth of the month because that's when most people typically get their bills. I wanted my customers and referrals in a good mood before they opened my mail.

Over the years, most people get to know their doctor, their insurance agent, and their banker quite well. And you should too. You're probably spending or sending a lot of money their way. But can you honestly tell me the last time you received a personal letter from any of them? I mean a personal note or card right out of the blue, more than once a year, simply saying "I Like You" or "Happy Valentine's Day"? Think about that. Makes you wonder, doesn't it?

Was it worth doing? Absolutely! Over the years, repeat business represented over 75 percent of my sales! Now that's what I call implementing a smart approach to successful business management. It was such a success that, along with my pricing and service, my direct mail program was a major contributor into my getting into the *Guinness Book of World*

Records. In fact, the Guinness people spent three days checking my handwriting and sales records for forgery, and calling customers to verify that I sold 13,001 retail vehicles. That's no fleet, no wholesale, and no used-vehicle sales. Every one of them was brand new, sold belly-to-belly in the showroom, one at a time. They just couldn't believe that many people could *spit my name out at the drop of a hat* and that they would all get in line to buy something from one person. They were simply astounded. *But it was TRUE.* They had me audited by the accounting firm Deloitte & Touche for three days. This was the same outfit that the dealership I worked at, Merollis Chevrolet, used to do their monthly audits. In the end, the Guinness people just shook their heads in amazement. They were satisfied with the results of their research and recognized me as the greatest retail salesperson. Period.

The Little Things That Count

When I sent out my direct mail, I made sure I didn't get caught up in sending out glossy mailings. My letters were not elaborate, gaudy, or anything like that. Anybody can put on a cheap show to get attention. What separated my mail from the rest of the heap was *sincerity.* When they opened up the envelope, I wanted them to see what was "inside" Joe Girard; I wanted to reach their hearts and touch their souls. To do that, you've got to remember to say "thank you" after the sale in a very personalized way with a handwritten card. They've got to know you care, that you're sincere and thoughtful.

That also applies to things like returning phone calls *promptly.* It's not that doing any one of these things will bring a customer in to buy something from you—that's not the point. Over time, you'll begin to recognize it's the *cumulative impact* of *all* the little thoughtful things you do that makes the difference. That's what shapes the image others have of you when you stay in touch with them in a personal and caring way. In the end, that's what counts. *That's* how lasting success is achieved. And *that's* how I became successful.

My approach with referrals and prospects was similar to how I handled my customers. The big difference was, of course, I didn't know these people, or not as well. Here, I was using direct mail more as a starting point. I was using it to build a bridge, to make a *connection*, not to talk to them. That would come in the follow-up, either by phone or with an appointment to meet in person. I still made my direct mail personal and tailored my messages to their needs. It might have been a referral I got that enabled me to find out something about them. That's where the little things I did for my existing customers became big things: when a referral turned into a bona fide customer. They "talked me up," and I would reward them for that lead with at least $50 (today I'd probably increase that) if they actually bought from me.

As I said, it's the cumulative impact of all the little things you do for a customer that makes the difference. It's also quite true that the little things YOU DON'T DO can make the difference between keeping and losing a customer. My favorite gripe is WHY anyone would think it's okay to take your time getting back to a customer who has a question about something, especially if this is someone who has a direct impact on your income. How stupid can you get? I just don't get it.

One day I was walking past a salesman's office in the showroom. I couldn't help but notice a rather large stack of pink phone call message slips on Greg's desk. The odd thing is that the stack looked either the same as it did the day before or slightly taller. He was obviously taking his time getting back to these people. Of course, I couldn't be sure, but I also began to notice that Greg was frequently paged on the loudspeaker in the dealership (and often by the service department). He would either ignore it or take his time walking back to his office, especially if he was in the middle of a joke with some of his "dope ring" buddies. I think it took about a couple of months before we rarely heard Greg's name called on the loudspeaker again and his pile of pink phone messages was reduced to one. It was *his* "pink slip" from the dealership letting him know his services were no longer needed.

We're all customers at some time during our day. Whether we're buying groceries, on the phone with a utility or credit card company, or in a department store, we all know and experience the feeling of frustration when we're ignored. So why would YOU do that to someone else? Why? Why? Why?

My point should hit home when you realize that everyone you ever meet knows at least 250 other people somewhere. And that's probably the bare minimum. I learned this from a funeral home director who once told me that 250 was the number of remembrance cards they would print up for a deceased person. That represented the average number of people who would come to pay their respects. Think of that for a moment: the pulling power, the influence, the impact a single person had on 250 other people he knew, all of them coming to pay their respects. And they, in turn, each know 250 people of their own. In case you think this is just a coincidence, I heard the same story from a first-rate caterer I did business with from time to time when planning typical weddings. My bestselling book, *How to Sell Anything to Anybody*, has a full chapter dedicated to this topic.

The message here is that you can't afford to jeopardize even a single customer or client because of the influence each person has on 250 other people. They will remember how you treated them and will tell everyone they know. If it's a bad impression or experience, it will spread like a contagious disease with your name on it. I call this *Girard's Law of 250*. It's not always easy either—I know. Sometimes you just want to give someone a *knuckle sandwich*. You just have to bite your tongue and roll with the punches. Don't ever forget this!

WRITE THESE THINGS DOWN NOW:

1. **Return all customer phone calls, e-mails, and faxes promptly.** If you don't, that's a good way to *burn a bridge*. In my book, *promptly* means as soon as possible—as soon as you can get the answer to their question. Get it done right away. Make it an urgent matter, even if it isn't—not two or three days from now or when it's convenient for you. The customer will immediately sense how you respond to them. They're always testing how you value them. Never let them down. Stay in touch and respond promptly.

2. **Never be late or break an appointment without first rescheduling.** Whether it's a meeting or a phone call, always be on time. Let the customer know *their* call or appointment is the most important thing in the world to you at that moment. Demonstrate it with *action!*

3. **Give your customers something they're not expecting,** a little something extra, something that says you really care about them. Be thoughtful. Trust me: they will remember. Almost three-quarters of my customers were repeat business. I gave them more than a "little" something extra. Maybe it was a little extra for their trade-in or perhaps a free set of color-keyed floor mats they weren't expecting. I loved them and they knew it. In return they made me number one.

The wolves are out there ready to "eat your lunch" if you disappoint. And you deserve to starve if you ignore your customers and assume they'll always be yours because of something you did one day in their life! Only a fool would believe that.

Even though your particular line of work may be different than mine, the basics will always remain the same. *Stay in touch* with your customers, clients, or patients on a regular basis, and do the little things well.

Most auto dealerships are pretty savvy about the importance of mailing out discount coupons for things like tires, brakes, batteries, and shock absorbers. One of the common strategies was to practically "give away" an oil change for a price no lube shop could touch. The idea was that once the car or truck was on the hoist, the service technician was bound to find something worn that needed replacing—and I mean legitimately.

Practically all of the big chain casual dining restaurants, such as Olive Garden, Red Lobster, Applebee's, and Outback Steakhouse, mail or e-mail "buy one, get one" coupons to their repeat customers as often as once a month to *stay in touch*. This is no small thing when family budgets are tight.

If you're in a corporate environment, then your customer base may be different than in a retail setting. Find out how successful individuals in your industry stay in touch with their customers and contacts. What are some of the little things they do that work well for them in your business? They are successful for a reason. Study their habits and patterns, and copy them. Adopt them into your routine. As I said earlier in the book, that's exactly what I did when I got started. I studied the habits of successful people in several industries before I chose a path of my own.

In Good Times and Bad Times

Staying in touch with customers can be a very pleasant experience if all it means is saying "hello" and checking in with them from time to time. However, sometimes staying in touch means having to possibly listen to something the customer doesn't like about the product they bought from you or the service they're experiencing. Now we're into a whole new ballgame of communication. They're the ones calling YOU. I'll tell you more about servicing customers in later chapters. But if an issue surfaces that is a problem for your customers, this is no longer a courtesy "keeping in touch" communication matter. Now we're talking about the potential loss of future business if this is mishandled.

I had a simple philosophy about how to handle unhappy owners. Whatever it took, I was going to *turn their lemon into a peach*. That's right. Sometimes this meant spending some of my own money (tax deductible, of course) to cover the cost of an item in service. For one customer, I think I spent less than $30 out of my pocket to cover the parts cost for a radiator hose and some clamps to keep them happy. My message to him was clear: **"Although the truck you purchased from me was out of warranty, my desire to please you was not."** In Girard's book, that's a *lifetime warranty*! Not only did that calm him down, but he came back four months later to purchase a new car for his wife. Thirty dollars well spent, I'd say.

For another customer, I remember how irritated he was because his power windows made a slight squeaking sound whenever they went up and down. I knew how much he liked the car, so I told the service department (my favorite team) to put any parts on me to fix the problem (the parts cost less than $40 out of my pocket). The window tracks were lubricated and checked. Everything worked fine. He was delighted, especially when he found out from the cashier the parts were "on me." He immediately came over to my office to thank me. Later that summer, he brought his daughter in to buy her first brand-new car to drive up to college in.

Why did I spend my own money? I saw it as an inexpensive "investment" opportunity to surprise them by turning a negative experience into a positive one. They were not expecting this level of care and thoughtfulness. As usual, the management of the dealership thought I was crazy spending my own money this way, but I knew precisely what I was doing. Besides, I never thought those customers belonged to anyone else but me. Those customers knew I wanted them to be happy. So when they called ME, they did it for a reason. They trusted ME enough to know I would help them with the problem.

It didn't happen very often that a customer was unhappy with their vehicle or service, but this is the time when I knew I had to "give a little" to retain them. They are *staying in touch with me* for a reason. I said, "I like you." Now I'm going to show them how much. *I was always careful to let them know, though, that I was doing this for them this one time as a way of thanking them.* This approach can work for you too.

Think of it as an opportunity to demonstrate your sincerity and gratitude for the business they've already given you. When you take this approach, you're giving them one more reason to stay with you in the future. It's a commercial—YOUR commercial. I wanted them to stay in this marriage for better or worse, in good times and bad, forever. No divorce here. No reason for it. I had the price, the product, and the service.

My job situation wasn't perfect. There definitely were some things I didn't like about how the place operated. But I knew how to look beyond that. Unlike a lot of other salespeople who drift from job to job every few months, I made the decision to stay put in one place for the long haul. I was committed to my customers. And they remained committed to me. We always knew where we could find each other. *If you want to see a tree grow and flourish, you leave it in one spot.* If you do that, it will bear fruit. If you dig it up out of the ground and keep moving it around, it can never get rooted anywhere and grow, so it never bears fruit. Use your head here.

Nobody could touch me because of the way I took care of my customers, and they knew it. That's why more than 75 percent of them came back to me time after time. Staying in touch with your customers means *servicing them to death*, not just talking to them. Get that into your head. Whenever you're in touch with them, nobody else has their attention but you. You've got a corner on them. *Monopolize them.*

And yes, sometimes this means listening to things that aren't good. You're going to hear about lost jobs, divorces, deaths in the family, kids with problems, and so on. It's all part of life. I've had people who came in to see me about purchasing a new vehicle, and after finding out their credit wasn't any good, they suddenly became depressed. One man in this situation went on to tell me about his having difficulties holding a job because of a drinking problem he was trying to correct. He then told me how this was affecting his marriage and how ashamed he was in front of his kids. He wanted to be a role model for them but didn't know where to start.

I listened intently to his story (knowing there was no sale coming today with him) and said, "Why not start right now, Harry? When you walk out of this dealership, Joe Girard thinks you're going to be a changed man. 'Does Harry believe that too?' That's the real question for you." He looked at me in a way that surprised me a little. His eyes were wide open, as if he had awakened from a daze. Why would a salesman spend the time listening to his troubles?

He said, "Thanks, Joe. Mark my words: I'll be back." It took almost a year, but sure enough Harry did come back, this time with a big smile and his lovely wife, Jean. As the new supervisor in a local manufacturing plant, he had no trouble getting credit for the new car I sold him.

If you're going to build relationships with your customers, you've got to be prepared for the possibility of getting involved in things like that. You may find yourself turning into a sounding board or counselor to some of them. Do it. They're simply telling you they trust you. This is your opportunity to show them you're a caring, compassionate, and sensitive person.

Listen, I'm not a certified psychiatrist or counselor, but my upbringing gave me a "degree" in going without lots of things. I can listen and show compassion with the best of them.

You don't have to have all the answers. Just learn to *be a good listener.* **Good things will follow.**

The Follow-up

After my third year of selling in the retail business, I was starting to get a taste of success. However, it was not without cost.

I was taxing myself so much physically that it was beginning to take its toll on my health. I was becoming a workaholic. I was wearing myself out, leaving little or no time for anything else. I knew I had to change something. I got some advice from my tax man who suggested I get some help, especially with the routine side of things, such as qualifying prospects, paperwork, and handling tons of incoming phone calls. This left me to concentrate on what I did best—interact with potential customers. I decided to take his advice. It was the smartest business decision I ever made.

I started out by calculating the number of additional sales I would have to close to break even (i.e., to cover the expense of adding employees). Then I added the additional sales I needed to make it worthwhile. Not surprisingly, it looked like the right time to do this since I knew I was missing out on some customers because they couldn't get in to see me. The decision was easy: GREEN LIGHT!

First I hired one man (at my expense); then it was two guys to handle all the follow-up detail and call-in responses to my direct mail. They would do all the probing and screening for me. They would "patrol" the service department for me to make sure my customers were being properly taken care of and even get financing approvals when necessary. I paid these two people a decent wage for the hours they put in. Having them on board made all the difference. As I said, it was a smart business decision.

Some of you may be asking yourselves, "How do you know when it's time to bring in help?" The answer is simple—run the numbers the way I did. If it doesn't compute to a positive number, you may be *jumping the gun* a bit and need to build up your business a little bit more first, like I did. The other way to tell is if you're working longer and longer hours and are not being able to manage or secure all the potential profits that are slipping away. That happened to me too. This makes the perfect scenario to present to your management, especially if you work in a corporate setting where a well thought-out evaluation and recommendation from you makes your case stronger. If they don't see the value in the missed opportunities of increasing profits, then your company lacks visionaries. Start looking to camp somewhere else.

I told you earlier, I never ate lunch with people in the dealership. When I did go out to eat, which was rare, it was with people who could help me—like bankers. It was a two-way street. I could help them too. I drove so much business into local banks that, on my name alone, I could have gotten credit approval for a dead man.

The Girard *machine* operated just like a doctor's office. "Doctor" Girard was always "in surgery." For the last 12 years of my 15-year career, if you wanted to see Joe Girard, you had to have an appointment. That meant you had to first be screened by the "nurse" for that appointment. Don't misunderstand what's going on here. I wasn't trying to be cute or "above it all." I was looking for a smart and efficient way to handle my customers (and soon-to-be customers) effectively.

AND I FOUND IT. By the time a prospect came in to see me, they had already been qualified and screened by my staff. I knew what they liked, what their tastes were, and what they were in the market for. I knew practically everything I ever wanted to know about the person almost as well as members of their own family. I knew what they did for a living, how much they made, the ages of their kids, what schools they went to, birthdays, anniversaries, and so on. I could have probably donated blood to all of them because I knew their blood types (just about).

This approach to handling customer traffic was a turning point in my career. **My direct mail program, my price, and my personal service are what made me.** Obviously, you need to have a certain amount of growth in your business before it makes sense to implement a method like what I used for direct mail and hiring additional help for handling my customer base. Do an evaluation on your situation like I just explained. Also, don't lose sight of the fact that my direct mail initiatives were only *part* of my overall approach to how I took care of my customers.

One of my favorite moments is the look on people's faces when I give them the keys to their new car or truck. It's all part of what I call Girard's Three "I Like You" kisses right after the sale:

Kiss #1. My guys would follow up with a high class, wedding-style "thank you" card after the purchase. In the card I would tell them, "You made a great decision. You bought a beautiful car. If you get a lemon, I'll turn it into a peach. Today you bought Joe Girard." **Always compliment people on buying from you, and compliment them for making a really good choice.**

Kiss #2. When the car or truck is delivered (usually in a couple of days) in front of the dealership, *next to my window* (one of *my* guys does this), I go outside to meet the customer. I place 25 of my business cards in the glove box as I remind them that I offer $50 for any leads they give me who actually buy. I say to them, **"I want to go where you go. I want you to have health, happiness, and success. Wherever you go, Joe Girard is with you."**

Kiss #3. Three days after delivery, I call the customer: "How's the car? How's the family? The kids (by name)? I want you to know I will never stand behind your product. I'll stand *in front* of it. I will service you to death until you're satisfied. Remember what I said, 'If you've got a lemon, just call me and I'll turn it into a peach.'" Then I add, "Did anyone see the car who liked it who might want one?" I ask for their names as I remind them, "If they buy, you get $50 from Joe

Girard!" I'd even give them a little more ($60) if they actually brought the person in to see me. Not only did that extend my chain of goodwill, it was a win-win proposition for the customer *and* Joe Girard. They picked up a nice *bird dog* (referral) fee, and I now had two locked-in buyers every three to five years—the original customer and their referral.

Staying in Touch Where and When It Counts: 5 Initiatives

I'm sure you've noticed by now that I used my own money from time to time to support my sales efforts. But I didn't just pluck silver dollars off a tree in my backyard whenever I needed some. Before I plunked down one dime, I carefully researched and studied the return I expected on that dime. *I only use money to make money.* As I said in the beginning of this chapter, *staying in touch* with my customers (the way I did it) wasn't cheap. But I saw it as an investment in me and my future; otherwise, I wouldn't have done it. And I made sure Uncle Sam and the dealer paid for most of it. Remember, in the end, I only paid 25 percent of the costs! You can do this too!

Sometimes it will be a long-term investment you'll be considering. This is especially important to remember when you're trying to build up a loyal customer base over an extended period of time as I did. Be patient. The return will come.

Here's a quick summary, then, of the five initiatives I've discussed that I used to keep in touch with my customers *and* enlarge my bank account:

1. My direct mail program was the key that really catapulted me into a high-profile sales success. Direct mail got my name in front of 16,000 people every month. Are you missing out on key exposure because people either don't know you or you've lost touch with them and they've forgotten who you are?

2. I hired two people to handle the responses to my direct mail and other administrative tasks so I could concentrate on closing the deals. Without them, I would actually have lost money because I was drowning in a sea of paperwork and missing out on new sales opportunities. Are you making the best use of your time? If not, it may be worth it for you to pay someone else to take on some of your more routine tasks. The key is to determine if you're missing added income opportunities because you're too tied down.

3. My *bird dog* fees "enrolled" many of my customers into Girard's personal extended sales force, all working for me. They got $50 for any referrals that actually bought from me. Think of people who could help you in your line of work that it would be worthwhile to reward, and consider doing it.

4. I would make it a point to wine and dine the local banks from time to time. I went first cabin, elegant dining with husbands and wives at Detroit's top-of-the-line restaurants like the London Chop House, and always brought gardenia corsages for the ladies. When it came to putting through loan approvals (and getting them done fast) for me, they never forgot my appreciation. As I mentioned earlier in the book, if you go out for lunch during your workday, have lunch only with people who can help you. You can have dinner with your pals after work.

5. This one is very important. I always remembered to recognize the importance of the team behind Joe Girard. They could make me or break me. A dinner once a month at a first-class restaurant for the 36 people in the dealership service department was my way of letting them know how much they meant to me. When I needed them most, there was nothing they wouldn't do for me. Think of the people who make a difference in your business, and let them know they're appreciated. They'll be there for you too when you need them.

Those are the things I did that jump-started my career. If you look closely, you'll notice all five have three things in common—they all put *money* and *people* to work for me, and they were all *tax deductible*. The old saying "Use it or lose it" certainly applies to money (as well as to the IRS). You'll get a kick out of this: the IRS couldn't believe I had such an effective system going. They were "in touch" with me regularly. Every year, they went over me with a fine-tooth comb. I had to show them all the receipts for my sales as well as prove that the *bird dog* fees I paid out to my customers were legit too. They couldn't believe anyone could achieve what I did. But I was clean as a whistle. *I was for real.* Whenever I heard from them, I took it as a compliment to my efforts!

It's very possible that all or several of these initiatives would also make sense in your business. Give them a shot. Don't be afraid to step out from the crowd and try some original thinking even if no one else is doing it. I did many things that the management either shook their heads at or laughed at. But I had the last laugh. As Liberace used to say, "I cried all the way to the bank."

The most successful people in any business are never going to be like everyone else. That's what makes them special. I'm proud to be a member of that select group.

The Telephone—as High-Tech as You Need to Be

With all the direct mail I was sending out, it would be practically impossible to make 10 to 14 thousand follow-up phone calls a month. But of the ones that did get back to us, and there were more than you can imagine, I would sometimes get on the phone with them myself, especially if it looked like they might be "on the fence" about buying. The beauty of the phone is that it can be a very persuasive communication tool if you use it properly. It's convenient, fast, and, compared to the cost of printing, very cheap. Remember, I'm using the dealer's phone here.

In fact, when I first got into retail automotive selling, I was basically provided with a phone and a desk. Period. That was it. I spent the better part of the day on the phone with a telephone directory next to me. I made at least 15 calls a day, mostly "cold" calls where the prospect was not really qualified at all. I knew nothing about them. I would call all the Browns on one day. Next day it would be the Joneses, or the Kowalskis, or the Smiths, and so on. I could practically tell you what day of the week it was by which letter of the alphabet I was on. It wasn't very scientific, but it was how I got started with my initial efforts to get in touch with potential customers. So my respect for the telephone has some very special meaning to me personally.

Even though the telephone hasn't changed much over the years, it's as hi-tech as you need to be when talking about building meaningful customer relationships. It should remain a primary tool in your arsenal of weapons to use for staying in touch with customers. The phone will never be a replacement for face-to-face interaction. In fact, it's the first thing I "turn off" when a customer is in my office. I had a strict policy that the secretary was to take all my calls. Remember my earlier comment—NO DISTRACTIONS. I want my customer focused.

However, when you're not with a customer in person, the phone is the next best thing and can still provide a powerful and personal presence. By using your voice in a warm, pleasant, and engaging manner, you'll stand a good chance of nailing that first appointment. *E-mail is not the medium of choice for this purpose!*

When I look at all the communication tools I used in my career to help me become successful, I realize they all had their place and value. But I also knew that what *really* made me successful were the principles I adopted that made customers feel special *all the time*—basically, all the things I did that are outlined in the chapters of this book. For example, all the things I talk about in how you organize and plan your day are critical when it comes to using your time effectively for *staying in touch with customers* and prospects. That's what got me to where I am today. No magic—just *dedication, ingenuity, and a burning desire to succeed.*

Touching the Ones You Love—the Unexpected

If staying in touch with customers and contacts is critical to your business success, then staying in touch with family and close friends is essential to living a purposeful life. You never know when you're going to be talking to them or seeing them for the last time. Unfortunately, that part of life is never written down in someone's appointment book.

How precious is the time you have with your family and close friends? If you truly love and care about them, you will never be able to put a price tag on it because your time with each other is priceless. I know it is for me and my family. All the things we've talked about that you should be doing to stay in touch with customers should go double for family. They are the reason you do what you do. Never miss an opportunity to let them know that.

Do the unexpected—a small bouquet of flowers for your wife for no apparent reason, a special candlelight dinner for a loving husband, perhaps a lunch date with your aspiring young professional daughter or son, maybe a special visit with parents who don't get to see you that often. Make it small, make it special, but above all, *stay in touch* with the people who form the bedrock of your life. They are the ones who energize the person within you and give you purpose each and every day you're on this planet.

RULE TEN
TELL THE TRUTH

If you tell the truth, you don't have to remember anything.

—Mark Twain, author and humorist

Truth leads to Trust and Trust leads to Success.

This is the last of the four chapters of *My 13 Rules* focusing on *interaction*. Nothing in this entire book will ring with integrity more than Rule #10, *Tell the truth*.

Living a Lie

Nobody likes the idea of having a negative label attached to their name. I'll tell you the one to avoid like the plague—**LIAR**. It's been said that even if you tell the truth for the rest of your life, **once you lie, you are known as a liar.** That's how much of an impact even a single lie can have on your character in the eyes of others. *You can never be trusted again.* The worst part about lying is that, once you start, you're on that slippery slope to the bottom. You then have to cover up your first lie with a second, then a third, and so on. At that point, you won't care if you destroy any innocent people who get caught in the *tornado* path of your lies. Pretty soon you're on a runaway stagecoach to self-ruin because others will soon figure out that what you said never actually happened.

Some people become so entrapped by their lies that they begin to believe they are the truth. But the real truth is, unless you can first be honest with yourself, you can never be honest with others. Your life becomes a "living" lie. You're a fraud—a complete fake. *You're nothing.* Here's a hammer to your head: **IF YOU ALWAYS TELL THE TRUTH, THEN YOU DON'T HAVE TO KEEP TRACK OF YOUR LIES.**

I remember being on a radio talk show some years back when the moderator said to me, "Joe, isn't it true that all salesmen are liars?" I said to him, "I can't speak for other salespeople, but I can tell you I'm not one. If you want me to lie, cheat, or misrepresent anything, then I don't want your business. Period." I'm sure that approach cost me some business over the years. I probably would have gotten away with it, and my sales record would have been bigger than it already is. That's not Joe Girard. I have to live with myself. I would have to go to bed each night for the rest of my life *tormented by the truth that I am a fraud.*

But I sleep well at night with peace of mind knowing that all of my 13,001 sales were *above board.* I think I am prouder of that than I am about the fact that it was a record-setting number that stills stands to this very day.

Nothing positive will ever come from anything you ever do if it's not based on the truth. If you don't believe that, then this chapter should rattle your skull. Yes, you can lie and get away with something for a while—but not forever. *YOU will get caught* because *a lie never lives to be old.* Sooner or later, you'll be tracked down like a filthy rat, humiliated before all your family, and labeled forever as the liar you really are. *TELL THE TRUTH OR DIE!*

If you really want to understand truth, start by looking at what's wrong with something first. You heard me right. If you study the bad things about something, trust me, it will leave a lasting impression on you. You'll straighten out in a hurry. It worked for me. I saw things as a kid growing up in the ghetto that I'll never forget, as grownup people fell under the spell of the *false promise of a lie*:

>> Observing the stupefying and violent effects of alcohol on grown men in the local bars as a nine-year-old shoeshine boy

>> Seeing the same bums on the same street corners looking in trash bins for their future

>> Watching people I recognized get picked up by the police for vandalism, theft, and gang fights

>> Coming home at night to a father who was interested only in how much change I had in my pocket

Once you understand the consequences of the dark side, you'll soon learn to appreciate the power of goodness and truth and how it applies to everything in life. Ask any soldier returning from combat after seeing death close up how much life is cherished now, something that might have been taken for granted before watching the violence of death snatch the life of a close friend in an instant right before his or her eyes.

Remember Scrooge in Charles Dickens's novella *A Christmas Carol*? His appreciation of goodness, compassion, and truth was realized only after his pathetic life was paraded before him by the ghosts of his past. That's when his eyes really opened up as he realized the truth about his ugly life. Scrooge got a second chance, but that was in a storybook. The rest of us have only one chance in life—and it's for real.

My Costly Education

When I was a kid, we didn't call it lying. We simply said we were "BS-ing" each other. Back then I had the good fortune of attending catechism (bible school) classes at a local Detroit Catholic church, St. Bonaventure. It was there that I learned about the importance of truth from a very special man, Father Solanus Casey. He was a very compassionate and inspirational monk (currently going through the review steps that will most likely lead to his recognition as a saint in the Church). Knowing about some of the trouble I got into growing up, you might be wondering if I skipped a few of his classes. Well, it's true my youth was certainly filled with a few left turns here and there, and I can't say I followed his wisdom every day, but *he did touch my life*. Father Casey taught me some things about truth that have stayed with me my entire life, not the least of which is self-respect—living with yourself. For that, I am eternally grateful.

My first lesson in appreciating the importance of telling the truth was a real wake-up call. In what I consider my first *real* job, I worked for Abe Saperstein, a small-scale home builder in the Detroit area. He was a pretty smart businessman who would buy vacant lots in different neighborhoods around town, build small inexpensive homes on them, and then sell them. Nothing fancy, but priced right.

As I mentioned in the Introduction, Abe was a decent man who took me under his wing and treated me like a son. In many ways, he was "the father I never had." He taught me practically everything I knew. I learned the business by working my way up from digging foundations to running construction crews. I eventually became the owner when Abe retired. It wasn't big bucks, but it was promising, and I made enough to feed three special people who had entered my life—my wife, June, and my two kids, Joe and Grace. Unfortunately, the one thing Abe never taught me about was how to balance good business judgment with *trust*.

I trusted just about everyone I dealt with. If someone said they were going to do something for me, I believed them. I actually thought people told the truth in business. I guess I was pretty gullible back then. I didn't have everything in writing from people, just their word or a handshake. Sadly, my trusting nature cost me a bundle as I fell victim to a salesman who was no better than a lying con artist.

It happened when I found a parcel of land at a bargain price big enough to build about 50 houses on it. I got excited! I could save money by spreading the construction startup costs over several homes at the same time since they were all next to each other. Now the reason the land was so cheap is that it was completely undeveloped, meaning no sewers were in. That was a big deal for Detroiters who wouldn't buy homes that had septic tanks.

The salesman representing the property assured me he had personally gone down to City Hall and checked. The sewers would be installed by the following spring, just a few months away. Fantastic, I thought! Once I bought the property, I would build a model and start selling from it. I took out a very high interest rate loan on the land to get started. I expected to have that loan paid off in no time since this was going to be a sure thing. I could only picture myself reeling in the dollars. Well, *not quite.*

I trusted, I believed, and I got screwed—and good. The truth was I was blind as a bat. I built the model, got the signs up, ran ads, and started to actually get quite a bit of traffic. People liked what they saw, and the price was right. But they all said the same thing: "We'll be back when the sewers are in." I sat there and waited and waited. No one was coming in to actually buy, and no one was putting in any sewers. That's a bad combination.

Pretty soon everyone seemed to be hitting me up for money I didn't have. I owed on the land, building materials, you name it. Before long, I was behind on everything. I even had to park my car away from my home at night to keep it from being repossessed and towed away by some collection agent. Things were out of control. I was in trouble.

Finally, I went down to City Hall to find out for myself what the holdup was on the sewers. Well, you guessed it. There were never any plans for sewers on that land—not now, not ever. I had been "walked downtown" as we used to say—screwed royally. And it was my own fault. I never bothered to check out the salesman's story, and I had nothing in writing. I was $60,000 in the hole for what amounted to a worthless piece of property. But that wasn't all of it! I dumped an additional $40,000 of my own money into building the two models along with a partially completed road! You might call it "my $100,000 lesson." That might not sound like a lot of money, but back in 1962, that was the equivalent of about $720,000 in today's dollars! Try that one out on your *attitude machine*!

Let me tell you, for a guy who was kicked out of high school, my *education* wasn't cheap. For what that cost me, I could have probably gone to Harvard back then, bought its library, and still had money left over to buy every house on that land I got sucked into buying. An interesting sidebar to all of this (as I mentioned earlier in the book) is that years later, I would be invited to speak before the student body at the Harvard Business School to give them a little "street" wisdom.

Everything I had done over the past 10 years to try and get my life back on track seemed as though it had just hit a brick wall. I felt like a truck going over a cliff. The pressure it put on me and my family was enormous. My house was foreclosed on. We were thrown out. Both of our cars were impounded. Even putting food on the table became a challenge. There I was with a wife and two kids—and we had nothing.

Whenever I read about today's housing crisis and the thousands and thousands of people who are losing their homes to foreclosures, I really feel for those families. I think back to my own living nightmare. Nobody came to our rescue. We had to do it on our own.

I went looking for a job by bus. *All I wanted was a bag of groceries for my family.* It was hard to come to grips with this. It seemed as though my reward for trusting was to have everything taken away from me, leaving me and my family empty-handed. Believe me, that can leave you feeling very bitter about doing the right things. I will never forget the moment when I realized I had been lied to. The face of that *snake* will live with me forever. Would you ever want to be remembered by anyone that way? If you lie, especially to a customer, they will bad-mouth you and your name to everyone they know. *Girard's Law of 250* will be your downfall. You're as good as dead.

I must confess, I did have a few fantasy thoughts about "getting" this guy who lied to me about those sewers. Thankfully (for him), I didn't. I think that would have been a slap in the face to the memory of my mother (and to Father Casey). That's not the example they set for me. Even though it seemed so unfair and wrong, I blamed myself for being so stupid. I was about as depressed as I could be. Although you couldn't have convinced me at the time, there would be a rainbow after the storm for Joe Girard.

Don't Stop Trusting

As bad as things were, that incident is where it really all began for me. I didn't become vengeful. I just learned to be a little bit smarter about how I went about doing things in the future. And it worked. The rest, as they say, is history. Without ever having sold a car before in my entire life, *in just three short years I would be the number-one salesman in the world!*

So what's the lesson here? For me, it's almost impossible to talk about truth without discussing trust and character. I learned just how deceitful people could be as I actually went into bankruptcy over that real estate deal. But *I was determined not to let it destroy or lessen my belief and trust in myself and others.* **THAT'S THE LESSON HERE!**

In fact, I actually became more determined than ever to become successful. It's been said that "you haven't met yourself until adversity is at your doorstep." I know I certainly met myself that day at City Hall. After a strong wind rips and tears away at everything that holds you together, if you're made of the right stuff, there's always one thing left that's still standing—*your character.*

Life has a funny way of taking sudden twists and turns and creating unexpected opportunities. Some people call it luck. I call it *Girard's destiny.* I believe it was meant to happen. The old saying "When one door closes, another opens" is very true. It certainly was in my case. Had it not been for that nightmare, I might never have achieved the success that I did. In spite of that experience, I never stopped trusting in myself or others.

You can't let one incident rule your life. Once you stop trusting and believing in the people who make a difference in your life, like your customers and business contacts (not to mention your family and friends), you might as well put your best outfit on and climb into a coffin because the end can't be far away. Only losers go down that road.

Nobody ever said life was fair, so quit blaming the world for your shortcomings. Just be smart about making sure important commitments are *in writing*. Learn from your mistakes and move on. Many people can't do this. They prefer to spend their time plotting ways to get even with someone who cheated them or lied to them. When that happens, you know you've reached the bottom. Soon honesty and trust are replaced by vengeance and hatred. If that describes you, congratulations— you've just signed on to work for the devil.

Stretching the Truth and the Art of Deception

A question we've all heard before is, "Are there ever times when a lie is not a lie?" That's not as easy to decide as it sounds. There are times when honesty can be a matter of degree. For example, telling a "white lie" or half-truth for the *better good* or protection of people, especially in life-threatening situations, or, for simply kind and compassionate reasons, is not necessarily wrong or a bad thing.

I've been in situations myself when I've had to *stretch* the truth a little. For example, I can remember complimenting a couple on how cute their son was when they were in my office. The truth was, he was a very ordinary and scruffy-looking kid. Sometimes common sense rules.

Stretching the truth is one thing; *deceiving* someone is an entirely different thing. Now you're trying to cheat someone out of something that's theirs—you're stealing. I once heard a story about a woman who was visiting the Leaning Tower of Pisa in Italy some years ago. She noticed a man handing a slip of paper to the tourists who parked their cars nearby. He asked for and received a sum of money from each driver. The tourists thought they were paying for parking. A woman, who spoke Italian, examined one of the pieces of paper and saw that the man was actually insuring the parked cars against damage in case the tower fell over. Even though it might have been legal, clearly this parasite was taking advantage of tourists who didn't speak the language, and he knew it.

Any way you cut it, *deception is still a lie*, no matter how slick you package it. Deception has many faces.

One in particular is a bit shortsighted and not a very smart business approach, although very commonplace. Believe it or not, the idea of "padding" the price with a few extra bucks is an everyday practice in every retail business. The customer isn't the only one trying to get the best deal. Right? Heed my advice here.

Instead of trying to squeeze every nickel you can out of a customer in one deal by cheating them out of a few bucks, why not take the *high ground*? Use your imagination and focus on the real opportunity on the horizon: **try to squeeze every year of loyalty out of them for the repeat deals ahead.** This is more than a matter of conscience. It's good business sense. Think about it. *You only have to sell them once.* After that, it's all about servicing them with care. Doesn't this make more sense?

Whatever a customer's experience is with you, that's the impression they will communicate to everyone they know. This is a classic case of where *Girard's Law of 250* kicks into high gear. If you've been less than above board with them, especially on what they paid you for something, it could cost you a bunch of money. Your reputation is now on the hot seat, and that could take years to repair (if at all). If you've cheated them or just taken "food off their plate" when they weren't looking, the world (your world) will know about it quickly! What do you want them to say about YOU? What don't you understand here? Tell me that isn't YOU.

By the way, I'm not talking about just what's bad business judgment. I'm talking about the difference between what's morally right and wrong. How would you like someone to nail you for a few extra bucks by inflating the price of a new flat screen TV you want to buy? How does it feel being in the other guy's shoes for a change? Not such a good fit, is it? Remember the guy who sold me that land? Well, that's exactly what you'd be doing to someone else.

Of all the dishonest things you can do to a customer, over-charging them—*swindling them*—ranks right up there with intentionally selling them a defective product. YOU'RE A LIAR AND A CHEAT! Why the hell would you do that to someone?

Every day we hear of people who continue to do this without giving it so much as a glance. Bernard Madoff, the biggest scam artist of all time, did it for 30 years! LYING FOR GREED will take your life down to the bottom faster than all the hard work you put into trying to get to the top.

Yes, it's a matter of *conscience and compassion.* If you believe in the Bible, Luke is very clear on this point in the New Testament: "Whatever measure you deal out to others, it will be dealt to you in return."

When I was in the Army back when I was 18, I could have exaggerated about an injury I received when I accidentally fell off the back of a troop transport truck and injured my lower back. For weeks the entire upper part of my body was taped up from my armpits to my waist. When the Army doctors inter-viewed me about the accident, I could have easily lied about never having an injury to my back before I joined the Army. But *I told them the truth.* I did have an injury to my back about three years earlier when I was practicing a dive and hit the diving board in our school's pool. Had I decided to just keep quiet about that swimming pool accident, I probably would have gotten away with it and received a discharge along with a disability pension.

But I would have had to live with myself and my deceit for the rest of my life. Every 30 days, a check would arrive in my mailbox, and each time I opened that envelope, it would *speak* to me in clear words, "Here's your '30 pieces of silver,' Girard." My brief stay in the Army ended with a medical discharge and, thankfully, without a pension. It was one of those times when getting nothing was better than getting something. But I did get something—a lifelong commitment to being truthful—and that's priceless.

You'll hear lots of reasons why telling the truth is the right thing to do. Some are obvious. It speaks well of your character and earns the respect of people around you. However, it might be the negative consequences of lying that provide the greatest motivation to tell the truth. A lie can easily cost you a promotion, money, or a friendship—maybe even create a dangerous situation for yourself. While it may be tempting to do it, you just don't want to take the chance of being caught.

You'd think anyone of average intelligence would realize this and start telling the truth. Unfortunately for many, the temptation is too great. Instead, they become pros at lying. They learn to "perfect" their lies so convincingly that they appear to be the truth. They've thought about everything: how it sounds, how likely is it to have happened, and, of course, the bottom line—how believable it is. Half-truths begin to look like the whole truth. This is where deception becomes an art form.

Over the years, there have been some very high-profile cases in the corporate and financial world where deception is witnessed on a grand scale. Executives are caught red-handed lying under oath during grand jury investigations where misdeeds cost investors and hard-working people billions of dollars in lost jobs, pensions, and life savings.

The Dos and Don'ts of Truth

Sometimes it's not what you say that determines whether you're telling the truth, but *what you don't say.* Let me explain. You might hear *someone else* say something that you know is not the truth. Maybe an important point was conveniently (or intentionally) "left out." By not correcting an obvious misstatement of the truth, *you too are indirectly lying.* This actually happens quite often. Many people will take the coward's way out when they hear someone lying because they don't like confrontation or might be afraid of losing their job. In other cases, they might see an instant opportunity for immediate personal gain.

For example, if the boss is handing out bonuses at the end of the year and accidentally calculates a slightly larger check for you by mistake, or gives you someone else's, by saying nothing and accepting it, you have just met *lying's* twin sister, *cheating.*

My Army experience is another case where, had I not said anything to those doctors, that wouldn't have meant that I wasn't lying. Yes, *silence can be a lie too.* I had an obligation to "fill in the blanks" about what really happened.

We're all human and tempted from time to time to compromise the truth, even just a little, because it's either convenient or we can gain from it personally. While I could give you many examples of things you should and shouldn't do, I think you're all intelligent enough to understand the obvious. Instead, I'd like to suggest a few guideposts that will keep you on the straight and narrow path of honesty.

Four Things You Should Do

1. **Be true to yourself.**
   > In order to like other people, you must first like yourself. Knowing who you are is being truthful to yourself. If you like what you see, self-respect will be your reward.
   > YOU CAN NEVER GET BEYOND THIS POINT BY "LIVING A LIE" ABOUT WHO YOU ARE.

2. **Think twice before speaking.**
   > Think carefully before you speak. Ask yourself, "Is what I am about to say the truth?" If it is, open your mouth and let the words fly out.

> I learned this technique trying to cure a case of stuttering I had growing up. It worked. It also works for telling the truth.

> If you think first, you won't rush into saying something you'll regret later.

> In the end, YOU ARE WHAT YOU SAY.

3. **Think of another way to say it.**

> Sometimes in a workplace situation, it is necessary to get a clear, truthful message across to someone, especially if a job situation is on the line. One way to do this is to mention the positive things about that individual.

> Encouraging positive performance can help to create change rather than resistance.

> Using this approach also avoids having to tell a lie.

4. **Temper truth with kindness.**

> If the truth in what you're going to say will hurt or embarrass someone, find a positive way to say it that still gets the message across without hurting them.

> Their feelings and emotions should be a strong consideration, especially if you know them to be sensitive.

> Putting someone down only makes them fail quicker.

Four Things You Should Avoid

1. **Don't exaggerate.**

> There's a fine line between exaggerating and lying. The truth is something that should be respected for what it is.

> If you develop a reputation as one who exaggerates the truth, people will become suspicious of anything you say. You will not be trusted.

2. Don't cover up for others.

> There may be times when you will be asked to tell a lie to cover up for someone. *Don't do it.* It's not always easy to resist, especially if the request is coming from a supervisor or one of the higher-ups. Your honesty will either earn you new respect or confirm you're working for the wrong company.

> Covering up and lying for kids is probably the worst thing a parent can do for a child. It sets the wrong example and gives the impression they don't need to be accountable for anything.

> Kids will always remember where they learned that from, especially when *they* get caught lying and it costs them a job or, worse yet, a marriage. This is not how you want your kids to remember you.

3. Don't ask others to cover up for you.

> For the same reasons you shouldn't cover up for others, don't put others on the spot by asking them to cover up for you. In many ways, this is even worse, especially if you're in a position of authority. The reality is, YOU'RE A COWARD! **Tell the TRUTH!** If you don't want to be bothered by a call, then tell your secretary you can't be disturbed right now, not that you're out of town.

> Unless you're operating in some illegal or immoral manner, you shouldn't have to lie!

4. Don't tell "little white lies."

> You have to use common sense in determining how to say something so that it is not a lie. We reviewed a few examples of that. But make no mistake: there's no such thing as a "white lie." *A lie can never be the truth any more than counterfeit bills are real money.*

> The danger is that "little" lies eventually become big lies. There's no stopping them then. When that happens, your character is on the way down. Soon you will not recognize yourself when you look in the mirror.

Here's the bottom line on the dos and don'ts of truth, short and sweet: *Truth leads to trust, and trust leads to success.*

Your Name and Your Word

This is the last of our three chapters on *interaction*—how we communicate with our customers, business partners, and other special people in our lives. In fact, this chapter, "Tell the Truth," is probably the most important of *My 13 Rules*. How you respond to this rule will most accurately define WHO YOU ARE ethically and morally as a person.

No matter what you do, if you want to stay ahead in the game, always tell the truth. The old saying **"TELL THE TRUTH AND YOU'LL NEVER GET CAUGHT"** is the simplest advice I can give anyone. If you want to sleep well at night each day of your life with no regrets, nothing will give you greater peace of mind than *living the truth*. You will never be haunted by nightmares of things you said or did that cheated or deceived someone out of what was rightfully theirs.

As you've probably sensed by now, "Tell the Truth" is more than just another chapter in this book to me. It's a very personal matter, probably because I have been lied to and cheated so many times in my life that it has taken on a very special significance. For me, telling the truth strikes right at the very heart and soul of who you are. When I see and hear people lying to each other, I get angry. When it's done to me, I feel violated. The truth is that sacred.

In spite of all the liars and cheats that roam this world, there are a large number of people who will never violate their obligation to be truthful. If you have people in your life like that, you are fortunate indeed, for they are living examples of hope for the future.

In my life, I had the privilege of knowing three such people who had *faith* in me:

> *Jack LaLanne*, the fitness and health guru, for his honest and candid remarks to me that changed my health habits for the rest of my life.
>
> *Dr. Norman Vincent Peale*, theologian and author of *The Power of Positive Thinking*, for his faith in my positive attitude and ability to help others.
>
> *Lowell Thomas*, world-renowned news broadcaster, writer, and global adventurer who, after hearing me speak, encouraged me to write a book about my experiences (which I have now done five times).

They are the special people in my life who pointed me in the right direction. Their inspiration, encouragement, and honesty played a significant role in helping me personally chisel my way through life to a rewarding and successful career based on truth and integrity.

One of the most important things you can do to make sure you always *tell the truth* is to look around you and take note of all the things you have experienced or attained in life that came from being truthful. These are truth's gifts to you.

» It might be something as simple as a car or a home that was acquired through your honest hard work.

» Maybe it's a family vacation you've saved up for.

» But most of all, think of the relationships you have made with others—a spouse, your kids, or maybe just a very special friend. Think of the honest and faithful relationships you have formed with them by being truthful and trusting, not because either of you had wealth or power, but because you were simply respectful of each other.

That's what truth will get you in this life: rewards and gifts attained with integrity.

When you look at all you have, think about ways to grow and expand those relationships and things you have attained *honestly* in life. And be sure to share your good fortune with others who have less than you. If you don't think you have much, let me tell you about something you do have that's quite valuable that you can share with others right now. *One of the few things you can always give in this life, and still keep, is your word. Cherish it. It has your name on it.*

PART III
CLOSE THE DEAL

RULE ELEVEN

LOCK UP EVERY OPPORTUNITY

If a window of opportunity appears,
don't pull down the shade.

—Tom Peters, author, *In Search of Excellence*

I had my customers locked in my mink-lined
handcuffs of LOVE.

Our first 10 rules focused on *preparation* and *interaction*. These next two chapters will zero in on the third section of *My 13 Rules*, "closing the deal," as I like to call it. As I said earlier in the book, *closing the deal* doesn't necessarily mean only completing a sale. It means achieving the desired outcome you're looking for in something. It might be improving a relationship with a friend, a relative, or a customer. Or maybe it means completing a project you've put on the back burner for a few months. Anything you set your sights on as a goal that you do achieve, whether it's personal or professional, means you've closed the deal.

Closing the Deal

n this chapter, I'm going to show you how to *lock up every opportunity*. By that, I mean getting yourself into the most favorable position to achieve any goal you set as an objective—personal or professional.

Now we all know how important and satisfying it is to achieve the goals we set out to accomplish in life. I spent an entire career in retail sales setting and breaking my own records. I achieved what I did because I never took anything for granted, even after I became number one in the world. I locked up my opportunities because my mindset remained unchanged from the very first sale I ever made. I remember it well. That customer sitting across from me that day was not a man in a brown suit. He was that "bag of groceries" I desperately needed to feed my family. I was hungry then. I was "hungry" during my 15 years of selling. And I remained "hungry" until I closed the last of my 13,001 sales. If there was one thing I WAS NOT, it was *complacent*—not a day in my life after that first sale.

I don't care what field you're in, there's too much competition out there to risk missing an opportunity you may get only one shot at. **You must be hungry.** Starvation is the great teacher of appreciation. If you like steak but haven't eaten a thing in a week, a piece of stale bread starts to look pretty good.

If you want to lock up every opportunity, you've gotta really want it. And if it's personal goals we're talking about achieving, even more so. What can be more rewarding than feeling the pride and gratification of knowing you raised your kids right: seeing them graduate from college or serve their country, being a special part of their wedding day, or being gifted with a grandchild? Now that's really special—mission accomplished.

Sometimes achieving goals can be especially difficult. You may be called upon to do what may seem impossible to you—helping a friend or relative through troubled times. Maybe it's a marriage on the rocks, drugs or alcohol abuse. In the chapter on *Girard's NO-NO's*, you'll recall I mentioned a couple of guys in our sales department who both had serious drinking problems. One of them, Jim, managed to break his addiction and went on to do fairly well in the dealership. I remember mentioning it to him once (using the other guy as an example of what not to be). All I ever said to him was, "Pretend you're looking in the mirror whenever you see Tom." I think it hit home with him.

Like me, you may not be an experienced counselor or an expert on any of that, but you can make a difference. This is especially true if it's someone you know personally.

That person you're helping believes YOU hold their "trust" card in your hand. They're counting on YOU to help them get back on track, so you've got to get it right for them. When you're faced with a mountain like that to climb, *closing the deal* can be really rough. But it's also a tremendous opportunity to see if you have what it takes to lock it up!

If you want to *lock up every opportunity*, here's my advice: *get your heart, your body, and your mind focused on the goal.* Block everything else out. Think, breathe, and live all of the first ten of the *13 Rules* I've talked about in this book. That's critical. You've gotta be at the top of your game whenever someone sees you or needs you, so concentrate on these rules. Soak them up till they become second nature to you.

The Other Guy's Shoes

The best way I know how to get yourself into a winning position with someone else is to understand their perspective better than they do. "How can that be?" you say. It simply means *putting yourself in their shoes* so that you fully understand what they're seeing, thinking, and feeling (except that you can be more objective than they can—they're too close to it). That's how prizefighters do it. They study their opponents until they "become" them. Then when they step into the ring with them, they know what to expect before it happens. They're prepared. No surprises. That's exactly what you need to do in life's encounters. That's your best shot at controlling and steering the outcome of a situation in your favor that I know of.

If I was nothing else, I was a master at studying people, their behavior and their habits. I already told you how much research I did on the background of my customers. Sometimes I thought I knew them better than they knew themselves before we ever met. Remember what I said in Chapter 7, "Listen." I told you to observe and *listen with all your senses,* not just your ears. Get to know what makes people tick. I got to the point where I could easily recognize the quality of watch they were wearing.

If you do it right, you'll learn things about your prospects that will help you steer things in the right direction—toward their comfort level. This will enable you to build the foundation for a relationship that could last decades.

If it's a customer we're talking about, you're looking to close more than a sale. You want to open the doors to servicing that customer for the rest of his or her life. That's repeat business waiting to happen. Service 'em to death with LOVE!

The same holds true for a personal relationship. You want to be remembered, respected, and loved for something you did in someone's life that made a difference. Whatever that may have been, you were there for them. You made an impact. You're a winner in their book. They'll never forget you. Sadly, many relationships never got to this level when they could have or should have. Just ask me. Every Father's Day, I think of that great void in my own life. But thank God there's a Mother's Day.

The Name of the Game Is Trust

Lock up every opportunity with TRUST. I stressed the importance of trust in Chapter 10, "Tell the Truth." In my opinion, if there's one thing a person wants more than anything else from another, it's trust. Yes, trust. If you have a relationship with a foundation based on trust, it can grow into respect and love. Without it, though, love and respect don't stand a chance. Our divorce rate is proof positive as to why marriage doesn't work without trust.

Learn to build those bridges of trust with your customers and special people in your life. Don't be afraid to encourage them to open up to you (or you to them for that matter). Just ask:

"Why did you buy from me?"

"What was it that I did that made the difference?"

"What can I do to make your experience even more meaningful in the future?"

I would often ask questions like these when I made my customer follow-up calls three days after the purchase (*Kiss #3* from Chapter 9, "Stay in Touch"). I made sure they knew I wasn't calling just to get flattering comments. While most sales reps wouldn't take the time to follow up with their customers after the sale quite the way I did, I had very precise reasons:

1. Making my customers feel better about their decision to buy from me *was* number one on my list!
2. I genuinely wanted to keep getting better and better at what I did.

Not only did they appreciate the thoughtfulness, but they were very open and responsive in telling me what they liked about the *Joe Girard experience.*

Keep building those bridges. Believe it or not, very few people want to do this. They're afraid to get "too close" to someone. They like things an "arm's length" away. That was fine with me. My approach was different. I didn't mind getting close at all because my goal never changed. I wanted my prospects to "walk in and drive out."

Don't ever take your customers for granted. *Lock up every opportunity* you have with them to build lasting relationships. Begin with trust and continue with outstanding service. If it's your family, *never let go.*

One of the things I used to do to build trust with my customers was something we called "spot deliveries." Insurance companies do this sort of thing all the time when they give you a temporary insurance binder until the real paperwork comes along in a few days. The important thing is you're insured immediately. In my business, if a customer wasn't sure they wanted to purchase the vehicle we had been discussing, I simply told them to take it home right then and there—right now! As long as they signed an agreement to bring it back in the same brand new condition they got it in, I gave them the keys and told them to take it home for a day or two. The fact that I trusted them that much said a lot to them.

I remember one customer in particular who was "on the fence" about committing to purchase. As he started to get up to leave my office, he said, "Joe, I'll give this some thought. But I need to go home and discuss it with the wife." Before he got two steps toward my door, I said, "Bob, I know it's a difficult decision. There's a fair amount of money involved. Let me take the pressure off." I handed him the keys to the car he just test drove as I said, "Here." He looked at me somewhat amazed. I continued, "Take it home for a couple of days. Let Noreen (I knew her name from the profile sheet) take it for a drive. Enjoy it together so you'll both be comfortable with your decision. Just bring it back the way you got it." I told him I'd take good care of the car he drove up in and have it washed for him in case he decided not to purchase the vehicle. He was not expecting this kind of treatment at all. He thanked me and happily drove the car home.

What was I doing? I was actually giving him and his wife "instant ownership." I was building trust and at the same time giving the customer an opportunity to reinforce his decision to buy and take ownership of the vehicle on his own. I wanted to put him at ease without any pressure. I knew that self-confidence generated decisiveness. Bob called the following afternoon and said they both loved the car and were looking forward to coming in to sign the papers to buy it (which they did).

The last thing I wanted was a case of "buyer's remorse." I was there to lock 'em up! I wanted my prospects to BELIEVE that, although the paperwork hadn't yet been completed on the vehicle, he or she already "owned" it. They were *already Joe Girard customers*, and now they were morally obligated to go through with the purchase. It was a mind game I almost always won because prospects in that situation were usually only at odds with themselves about closing the deal—they already loved the car and, almost always, me too. I was there to help keep the ship on course, safely steering it into Girard's "harbor" in case things got a little stormy.

HERE'S THE KEY LESSON: If you want someone to be persuaded that your advice or recommendation is best for them (whether it's buying something from you or embracing an idea you have), make accepting the outcome *their idea*, not yours. Get them to believe that you didn't sell them anything; what really happened is *they* bought something. It's not as confusing as it may sound. What I did do better than anyone else is *persuade people that they should consider making a decision to buy a product from me. But it was always their decision.* And the record shows that several of them agreed and said "yes"—13,001 to be exact. And I complimented every one of them on their decision. Congratulate the people you do business with on their choice. Be sincere and mean it. *They trust you.* Don't let them down.

I can honestly say that I had maybe one case in 15 years (if that) of someone actually returning a vehicle to me without agreeing to purchase it—one in 13,001 sales. Now there's a top-of-the-line track record with unbelievable odds stacked in my favor.

I knew the dealer wasn't too crazy about the idea of a customer driving off with one of his cars without a commitment to buy, but the fact was, IT WORKED.

Quite frankly, I was used to the idea that the dealership management wouldn't go for some of my leading-edge thinking on how to take care of customers. Why did they go along with it? Simple—I brought more sales and profits into that dealership than all the other salespeople combined, and they knew it. They also knew that the customers who bought from Joe Girard were *MY* customers, not just people who purchased something from their dealership. I was the link to their success, and they never forgot that. My numbers spoke loudly to them—I held the trump card every time they objected.

It was that narrow-minded thinking that prevented many dealers and salespeople alike from really becoming successful. Once again, Girard was way ahead of the curve and looking *down the road* at a relationship-building opportunity, not just a one-time sale.

Even if you don't have a big following at first, don't be discouraged by not getting the support of the management in your company. Learn your business thoroughly. Demonstrate your techniques and approaches, and show the leadership in your company how your methods are helping grow their business and making them more profitable. When they see that positive vibes about the company are beginning to spread whenever you are handling their customers' needs, you will most assuredly be recognized for this. By the way, if that doesn't happen and you are essentially told to get in step with the old company ways, dust off your resumé immediately. *You know what you are doing, and others will surely want you on their team.* Be patient, though. I didn't achieve what I did overnight.

I also went out of my way to build the trust of women, many of whom had difficulty getting credit, partly because of the low wages paid women back then. I felt for them and their situation. I know what it's like not to have anything. I've stood in that pair of shoes before. It's a miserable feeling. Still, most guys in our sales department wouldn't touch a deal like that. They always thought dealing with single women customers and trying to get credit for them was a complete waste of time. Not me; I found a way to help them and myself at the same time.

I remember helping out a recently divorced young lady who needed help establishing credit. I contacted one of the banks I did a lot of business with and asked them to get me the names of some reputable firms who dealt in the business of buying diamonds and jewelry. I passed these names onto my prospect and showed her how to turn her diamond rings and other jewelry into credit to be able to afford the vehicle she wanted. I could see my encouragement all over her bright smile (which I reflected back to her). We were able to put a deal together in a few days with her credit so she could get her life rolling again (and in a new Chevrolet from Joe Girard).

If there was any way at all to get ladies credit, you could bet that I knew how to do it better than anyone else in the business. I had a reputation for that. They trusted me, and I made it happen. I was connected to banks, and banks were connected to me. Those women never forgot me. Many of them became repeat customers of mine till the day I retired. The only losers were all those jealous people in the sales department who ignored them.

Keep 'Em Coming Back

Do your homework before you get with a customer or person you're trying to help or influence. Don't do what so many people in retail sales do. They assume they just have to "meet and greet" and look happy to get the business. They do nothing to prepare for a potential customer or sale. They don't know anything about the customer and, worse yet, they don't know their products or services the way a customer has the right to expect they should. In other words, they know "nothin' about nothin'." They're so ill-prepared, it's no wonder nobody ever comes back to them for a second look.

I've had this experience countless times when shopping myself as I'm sure you have too. I recall one particular incident when a salesman in a cellular phone shop (that I had bought from before) couldn't tell me if I would be able get good coverage in the area I lived in. The store was only three miles from my house. I live in a well-populated suburb, not out in the sticks where reception might be an issue. When I asked about which phones he had that would give the best reception and had the best features, again he seemed lost. He couldn't tell me the differences between the phones I was looking at. I looked at him and said, "Don't you have a manual or something you can check?" He said he did but would have to locate it. He excused himself and then began a desperate search for the manuals, practically emptying any drawer in his path. If it wasn't so pathetic, in a way, it was actually quite amusing to watch. I finally called a halt to the "search" and told him not to bother and that I'd be back. Needless to say, I never returned and purchased my phone elsewhere. Part of the problem here is obviously poor training, but mostly it's lack of common sense.

If you expect to have repeat customers or people wanting to continue a relationship with you (personal or professional), then you had better be considerate of them and show an interest in how they see things. Forget about your point of view. Concentrate on theirs. If you don't, you'll fail miserably.

Although I was very successful at what I did, I don't want you to get the idea that everyone I ever sold anything to was a piece of cake. That kind of luck didn't exist in the business I was in. You had to work at it. You had to understand, respect, and anticipate the kinds of concerns customers would have about what you were selling.

For example, I can remember that quality was always a big issue. Even though, for the most part, the products were pretty good quality and reliable, there were occasional problems. Sometimes it was cosmetic, like the pinstriping on the side of the body would begin to peel off. Other times it might be more of a mechanical issue, like the power windows wouldn't align properly or the radio seemed to have electrical connection problems.

Whatever it was, you had to be prepared to deal with and overcome the legitimate concerns customers would have about the product and service they were getting. If you were prepared and looked at things from their point of view, you were able to anticipate how they would react to anything you told them. Because of that, I was almost always able to control the outcome before it happened. That's how I kept them coming back for more. They trusted me, and they knew I would deliver because I always did.

If it was a service issue, I saw it as the first opportunity to get them back on my Ferris wheel for the next sale. I know this may sound odd to some of you, but I actually relished the opportunity to make things right with a customer. While most of the salespeople would look for a rock or another person to hide behind when a disappointed customer approached them, I saw it as the first step toward securing the next sale. I loved it!

One customer came into the service department angry about a rattling sound that just wouldn't go away in the new car he'd bought from me. He vowed never to buy a vehicle there again. I thought I'd never see him again after that visit.

I calmly told him he had my word I would get it taken care of and asked him to join me for a cup of coffee while the service department took care of his problem. He calmed down some and agreed.

I looked him sincerely in the eye and said, "Carl, if the second dealership I went to work for didn't hire me, I might have looked into another line of work. I would never have gotten a second chance to prove I was not only a competent salesperson but the very best in the world at what I do."

I walked him down to my office to finish our coffees as we sat both facing my desk with my empty chair in front of us. (I wanted to be on the same side with him—a more relaxed arrangement.) I gestured to the wall of framed sales award plaques in front of us that I had received over the years, and there were dozens. I told him, "Carl, you might say this is my 'wall of second chances.' That's what a second chance can get you if someone will just give it to you."

He had seen that wall of plaques before when he bought his car from me. However, he never thought of them in quite that way. Carl was duly impressed. More importantly, he understood my point. I was basically asking him to do the same thing for me. I was careful not to get defensive or blame the factory for what was wrong with his car. He learned I had the guts to "take the hit" even though it was a factory issue. He learned something about ME at that moment. I wanted to make it right for him.

The car was properly repaired and never squeaked again. How do I know? I called him every week for the next six weeks as I said I would to find out how it was doing (cementing our relationship for the next purchase in the process). He really appreciated the follow-up calls, but most of all he appreciated the unusual commitment I demonstrated to him. His brother-in-law bought a new pickup truck from me four months later on his recommendation (for which he picked up a nice $50 *bird dog* fee). That's how you keep 'em coming back for more.

I wanted to keep 'em coming as long as I could keep standing. And in the shape I'm still in today, I could pick up where I left off in a heartbeat if I wanted to. How's that for staying the course?

To me, keeping a customer was like clutching the string attached to a beautiful balloon. If I let go, it would just fly away and eventually burst—opportunity lost. There was no way to get it back. Let me tell you, it would take one helluva tornado or hurricane before Girard would ever let go of a customer. That's how I played the game of retention. My customers were like family to me. I was in it to win and to make winners out of my customers. I kept 'em coming back for more and more. I really didn't have to "lock them up" at all. They placed their hands in my handcuffs willingly because they were the "softest, mink-lined, LOVE cuffs" you ever saw. And I made sure they enjoyed the experience over and over, again and again. Nobody in history ever turned more retail customers into gold the way Joe Girard did—not even King Midas! Midas was a myth; Girard is for real! How about that for a "golden touch"?

Diamonds Are Forever

Many of us are fascinated by the dazzle and mystique of diamonds. Remember the James Bond movie *Diamonds Are Forever*? Those gems had such a grip on people in that film, it seemed as though they were obsessed. They would kill or die for diamonds before surrendering even a fraction of a single carat of those spellbinding precious stones. It's no wonder that many people put diamonds right up there with gold and good health as possessions they'd like to have most. How about you?

I want you to close your eyes for a moment and imagine the feel of a large cut diamond resting in the palm of your hand. Now slowly open your eyes and look down at the dazzling brilliance of the gem you hold. Now gently close your hand as you protect that precious jewel from ever escaping your grasp. You must believe in your heart that no one is permitted to take that away from you. It is your treasure to keep forever.

That, my friend, is not a diamond you have in your hand. I want you to think of it as a *relationship*, a special bond you have with someone. It could be a friend, a relative, or a customer. It doesn't matter. It is as priceless as the most brilliant of gems. If you treat special relationships with the thoughtful and caring consideration they deserve, like diamonds, they are forever—but not for everyone. If you take your eye off the ball and loosen your grip on the treasures in your life, they will surely be lost to someone else. *Never forget to reinforce those special relationships.*

If it's customers or business colleagues we're talking about, they represent more than just the means to buy a precious stone. They are the source of what you need to provide everything else in your life—a home for your family, education for your kids, and a source of income to maintain your good health well into your golden years. So why treat them as though they don't matter? LOCK THEM UP! *You need them!*

Customers always want to be reassured that you really do care about them. Nurture those relationships and do it often. *Constant reinforcement* is the key. Let them know how important they are and that you are thinking about them. Take nothing for granted. Send them a personalized card or make a two-minute phone call. You heard it right. In two minutes, I can tell a person everything I need to say. How do I know?

1. **It's all written down** on an index card! Short, sweet, and to the point.
2. **Experience**—I make dozens of these kinds of calls practically every day.
3. **I am motivated** to constantly surround my customers with deep water. No one is permitted to get near Girard's customers.

Don't wait to be asked if YOU'RE "still alive." If they have to initiate the contact, you might as well be dead as far as that customer is concerned. Expressing sincerity at that point is like chasing the truth—your trust is on the line and you've lost.

I know that some business and personal relationships don't always go the way we want them to in spite of our best efforts. But don't blow it by letting the opportunity slip away because you failed to do the basics of keeping in touch. You'll stay up night after night tormenting yourself once you've lost something that was special to you because you just failed to pay attention. There's plenty of time to think about something you let get away once it's gone. Don't put yourself in that position. Never, never let someone pick your pocket while you're not looking. These are your treasures to keep forever.

In life, treasures come in many forms. If someone asked me what the most precious thing in the world is to me, I would say, *"A loyal person who would be faithful to me forever."* You know who those people are in your life. In my world, I had a grandmother, a mother, and a wife who spent a good part of their lives reinforcing and selling—*reinforcing and selling* ME—on the idea that I was worth something until *I decided* that I could be someone. They were all like precious gems to me: my wife, June, whose life was tragically cut short at age 46, and now my wife, Kitty, a diamond whose brilliance glitters as brightly as ever in my life. These are the reinforcements in my life that helped to make me what I became and what I am. Believe me when I tell you this: I have received more than I could ever give back in return. I have truly been blessed.

Losing a Sure Thing

We've seen it happen before. Something looks like a sure thing—it just can't lose, no way no how, it's in the bag, a slam-dunk. And then suddenly it's gone—it's lost. The worst nightmare realized in full living truth. What was supposed to be an almost forgone conclusion ends in shocking disbelief. How can that be?

How could a magnificent "unsinkable" ship like the *Titanic* actually sink? As unbelievable as it may seem, it did. We all know the story and the reasons. Let me give you my take on this: *arrogance* and *incompetence*, not to mention *stupidity*. When you put those three bunglers together, you've probably got the worst combination you could come up with to get anything done effectively. But it happened. Human beings did it, and people died.

Just when something seemed like a lock—a sure thing—disaster struck. It often does to those who are "asleep at the wheel." What quickly follows then is the embarrassment and humiliation of failure and, in some cases, a legacy of shame and guilt. Sometimes even time does not forgive or forget; a century later, the saga of the *Titanic* is eternally sentenced to retell its sobering story over and over.

Although the *Titanic* was the most magnificent engineering and design feat of its time, the grandeur of this ocean liner is ironically but a footnote in its history. It will always be remembered for what was lost, not what was achieved. There were no winners. You'll never read anything praising the great iceberg that took down the *Titanic*!

There are some who would say that it was just bad luck that this happened. Only a complete fool would think that. But they're out there. First of all, I don't believe in luck, as you know. As I said earlier, "Luck is for losers." I believe in controlling the outcome by paying attention and never taking your eye off the ball.

Pay Attention Now!

HERE'S THE LESSON: You can never assume anything about how locked up your opportunities are in life, whether it's personal or professional. You have to work at a marriage with the same intensity as you do trying to land that big account. Only death is certain. Everything else is up for grabs and goes to those who use their heads and learn to anticipate, to "look around the corner" with a plan to deal with the unexpected. Very few people actually do this. **If you learn to look ahead and anticipate things, you will have discovered what the real edge in winning looks like.**

When you reach that point, there will be no doubt in your mind that you have arrived. Your confidence will soar. Losing a sure thing will not happen to you because you know nothing is certain, and you will take the necessary precautions to insure it doesn't. When you close your hand on that brilliant diamond, it will never be allowed to escape—not now, not ever. Period. Congratulations. You've just separated yourself from the pack.

Silence Is Golden

Another common mistake people in sales make is overselling a customer who has already decided he or she wants to do business with you. I've actually watched other salespeople sell themselves out of a sold deal by talking too much and at the wrong time. There's a reason **SILENCE IS GOLDEN**. Once you've given your remarks or explained what you have to offer to an individual, it's now time to let them respond. STOP TALKING.

Sometimes, it takes a fair amount of discipline to not break the silence between you and another person, especially when it feels a little awkward. Seconds of silence seem like minutes. Even though it's tempting to break the ice, you must learn to remain silent. *It's their turn to speak.* If you're meeting with the individual in person, then just make polite eye contact and await their response.

You'll never get their feedback or response to what you are asking for if you continue to talk. Furthermore, that could jeopardize your relationship if they feel you're taking too much control of things. Before you know it, you've let go of the string attached to a beautiful balloon that could have been yours. Your locked-up opportunity has escaped and all because you weren't paying attention. Never forget: *the person you're with must always feel like they're in charge*, even if they're not.

I'd bet that more sales and relationships are lost because of things that were said rather than because of things that were omitted. I once sat down with one of our salesmen after work as he told me a story about how he had lost what he called a "done deal." He said the customer was just getting ready to sign the purchase agreement when, in his excitement to show off the service department, he told the customer to first take a moment and come with him so he could show him the operation. All he did was brag about it and the great products that Chevrolet was producing. In his haste to make a good impression, he found himself talking more and more about everything and forgot about the upcoming factory recall that was taking place all over the country. When they arrived at the service department, there it was in full swing—a line of recalled vehicles in to fix some faulty electrical switches. It was minor, to be sure. However, the customer saw it very differently. He pictured the car he was about to buy as showing up in a long line for repairs. His hesitation quickly turned into a decline to buy. The lesson is clear: *Never take the pen out of the customer's hand when a purchase agreement is being signed!* You could say he *talked* himself out of a deal. It was a costly lesson, but he learned.

You'll never "put your foot in your mouth" because of something you didn't say. Quite often the wrong things are often said *after* the desired outcome has already been reached with someone. Once a person achieves what he or she set out to do, and the goal is in their grasp, they tend to let their guard down. They stop paying attention to small things. In their mind, the deal is signed, sealed, and delivered. The reality is, it isn't. It can still be lost. That's the time to really knuckle down and prevent stupid mistakes from happening. That's not the time to slack off. The less you say, the better chance you have of closing the deal and locking up the opportunity.

And this concept applies to everything we're talking about here: sales, service, and especially relationship-building. You've heard the expression "lock and load" when referring to guns? I'm introducing "listen and lock." If you pay attention to the person you're with and *spend most of the time listening* to their concerns and understanding their perspective, you'll be in a stronger position to *lock 'em up*. Another way of saying "Silence is golden" is "If you want their gold, then shut up."

Getting Positioned for Success

At the beginning of this chapter, I stated that the idea behind *locking up every opportunity* was *"getting yourself into the most favorable position* to achieve any goal you set as an objective." Unfortunately, there's no guarantee it will always be accomplished. We all have our bad moments and bad days. Even the very best major league baseball players have their share of strikeouts. You can't judge an athlete by a single game. Instead, you have to look at your total performance over an extended period of time to get a better picture of how you're doing, not at a single bad day. You'll have them. It's part of life.

In a very practical sense, the real goal of this chapter is to prevent you from shooting yourself in the foot before the "hunt" even starts. That's where most of the mistakes occur when dealing with other people—at the outset, not at the end. If you want to improve *your batting average* of locking up opportunities, you must prevent stupid blunders from happening at all costs. The first 10 of *My 13 Rules* are explicitly designed to get you into the best shape possible so you don't make those kinds of mistakes. The competition is stiff enough without adding your own stupidity to the list.

Get yourself in the right position to succeed by first making sure that all the basics are covered. Keep rereading the previous 10 rules until they stick like glue to you. When you "become" those first 10 rules, you'll be ready to lock 'em up for good.

When I retired from the business of retail selling, I was 49 years old. That's right, there's no typo here. I was 49 when I launched into a whole new career as a motivational speaker, sharing my experience and know-how with audiences from blue chip corporations and organizations all over the world (which I do to this very day). You see, I never really "retired." Joe Girard retiring would be a little bit like not seeing the sun rise. *Overcast days are not permitted in my life.* I know all too well what days without sunshine look like.

I remember the first time I appeared before a sellout crowd. At the end of my presentation, I left the stage to a standing ovation from a very enthusiastic audience. When I got off the stage, I said to myself, "Joey, you've come a long way, baby." I had the audience locked in my "mink-lined handcuffs of LOVE" just like the customers I had locked up all those years. I could feel a smile coming on as I heard the echo of my father's voice ringing in my ear: "You're a bum, Joey. You'll never amount to anything. You're no good. You'll always be a bum." I could still hear the audience applauding as I looked up at the ceiling behind the curtain and whispered, "You're right, Pa. I am a bum. I don't even have a steady job anymore, Pa. I am a bum." I turned and smiled as I looked back at the audience from the stage wing. "BUT I'M A RICH BUM." Case closed.

RULE TWELVE

STAND IN FRONT OF EVERYTHING YOU DO FOR OTHERS

Character is like a tree and reputation is its shadow.
The shadow is what we think it is;
the tree is the real thing.

—Abraham Lincoln, sixteenth President
of the United States

I get between *my customers and any problems
they might experience.*

S am Walton, the founder of Walmart, once said that the two most important words he ever wrote were "satisfaction guaranteed." They were on the company's very first sign. Customers knew that from the moment they entered the doors beneath that sign, they could feel secure in any purchase they made there. The company stood behind those two words. Their reputation and future were locked together in that promise, and, in my opinion, it's the main reason why Walmart became one of the most successful companies in history. Simple but brilliant—that's the kind of stuff I like. *Satisfaction guaranteed.* Just two words! What a combination; what a smart business plan.

I take a slightly different approach than Sam Walton did, but we come out the same way. I don't stand *behind* anything I do for my customers. I stand in *front* of everything I do for them. By that, I mean I get *between* my customers and any difficulties they may be having with the products they buy from me. I don't want them anywhere near problems. My goal is always to shield and protect them from anything bad at all times. In this chapter, I'm going to show you how to do that.

As I said in the Introduction, my first six rules focus on *preparation.* The next four center on *interaction.* Rules #11 and #12 are all about *closing the deal.* This, then, is the second of that last set, Rule #12: *Stand in front of everything you do for others.*

The Power of a Promise

The way I look at it, taking care of customers is more than a matter of good business sense. It's a matter of good conscience. I couldn't go to sleep at night knowing I could have done something to make a customer's day end a little bit better than how it started, but didn't, because I decided to either ignore them or get involved in something else. But it did happen to me—ONCE.

Whenever I got busy, which was more often than not, I would sometimes get so focused on making the most of my time that I could disconnect myself from anything else going on around me. While that was a great discipline and asset for me, it could also create a small problem. I remember one instance when a prospect caught me going out of my office, heading to the finance department. He said he had a question for me. I was moving quickly as I usually do when I work, especially when I have a customer in my office. I glanced at him and said, "I'll get to your question as quickly as I can, but right now I have to take care of what I'm doing at this moment."

By the time I got around to that prospect, he was nowhere to be seen. I remember the anxious look on his face as I passed him by. He wanted help. I could have stopped, taken one minute, and answered his question, but I was focused on my mission of the moment. I felt bad not because of the potential lost sale but because I had an opportunity to make his day a little bit better than when it started, and I didn't.

That evening, I gave myself a good lecture for ignoring him. That was not like me at all. "What kind of attitude is that?" I asked myself. It never happened again.

If you ignore someone who is crucial to your livelihood, and you're right there and know exactly what to do to help them, then what the hell are you waiting for? Where is your common sense?

When I shook the hands of my customers as I gave them the keys to their new vehicles, I complimented them on their purchase decision and reminded them, "Today, you also 'bought' Joe Girard." I made a promise to them right then and there that I would be there for them if ever they needed anything. And I meant it. *I gave them my word.* I knew what the *power of a promise* could do for my future relationship with a customer. I also knew how it could backfire on me if I ever violated that trust. Don't ever make a promise you can't keep. It will come back to haunt you and kill any chance you have of generating future business or referrals. You must take your commitments very seriously. If you stand in front of your commitments to your customers, they will follow you to the ends of the earth. Watch the *Girard touch* here.

If ever a customer of mine had a problem with their product, they were instructed to call me first, not the service department. I know what you're thinking: "What? Why not let them go right to the service department? After all, that's what it's for, right?" No, no, no—not in Girard's world. If they're coming in for normal service maintenance like an oil change, I probably wouldn't get involved. But if they're having problems with their vehicle, I'm in the loop immediately.

The service department (remember, these guys are on my team) understood that all those types of calls were to be channeled to me first. If I'm the one making the promise, then I'm going to be the one controlling what and how that customer is handled. One of my people (I'm talking about the two guys I hired that *I paid* to assist me, not the dealership) would be the contact point for all my customers. I always got between my customers and their service needs. I left nothing to chance. That's the way I operated. I was the ONLY salesperson that did that. But listen up! I was also the most successful retail salesperson of all time.

I knew how to keep the customers I had already sold. ARE YOU GETTING THE MESSAGE? This is one of the reasons you bought this book, so pay attention here. Nothing would anger me more than finding out that one of my customers had to come back a second time to correct the same problem, especially one I could have prevented had I been involved. The fact that this had happened on a few occasions is precisely what prompted me to set up my own system for servicing my customers. As far as I was concerned, those customers (that I had already sold) could be lost in the service department if things weren't done the way they should be.

The entire service department understood my position on customers; I never ever thought of a customer coming in for service as being anything less than a sales opportunity. I've always been a firm believer that excellence in how customers are serviced has everything to do with closing sales—*future* sales! To me, *there is no such thing as a "routine" service visit— even for an oil change.* **All customer visits are special.**

Don't get me wrong here. **We had an excellent team of professionals in our service department** who I knew could make me or break me. I wanted them on my side, so I took good care of them. As you know from reading Chapter 9, "Stay in Touch," I respected and appreciated them very much, and they knew it (36 people, wined and dined, every month, by me—and, of course, Uncle Sam). There was nothing they wouldn't do for me. Those service reps and technicians stood *behind me* every step of the way in much the same way I stood *in front* of my customers. *We worked together, not against each other* (unlike what you often hear about sales and service departments in many businesses). As a result, *my customers were always "special" cases.* THIS IS A VERY IMPORTANT CONCEPT YOU MUST GRASP. More of the *Girard touch* in action.

As I mentioned earlier, there were even occasions when I actually paid for parts out of my own pocket for customers on minor service repairs, like a wheel alignment, for example (and touched Uncle Sam for it later with a write-off on my tax return). Even when their warranties expired, I might say to them, "Come see me." I'd work something out for them. The dealership management thought I was insane for doing that. NOBODY, I MEAN NOBODY, EVER DOES THAT! BUT I DID.

Once again, I was way ahead of the curve on this. Although I didn't have to do it that often, I remembered that I made a promise to these customers, and I was going to keep it! This small measure of goodwill had a major impact on securing my relationships with them. I saw it as an inexpensive, personalized commercial, tailor-made just for them—chump change (I don't think I ever spent more than $30 or $40) for building a long-term relationship. They never forgot how I made them feel—*special*. They jumped back on my Ferris wheel so fast it would make your head spin.

Those customers never belonged to the dealership or anybody else! I was the key human contact they had in that place. That's the way I set it up. They belonged to me. They were mine as long as I protected them! Period. That's the power (and reward) of *keeping* a promise, pure and simple. Winner—Joe Girard! This is so simple and logical to me, it makes me laugh to think that nobody else would do it. Here it is in "Girard-speak": **PUT A NICKEL ON THE TABLE TODAY TO MAKE A DIME TOMORROW.**

Nurturing Relationships

I know you know I don't care for tattoos any more than I like earrings pierced in the tongue. But when someone meets me, they're introduced to a different kind of "tattoo." This one shines so brightly, they never forget it—my smile. It's the one that says, **"I LIKE YOU."** They see it in the way I treat them, in the way I follow up with them, and in the way I care for them. Many of my repeat customers (some on their third and fourth vehicle purchases) know the first thing they see whenever they come in to select their new vehicles is the welcoming smile that sold them the first time we ever met. One customer told me they felt so relaxed and at home when they were with me that I made buying a new car feel like a visit with family. I took that as a high compliment.

No matter what line of work you're in, every time you come in contact with a customer or client you've sold something to, or entered into a business agreement with, your goal remains the same—*add a layer of glue to your relationship.* Never take them for granted any more than you would a spouse, or you will surely lose them. And, yes, you have to work at it. Everyday life may never be as grand or as beautiful as that wedding day, but you must never forget the promise and commitment you made, whether it's personal or professional. *Stand in front of what you said you would do.*

A lifetime commitment is never realized because of a single gigantic act. It is attained by never letting up on the constant day-in-and-day-out attention to and nurturing of the little things that make up the whole. That's what really makes the difference. If you've been ignoring this approach up to now, it's time to get on board! A relationship can grow into the most beautiful tree you ever saw and bear the sweetest fruit you ever tasted for *as long as you care for it*. Nurturing relationships are at the very foundation of *My 13 Rules*. They are the way to make living life to the fullest a reality, not an empty dream or wish.

Becoming a Believer

There's an old saying: "If you want to dance, you've gotta get on the dance floor first." In other words, you won't get a thing done if you don't have your mind and your heart fully committed to the task at hand. *You must believe in whatever it is you are doing* to be successful. The folks at IBM understood this idea very well. They had three basic beliefs that governed everything they did. They started out by first getting everyone in the company on the same page *right up front*. We're talking about thousands of people here.

1. Everyone had to *respect the individual*. Success was achieved by getting all employees pulling in the same direction.
2. They were almost fanatic about becoming global leaders in providing the *best customer service possible*. They understood the value of customer retention.
3. They expected to achieve all their goals and objectives through the *superior performance of all their employees*.

There are some people who think company beliefs and mission statements are just there for the amusement of corporate management. The reality is, it's the people on the front lines who can make or break a company, and that's serious. What I like about the beliefs IBM adopted is that *they all center on the individual.* They're about making believers out of individuals. So what does this have to do with getting customers and other people, perhaps in your personal life, believing and trusting in you? Well, it's IBM's second belief that got my attention: *providing the best customer service possible.*

Once you become a believer in its power, *the reward for customer service is customer retention.* People will always be grateful for any extra effort or service you give them to let them know how important they are. This is especially true when a product or service you sold them is in question. Now's the time to "turn that lemon into a peach." That's the opportunity to really shine and make your mark. And if you do a little something extra the way I did, they'll never forget how you made them feel. It's when they least expect it that makes it special. They know you don't have to do it! That's when it counts the most.

Don't let others talk you out of doing something extra for people you care about. Don't let their jealousy take you down. Stay away from losers, and separate yourself from the pack. The truth is, when people see how much you believe in what you're doing for them by standing in front of your commitments, they'll respond by believing in you. It's human nature. You don't need a degree in psychology to figure this out either. *"Dr. Girard" has spoken.*

Leave a Legacy

Once I got rolling in my sales career, I made up my mind that, when I was through, I wanted to leave a legacy of compassion and commitment to all my customers. And, since most of them came back to me time and time again, I think I did. When you needed Joe Girard, he was there for you. He didn't "hit you when you were down." He stood in front of everything he ever did for you. I think I am most proud of the fact that that's what made me successful. Believe it or not, not everyone agrees with this approach. Some are doing nothing and apparently don't seem to care much about it.

When I think of the health care and pharmaceutical industries, I can't help but be outraged at what charges, even for the simplest of services, are being heaped on the majority of American citizens—yes, right here in the USA. What kind of legacy are those industries leaving in the minds of the average person? What about the elderly in our society who have the greatest needs? And what impression are they giving to the young people growing up today? When people have to decide between food, clothing, and a flu shot for their families, the flu shot loses every time. It seems as though no one really cares. In my opinion, the legacy of these industries is clearly one of shame. And, yes, it will eventually take the government to rope them in like all other rogue industries that just can't find the conscience to do the right thing on their own. Remember the tobacco industry?

Listen, I'm not trying to make a political statement here or get on the case of doctors, nurses, pharmacists, or anyone else in those industries. I know there are very dedicated and wonderful people in all professions. But the facts speak for themselves: when people are going without basic medical services because they can't afford them, and the profits are stacking up higher and higher in the health care and pharmaceutical industries, something's wrong with this picture. If I took care of my customers that way, they'd walk so fast I'd be out of business in no time.

How you handle the people you care about most in this world—your family, your customers—has everything to do with whether or not they will stay with you or come back to you. People don't forget how you treat them. Fortunately, you get to decide your own fate here.

HERE'S THE LESSON: What people will think about your character and reputation in the future is forged now—*not tomorrow but right now.* What are you doing about your legacy? Here are some guideposts for you to follow:

1. Always remember the time you spend cultivating customers today is the fruit that will keep them for tomorrow.
2. Do thoughtful little things for your customers to remind them you care. Send a birthday card; congratulate them on a new baby or a new job.
3. It is the unexpected little things you do that will register the most (reread Chapter 9, "Stay in Touch").
4. "Give them what they want—and a little more," as Sam Walton used to say. They'll remember you and return your kindness many times over.

Building the Power Reputation

No matter what industry you're in, your reputation for standing in front of your products or services is the lifeblood of your business. If it isn't, it should be. It's the power in your engine. We had a butcher in our neighborhood some years back who was known for selling fresh quality meats. He had been in business ever since I can remember, working hard to build it up to what it was. It became so successful, he moved into a larger facility and expanded his staff to meet the demand. Unfortunately, some of the new hires didn't have his passion for quality. Pretty soon the reputation of his market began to slip. Some of the meat he was selling was starting to "turn." Once the word spread, he was finished—"deadski," as I like to say. None of his regular customers would shop there again. A lifetime of hard work down the drain because he failed to manage his growth and success properly. His business never did recover to what it once was.

If your reputation is suspect, that can put your business "out in the street" in a split second—and that's *for real*.

When I say *stand in front* of everything you do for others, I'm talking about backing up the commitments and promises you made. Your reputation and character are on the line now. Here's the good news: when a customer or person has a question or issue with a product or service you provided, don't think of yourself as being in the service department where you work. I want you to picture yourself as though you are standing in front of the sales department door where you work, and you're about to write up this customer for another order. That's exactly what's going on here. **This is your opportunity to flex your reputation muscles.** You're servicing them to death so they'll get in line, one more time, to buy again. You want them leaping onto your Ferris wheel for yet another ride. **Close the deal.** That's the kind of power a positive reputation commands.

Here are some things you can do to help *stand in front of everything you do for others:*

1. **Make sure you're the primary contact for everything your customers or clients need.** If it's a service matter or a product issue, you can send them to someone else if you like, but make sure the initial contact always begins with you. You're in control. No surprises.

2. **Ask yourself, "What's it going to take to retain this client or customer?"** What's this customer worth to you over the next 10 years? This is a value judgment. Do the math. I'd bet that, in most industries, keeping a customer for 10 years or more will weigh in heavily for "putting that nickel on the table today to make a dime tomorrow." As you know, I would occasionally put up a little of my own money to keep a customer happy. Does it make sense for you?

3. **Make them feel special.** Whatever it is you're doing for them, make sure they know you don't do this for everyone.

Make them feel appreciated. Once you accomplish that, it is they who will appreciate you!

4. **Follow up personally.** After doctors perform surgeries, they typically contact the patients directly for a person-to-person discussion about recovery and next steps. You should too. Always check with your customers or business clients after you've resolved some issue to make sure they're happy and satisfied. You can't get your name in their minds too often at a time like that. **You must know that all is well.**

As you know by now, *My 13 Rules* apply to your personal as well as your professional life. The *power of your reputation* works the same way except that it's even more important here because it impacts a personal relationship.

It should be obvious by now that building a power reputation is a significant step toward establishing the character of who you are and what you stand for in life whenever you are seen or others mention your name. This isn't about being famous or anything like that. It's about representing yourself to others with the same honesty and respect you would want from them. When your character achieves that status, your reputation cannot reflect anything other than a positive image. **You are now the complete person.**

Creating the Complete Person

When I talk about being the complete person, I'm not referring to anything that suggests you, I, or anyone else is trying to become the perfect being. Far from it. We're all human and subject to making mistakes. My ideas about being a complete person are simply to *make you aware* of how others see you. When you are interacting with people who are either counting on you to stand behind your commitments or to provide some needed assistance, this is your opportunity to make a difference and step up to the plate. *Stand in front of every-thing you do for others.*

It's one thing to show a caring nature and help customers and other clients through some issues so that your relation-ship remains intact with them. You should do that. It's quite another thing to let anyone (prospect or customer) who comes in to see you about something think that "it's all free." It's been said, "If you help someone when they're in trouble, they'll remember you when they're in trouble again." Once in a while, you'll run into someone who'll try to take advantage of you, especially if you develop a reputation for being a person who demonstrates a caring attitude toward others. There are some conniving thieves out there who will see you as a "soft touch" when it comes to getting favors. Be prepared for them. They have only one goal—to cheat you out of something. Trust me, as your success grows, they will come. This is something that, unfortunately, you might also see in your personal life with family and friends. It happens.

As I mentioned several times, I often "gave a little" to help customers out to let them know I cared about our relationship. For the most part, they were all very appreciative. Once in a while, though, I'd run into a person who was interested only in taking advantage of me and not really sincere about being a loyal customer. They were interested only in what they could get for free—nothing else. Even prospects would occasionally come in and ask for free oil changes for the life of a new car as part of the deal because they heard Joe Girard never says "no" (which was not true).

I remember a certain customer who bargained so hard with me on the value of a trade-in car they were putting down on a new vehicle that the sale was almost not worth the time and effort I was putting into it. It was this same customer who, after I provided a free oil change and tire rotation a year later as a way of letting him know I cared about his business, wanted a set of new floor mats thrown in just to see if my interest in him could be stretched a little bit further. I was offended, to say the least, that someone would have the nerve to suggest that, but I handled it with dignity (although I had to shame him a little).

I said to him that I was quite sure a man of his stature was used to high-level business dealings that far exceeded the paltry value of a set of car mats. He didn't press me on the car mats.

Don't be a patsy. Here's what to do if someone comes looking for something for nothing:

1. **Don't be rude or impolite.** That's not who you are. The complete person does not take that approach.

2. **Let them know you are flattered that they know of your reputation for taking care of customers.**

3. **Tell them that all your customers are special people and deserve special treatment.** What you do for them is reserved for them only.

4. **Close the conversation by telling them you'd love to add them to your list of special people too.** Now you're calling their bluff. The ball is in their court. You're getting right to the point—"Buy a new vehicle from me"—but you're doing it politely.

Chances are they'll walk, but your dignity and self-respect will remain intact.

Or who knows? Maybe you'll convert someone! That's the classy way to handle a situation like that.

With family, I think it's a little bit more delicate. While I firmly believe in sharing what I have with others, you have to be aware that some may just be looking for a handout and will send you on a guilt trip if you don't come across with some cash. I know there are situations that require more than a compassionate heart, but I have always been a believer in the old proverb, "Give a man a fish and you feed him for a day; teach a man to fish and you feed him for life." I believe *My 13 Rules* are very much aligned with this idea—both for you and the people who are important in your life, whether they're customers, family, or friends. If you do something that impacts the direction of someone's life positively, there's so much more to feel good about than simply putting a piece of bread on their table for the moment. The complete person understands this concept very well. *Could that be YOU?*

Becoming a Visionary

I believe one of the most important reasons to *stand in front of everything you do for others* is to unlock the potential that lies ahead as a result of seeing the possibilities we've been discussing for repeat business, mending relationships, or just plain giving someone a helping hand when they need it most. Each outcome carries its own special form of gratification. Once you begin to see things in this fashion, you're on the road to becoming a visionary, one who has developed the skill and instincts to think with imagination, or "outside the box" as some people like to say.

Ordinary, predictable, and hard-headed behaviors are not the traits of a visionary. That sounds more like some of the people I worked for during my sales career. I finally came to the conclusion that some things and some people are just not meant to be changed. The stubborn positions of people like that actually made it easier for me to succeed and stand out in the crowd.

As my sales began to grow and grow, I discovered less and less competition. I found myself quite alone because I was so far ahead of everyone else in the industry. Somebody once said, "It's lonely at the top." As far as I was concerned, nothing could be further from the truth. I loved it up there by myself. Try it; you'll like it. I did.

Although I never felt especially gifted, I did know how to "look around the corner." I anticipated with the best of them. I developed a visionary's approach to finding opportunity. I dared to put my money where my mouth was when everyone else curled up in a ball and hid. My words to my customers echo in my head to this day: "I will do whatever it takes to *turn that lemon into a peach. I will stand in front of everything I do for you.*"

No one else had the vision or audacity to do what I did. Yes, I took a risk, but it was well thought out. I knew how people wanted to be treated. I also knew the power of doing something a little bit special for them when they least expected it—no magic, no mystery, just common sense and, yes, *vision.*

The opposite of being a visionary is being narrow-minded. Everyone in the industry saw what I was doing. I never kept my approaches a secret. It was there for the taking. Anyone could have copied what I did with customers. Unfortunately, many didn't want to put in the time or make the effort that I did. Some weren't willing to "give up a little today to make it up and more in the future."

If you can latch onto this idea of having vision and not be afraid to try some imaginative approaches, you'll grasp the idea behind why *standing in front of everything you do for others* is not difficult to do at all. It's the smart approach.

Girard's recipe is simple:

TAKE A CUP OF CONFIDENCE
ADD A PINCH OF IMAGINATION
LACE IT WITH LOVE
STIR REPEATEDLY UNTIL THE VISION IS CLEAR.

PART IV
REENERGIZE

RULE THIRTEEN
REWARD YOURSELF

The highest reward for a man's toil is not what he gets
for it, but what he becomes by it.

—John Ruskin, poet, artist, and social thinker

*Kitty and I celebrate our successes with many
trips to places like Las Vegas.*

REENERGIZE YOUR ENGINE

You've now reached the fourth and final phase of *My 13 Rules—reenergize*. This is Rule #13, where you take time out and *reward yourself.* It's the final leg on your climb to the top of the mountain. When I talk about rewarding yourself, I don't mean just giving yourself a pat on the back for a job well done with a trip to Vegas. I'm talking about making sure that your engine doesn't *overheat* because you didn't give it a rest. This is your time to cool down, slow down, and enjoy life.

Whenever I watch Olympic-class sporting events, I especially admire seeing the distance-event athletes in action. The marathons they compete in are the ones that really put the inner strengths and endurance of competitors to the test the most (and that's right up Joe Girard's alley). You really see who has what it takes to go the distance. Whether they're swimmers, runners, or cross-country skiers, one thing they all have in common, besides being highly motivated, is smarts—a keen sense for knowing how to balance and pace themselves to make sure they finish, and finish as strong as they possibly can. They know when to go all out. But like a jockey and a racehorse, they also know when to hold back. This same idea is true of how you work. If you don't take time out to reenergize, you'll eventually burn yourself out. What good is that? Well, here's the temptation.

Quite often you'll see someone "get on a roll" and they just can't stop. Things just seem to fall in place for them. They're afraid to stop—they're "in the flow" or "in the groove," as we say. They're making money. Or maybe they're a hit on the social scene. Whatever. All they want to do is to keep going and going until they finally run out of gas—until what? *They drop dead?*

If we're talking about work, and maybe you in particular, pretty soon you find yourself putting in 10–12 hours a day. Your family has practically forgotten who you are. You're on a runaway stagecoach, and you can't get off. I know. *I was on that runaway stagecoach myself.* As I mentioned earlier, in an odd sort of way, success almost killed me. My success was taking a toll on my health until I finally got smart and got help. That's when I hired those two guys to come work exclusively for me. I *rewarded myself* by using my head. *You must take the time to reenergize your engine.*

The Reward You Give Yourself

There probably isn't a better feeling than that moment of personal triumph. Victory is finally in your grasp. You've just won the battle. You've closed the deal. You've met your goals. When everything seemed like all was lost, you knuckled down and stayed the course to come out on top. Or maybe he "popped the big question to you," or she just said "yes" to your proposal. Whatever it is—YOU'RE THE BIG WINNER TODAY! As they say at McDonald's, "You deserve a break today." So take one! REWARD YOURSELF! "Okay. What should I do?" you ask.

Rewards and success are all relative. I mentioned earlier that as my success grew and I exceeded my goals (which was most of the time), my wife and I rewarded ourselves with trips to Las Vegas for nice long weekends, usually every month. It was a great way to spend some personal time together, relax, and celebrate our successes. We'd often stay at the Dunes, one of Las Vegas's premier hotels in those days. We had a ball back then, and today we still make frequent trips to Vegas to take in the shows, the energy, and the excitement of The Strip. Now maybe that's not your thing. Maybe you'd like a quiet weekend in a log cabin up north. Or perhaps golf, fishing, or boating is what you like to do. Maybe you're an artist or a concert-goer.

Whatever it is, make it *special*, and do it with someone who is *special* in your life. Celebrate the moment. You deserve it!

When I first got started, though, those kinds of rewards were just out of the question. It took me some time to get back on my feet after some of the earlier financial disasters I experienced. Whenever I made a few extra bucks, I was just happy to see my family feel a little bit of security for the first time. Perhaps a new dress for my wife or a new pair of shoes for my kids was all I could manage at first. I was just happy to see the smiles on their faces and love we all felt as my confidence began to grow. I think I'll remember those days of "small rewards" more than the bigger ones that came later.

You may be in the same situation I was in. Be patient. It'll get better. Trust me. Most of all, *trust yourself.*

You have to decide what's important and what you can afford. A good rule of thumb is to make sure you remember to put some of your reward away for a rainy day. It'll come as sure as night follows day. It's just the way life is. Someone will need some unexpected dental work. You may have a leak in your roof or basement. Or maybe a car needs fixing. Whatever it is, *try to stash some of that success away* in the bank. Take the pressure off yourself and plan ahead. That's the smart play.

If you have a family, let them all share in the fruits of your labor. After all, they are the reason you do whatever it is you do. They should be your reason for being. If they are, you have a loving family. Take them out for a day at a local amusement park, or maybe a ballgame, or perhaps it's a night out on the town with your spouse. They'll return the favor to you over and over by providing you with all the motivation you'll ever need to continue to grow your success in the future.

If you reward yourself with things you can see in your home, like a big TV, some new furniture, or even a second new car in your driveway, they serve as constant reminders to you and your family of your achievements. In turn, they also become your motivators to reenergize yourself to continue your successful growth pattern. I can remember buying our first large television, doing some remodeling to our home, and eventually even receiving a top-of-the-line Airstream motor home for my professional services. I also remember how good I felt seeing my family well-dressed because of my efforts.

Whenever I would see these rewards around my home, not only did they tell me I was doing a good job, they reminded me over and over *how* I did it: *following My 13 Rules.* That is precisely how it happened. No secrets. *Just doing the basics better than anyone else!* That'll make you feel like a million bucks every time.

Personal success also brings other rewards, the satisfaction of which almost goes beyond what words can describe.

The Reward You Give Others

Perhaps the greatest reward of all is sharing your good fortune with others—the gift of giving. For a guy who grew up with practically nothing, this one is especially *close to home* for me. While it's nice to receive tangible rewards for your achievements, especially like cash so you can buy things for yourself and your family, it's also a very special experience to be able to give something back, to share your rewards with those less fortunate. That is a feeling that has to be experienced to be fully understood and appreciated, especially when you can see it in the eyes and smiles of others you have touched.

It must have been quite a few years after I left home and started working on my own that I was finally able to enjoy some of the rewards of independence and hard work. I really first saw it in the way my young family responded when I finally got my head above water and had a few bucks to actually surprise them with some things they weren't expecting that they really needed. For me, charity really did begin at home. It brings a tear to my eye to this very day.

Even when I think back to my own childhood, I try never to forget that there are a lot of people out there who are so much worse off than I ever was. Probably because of that, my most favorite charity is the Save the Children Foundation. They provide food, education, and medical care to needy children all over the world. Nothing makes me feel better about giving than giving to that organization.

To this day, I donate copies of my books to many prisons all over the country free of charge. There are forgotten people in there who, in many cases, have little or no hope of ever amounting to anything in life. If I can help some of them turn their *attitude machines* around and get focused in the right direction, I might be able to provide just the spark they need to get their lives in order and on track in preparation for the day they walk out of there as free men and women. And I'm very gratified to have received several testimonials over the years from prisoners who said, "Thanks, Joe. You turned my life around."

One year I decided to give my entire speaking engagement fee at Oral Roberts University as a contribution to the new school tower the university was constructing. I wanted those kids to know the importance of sharing their time, talent, and treasures with others in this world while they were still in their learning years. If I could impact even a handful of them, they, in turn, would impact others. I saw it as *Girard's Law of 250* (see Chapter 9, "Stay in Touch") doing something really special for the community. I think I got back more than I ever gave that day.

Listen, I'm not telling you all this because I think I'm some kind of special philanthropist or because I'm on a fundraising campaign here to send you on a guilt trip if you don't part with some of your cash from time to time. *I am* on an *awareness* campaign, though. If you haven't figured it out by now, this whole book is about *awareness*.

HERE'S THE AWARENESS LESSON: I'm not the richest man on earth, but I have more than most. And because of that, I believe in *giving something back*—giving to those who have less. In your case too, I'm sure there are those who have less than you. Think about it.

What are the top three organizations or people in this world that command your highest respect and admiration for what they do for others? Who is special? Who are you willing to help? Start somewhere. Pick one and make a commitment to share something, even if it's small at first.

Don't ever forget where you came from. Once you become successful, you must always remember that you too started somewhere. And for most of us, that's at the bottom of the mountain. For me, I was practically one step out of the gutter. *I'll never forget where I came from.*

Sadly, many people do forget their roots. They become intoxicated with their success. They hoard their wealth and share nothing. That's what people will remember about them. What a legacy to leave behind.

Sharing your reward doesn't necessarily mean giving only money. Sometimes it means *sharing your time* with someone special or in need. Maybe it's a personal relationship that needs reenergizing that's been a little bit neglected. When you have the opportunity to mend a fence, make sure you do it. The gift of your time can be as special and precious as anything.

Perhaps the gift you give is simply *listening*. It means you are sensitive and care about someone or something more than just yourself. Nurture those special relationships by holding them firmly but gently in the grasp of your hand. Don't choke or squeeze them to death. Give them room to breathe. They know you're nearby if you're needed. Why is this so important?

In the end, I believe we will be rewarded not because of the *number of "sales"* we made but because of the *number of faces* we were able to put a smile on besides our own. Think about that.

A Critical Difference

It was the great French writer and philosopher Voltaire who once said, "Rest is a good thing. But boredom is its brother." He was cautioning against falling into the trap of DOING NOTHING. In my opinion, if boredom is the brother of rest, then *laziness* must be his twin sister. Don't confuse rewarding yourself by relaxing and enjoying some time off with being lazy! The difference here is huge. If you've worked hard to achieve your goals, then you deserve everything that recognizes that effort.

There are some people, though, who haven't accomplished a damn thing in their lives, yet all they ever seem to do is "reward" themselves. We had a lot of them in our business: extra-long lunches, leaving work early, heading to the bars with the other losers in the "dope ring." The reality is these are the flunkies in life whose only accomplishment is to deny their families of any opportunity to experience the joys of a quality home, a quality education for their kids, proper health care, and a secure financial future—all denied to the people who were counting on them because of their selfish laziness. And wasted time is something you can never recover.

I was always troubled by people like that. On the one hand, I almost wanted to cheer them on because each one of them represented one less person I had to compete with to provide for my own family. Yet on the other hand, I recognized the sad reality that somewhere out there were families who were being denied something that month because of the lack of work ethic I saw around me and in other many retail businesses. In my book, that's not just laziness; that's not just failing to live up to your responsibilities and obligations as a spouse or parent. *That's Cheating with a CAPITAL "C."* The only reward that's being enjoyed is the one being stolen away from a deserving family member.

Here's what gets me. When you stop to figure out how much time and energy is wasted trying to scheme up anything possible under the sun to avoid thinking, planning, or any hard work of any kind—always looking for the "easy way out"—you probably could have spent the same amount of time doing it the right way in the first place. Let's face it: even the most conniving person around has to stop and figure out how he or she is going to hide the fact that they're really doing absolutely nothing at all at work, all day, every day. I hope that's not you. I mean, sooner or later someone is bound to catch on to the idea that you're dead weight where you work and everyone is carrying YOU. In fact, YOU'RE AS GOOD AS DEAD. YOU WILL BE FIRED. And, as always, your family will take the hit (again) for you.

Indeed, reenergizing and taking time out for a job well done is a very different proposition than doing nothing at all from the time you crawl out of bed every day of your life. That is the best definition of *misery* I've ever seen.

Don't "Dance" on the Mountaintop Too Long

Remember, *rewarding yourself* is about reenergizing. As I said in Chapter 1, "If you dance too much at the top, you might slip and come crashing down to the bottom." Keep it balanced. Savor the moment, but be ready to get going again. There will always be more mountains to climb. But by all means, enjoy your reward.

I took my play time very seriously and very personally. First of all, *I never went anywhere without my wife.* When we planned our time off, I didn't want to hear from anybody about anything. I didn't check the office to see who called. I didn't have my mail forwarded. When it was time for me to reenergize, I didn't want anything to interfere with the quality time I had set aside for that. Period. Everything was put on hold. Why was I so insistent on that? Anyone who knew me knew that when I got back to the office the day after a vacation or trip, WATCH OUT!

They would witness a recharged, reenergized JOE GIRARD "on a full tank of gas" as he broke into the front door of that showroom, *ON FIRE* and ready to take on the world unlike anything they'd ever seen before! That's why.

Everyone knew when I was back in town. I had come down from the top of the mountain, and I was ready to go. That's the way I played the game! *I never sat on my reward.* The moment I got back on the front lines, I was all business again. It was as though I never left. When you recharge a flashlight with a brand new battery, it shines brighter than ever. To do that, though, you have to turn the flashlight off for a moment so you can replace the old batteries with new ones. That's exactly how I operated. It was a routine that became part of my life. While we had a few lazy people around the office, the funny thing is, because of my work ethic and commitment to hard work, I probably actually had more really truly relaxing and fun time in a year than they did. The difference was I didn't cheat. I EARNED MY REWARD.

Life's Reward

We've been talking a lot about short-term goals and rewards that give you the opportunity to recognize your achievements and provide a chance to reenergize as you work your way through the year. But what about something more long term? How about a *lifetime reward* for achieving what you set out to do in your career? Now that sounds like a plan to me. Although I never really retired (and never will) since I'm still very active giving presentations and motivational speeches all over the world, I think I can safely say that I have rewarded my wife and myself with a pretty nice standard of living. I set my goal of doing that a long time ago and I achieved it, so I have every intention of enjoying it, and I do.

If you want to set a long-term goal for yourself that has a special *lifetime achievement reward* at the end of your career for yourself, I think that's great. Maybe it's a home in a tropical climate. Or perhaps world traveling is your thing. Whatever it is, get that reward in front of your face early on, and set your sights on achieving it just as though it were a sales objective or a special assignment you're taking on. Quite frankly, I can't think of a more important project than that one. Can you?

Get excited about this! Look forward to it just like when you were a kid counting down the days till Christmas. Dangle this reward in front of your eyes every day. Put a reminder or a picture on your desk, in your car, or wherever you work. Never lose sight of it. The reason you want a long-term reward like that as an incentive is because when that day comes, you'll be making the biggest change in your life since you learned how to walk. It's finally time to *cash in your chips for the good life.*

Now you can swing in your hammock, at a night club, or with your golf clubs—it's your choice! You've earned it. Take a deep breath and give a big smile because you're loved, respected, and fulfilled. *My 13 Rules* have put you ON TOP OF THE WORLD!

The Ultimate Reward

In the final analysis, perhaps the most gratifying personal experience and ultimate reward of all is simply knowing that *you did your very best.* And that's really all one can ask of oneself. Doing all that you could possibly do has enabled you to provide the very most you could for yourself, your family, and other important people and causes in your life.

President Calvin Coolidge probably said it best when he said something like, "There is nothing more common than unsuccessful people with talent, genius, and education. Nothing in this world can take the place of *persistence.*" Thank you, Mr. President. I couldn't agree more. I'll use myself as a good example. I never thought I was particularly smart or talented. As far as education goes, I never even finished high school. But

I am successful because I NEVER STOPPED TRYING. I never gave up on myself. I WAS PERSISTENT. I was DETERMINED TO SUCCEED—AND I DID! As I've said, over and over again, to thousands of people all over the world—"IF I CAN DO IT, ANYONE CAN!"

Have you ever said to yourself or to your spouse, "What ever happened to our old friends Jack Jones and Jane Smith? It seemed like nothing could stop the success train they were on. We never hear a thing about them. It's like they vanished into thin air."

Believe it or not, there are actually lots of people like that out there, in all fields, who enjoyed some success but somehow never even came close to accomplishing what they could have.

There were mountains they had the talent to conquer but didn't. There were lives and people they had the resources to touch but didn't. There were goals that were easily within the grasp of their capabilities but were left in the distance on the road just ahead. They never lived up to any of their expectations because, at some point, they decided to take the path of laziness and idleness. They decided they'd had enough. They didn't want to expend any more energy on anything. For all intents and purposes, their lives were over. They just drifted into the alleys of life as the rest of the world raced by, empty lives filled with the regrets of what could have been. *Failure* has never been defined more clearly for me than that.

By comparison, people of lesser talents and natural abilities who give it everything they have to be successful often surpass these so-called "fast-trackers" in both achievement and in living life to the fullest. Yes, it means giving 150 percent. Anyone can give just 100 percent. It means accomplishing what you set out to do or possibly even *exceeding your expectations* of what you could do. Now that's sweet. It's even sweeter when you exceed the expectations other people have of you.

When I give motivational presentations or get feedback from my books, nothing gives me greater satisfaction than knowing I reached or touched someone in such a way that they're now energized to turn their lives around and become something they never dreamed possible—and all because I had an opportunity to get my message in front of them. How do I know when I've "reached" someone? They tell me.

You were inspirational! You really connected . . . a positive impact!
Harvard Business School

Girard captures the essence of rising to the top.
Mary Kay Cosmetics

Loved Joe's enthusiastic, catching style!
General Electric

An absolute "TURN-ON" . . . bar none!
PPG Industries

Joe will empower you to become tomorrow's entrepreneurial legend.
Avis Rent-A-Car

We definitely overachieved our objective!
IBM

Joe Girard is something special!
Newsweek

YOU ARE TRULY #1!
John Deere & Co.

My friends, rewards like those are the priceless gifts in life that make it all worthwhile. Yes, it's great to be NUMBER ONE. But there's something even more important than that. It's not so much about *some day* being the best as it is about *always being the very best that you can be.* If you can manage to do that, you're a winner every day. *That is the ultimate reward.*

THE NEXT STEP

**Failure is simply the opportunity to begin again,
this time more intelligently.**

—Henry Ford, automotive industrialist and innovator

*Through all my achievements and success, I
never forget where I came from.*

Joe Girard's 13 Rules—the Real Deal

Well, you've done it! Congratulations! You're now ready to take that critical next step—to launch the *new YOU*. You're already a WINNER for choosing the path of prosperity instead of the road to nowhere by doing nothing. By the way, you'll be pleased to know that *most people don't* do what you've decided to do. They *don't* want anything to do with something that pushes them off their sofa and into action. That's why the world is filled with ordinary people achieving ordinary results and living ordinary lives. But that is not you. You see the value in *My 13 Rules*. You've decided to embrace them. They are now an inseparable part of your life. YOU *ARE* THE 13 RULES.

Anyone can write a light, fluffy book filled with empty ideas that sound good in a textbook. But the test is when you put them into action on the front lines; then it's a whole different thing. That's where experience and firsthand knowledge come into play.

Welcome to the World of Joe Girard

Although I was in automotive retail sales, *My 13 Rules* are just as relevant in the insurance business, real estate, the medical profession, the construction industry, teaching, building a happy home, or anything else. No matter what you do, whether you're in sales, service, a teacher, a technician, a designer, a decorator, a doctor, or a homemaker—I don't care—you name it and *My 13 Rules* will form the foundation and roadmap to accomplish anything you set your sights on. That's the beauty of them. You decide where you want them to take you. If you want to get to the *TOP OF THE HEAP* and become *NUMERO UNO* in your world, on the job and at home, this is the place to start!

When I decided to write *My 13 Rules*, I made up my mind that I wanted to create a book that was more than a one-time read. I wanted to give you the gift of a lifetime, something that would be filled with *specifics*, things you could do that would really help you. THIS IS THE REAL DEAL.

I didn't want my name on something that was filled with a bunch of empty theories that sound good but don't give you anything specific you can actually do. I wanted this book to have some *teeth* in it—real approaches that work. I wanted to help you build a foundation. I believe *My 13 Rules* have succeeded admirably in accomplishing that.

You now have in your possession a very thorough yet practical guide to help you get ready for both the professional and personal challenges life throws at you. Every rule has been carefully thought through to give you just what you need to survive and succeed in today's world. You're now armed and ready to take on whatever life throws in your path. If you feel a weak moment along the way, you know the drill: reach for *My 13 Rules* to light the way and give you the strength and determination to stay the course.

From the moment you get up in the morning to "take on the world," you'll know exactly what to do. If you're smart, you'll reread the chapters of this book over and over again until all 13 rules become permanently encased in your heart.

To be successful in life, you've gotta be at the top of your game whenever someone comes in contact with you. Concentrate on how you can apply *My 13 Rules* to your everyday routines. Meditate on them. *Make them the foundation of WHO YOU ARE.*

Pushing Your Way Forward—Give It All You've Got

I'm sure there are some of you who felt that I pushed you pretty hard throughout this book at times. Some of you may even have been a little bit offended at how I said some of the things I said. If you're looking for an apology, don't hold your breath. I warned you up front that I was going to get your attention, and I was going to "tell it like it is"—no pulling any punches.

Why do I have such a hard-line attitude about hanging tough? There is only one reason I take this approach: *I am so absolutely passionate about winning* that, if you don't catch my *fever* here, you aren't going to have enough *gasoline in your engine* to make it across the finish line. What I'm talking about is high-octane efforts for *high-octane* results. *I want you to be as passionate as I am!*

Yes, there are a few quitters out there who couldn't take it. Clearly, they didn't have what it really takes to make the grade. As a result, they never got far enough into the book to read this. That's okay, because while I wrote it for everybody, *it's not for everybody!* Only the select few who have their heads screwed on right will get something out of it. *My 13 Rules* will separate the strong from the weak (as they should). We don't want any second-rate players on our team. This book is for *positive-minded* people who know that being *positive* and having *determination* are the most important factors all successful people count on to smash through life's obstacles.

If you really want to be successful, and if you really are ready to make a change for the better, you have to knuckle down and *push, push, push* yourself. THERE IS NO SUBSTITUTE FOR THIS. You must take this approach. And I'm here to push you every time you open this book.

No one's perfect. We all need encouragement and want to know we're making progress and that what we do counts for something. However, you don't get better by having someone "stroke your ego" when you continue to make mistakes. You want someone to step up to the plate and tell it like it is. Right? Only a true friend will tell you what's *really* happening. Never forget that in decision making there are two kinds of pain—the *pain of discipline* and the *pain of regret*. What's your choice?

Remember, you want to be where no one else is: AT THE TOP. This book is your ticket to the "big dance." Are you ready to show off your moves?

When someone asks you what you did with your life, wouldn't it be wonderful to be able to look back at them, smile, and say, *"I exhausted all possibilities of what I could have achieved."* What will your response be?

Only you will ever know the truthful answer to that question. You never want your life to be about what you *could have* or *should have* done. Let it be only about *what you're glad you did!*

My 13 Rules will show you how to live a purposeful life so you can answer the question of what you did in life with pride and a sense of accomplishment.

Even though we may achieve the goals we set for ourselves in life, that isn't to say that any of us quite reaches the point where there's nothing left to live for. That would really be a tragedy. If you really think there's nothing left to be done, let me remind you of what the great Irish playwright George Bernard Shaw once said: "Life is no brief candle for me. It is a sort of splendid torch which I have got a hold of for the moment. I want to make it burn as brightly as possible before handing it on to future generations." Now that's living life to the fullest. And he did—94 years' worth.

May YOUR TORCH burn as bright as a star-filled night! And keep it lit; there's lots of living to do!

At the end of the day, it's all about managing to achieve and experience a rich and satisfying life that is shared with those who are special to you. You will not get there with a half-baked effort either. You can't fake success. You have to *give it all you've got*; otherwise you'll fall short of the mark every time. And don't put it off. If you lack the courage to start, you have already finished. Replace *some day* and *one day* with *today*. *Hit the bricks running.* Make each day, each hour, and each minute special. *Live for today.*

In all likelihood, in the beginning you won't hit your goals on the first, the second, or maybe even the third try. Don't be disappointed. It may take years to finally get to where you want to be. That's all part of the journey. It's all part of the experience. It took me more than three years of tireless work to finally become number one in the world. But once I did, I never looked back. I stayed on top of the world for the next 12 years, unchallenged, until I finally retired from active retail selling to pursue motivational speaking and sharing my experiences with others.

Through it all, I was patient. I never gave up on myself. Remember, there is no such thing as *failure*. There is only *success* and *quitting*. Those who are the very best at what they do move on from failure, and that's the measure of a true champion. (Remember Joe Louis getting up from the mat.) If you wallow in self-pity, you cannot move forward.

I've said this many times: "You are in control until you have no mind left." So *give it all you've got* because winning is closer than you think.

Have No Regrets

Albert Schweitzer, the noted philosopher and missionary physician, once said, "*Success* is not the key to happiness. *Happiness* is the key to success. If you love what you are doing, you will be successful." He had the right idea. You see, only if you actually do *have* a great life can you then say I *had* a great life. So *have a great life*, then you won't have to wish for a thing because *you did it.*

How complete a life are you living?

Any regrets?

Are you truly content?

Are you satisfied?

Are you happy?

Happiness alone will give you the chase of a lifetime! And that "chase" *is the next step.*

So take what you have learned about *My 13 Rules* and commit to putting them into action—today. And if this is a second chance for you, even better; grab it with all the gusto you can. *It's never too late to become what you might have been!*

When you look back on what you did in your life for yourself, for your family, and for your community, HAVE NO REGRETS. I know in my own case, even with all of life's shortcomings and left turns, I wouldn't change a single thing about what I did because, taken all together, my total life's experiences are what made me what I became—and I continue to add to that every day!

Let me leave you with some words of wisdom to put on your nightstand; better yet, memorize them. After you've said a prayer and kissed your spouse goodnight, let this be the last thing you recite before calling it a day.

> Life is too short to wake up with regrets.
> So love the people who treat you right.
> Forget about the ones who don't.
> Believe everything happens for a reason.
> If you get a second chance, grab it with both hands.
> If it changes your life, let it.
> Nobody said life would be easy.
> They just promised it would be worth it.

If you follow *My 13 Rules* just like I've laid them out in this book, you'll quickly get yourself on the right track to success and avoid the mistakes and pitfalls I fell into during the early part of my life. Believe me, if you do that, you'll save more than just a few years and a few bucks. I think *My 13 Rules* will probably turn out to be one of the wisest investments you ever made. And nothing could make me any happier than that.

May you succeed in conquering the summits of every mountain in your path.

My best wishes to you and those you love.

I did it MY WAY.

INDEX

ABOUT THE AUTHORS

Joe Girard

Joe Girard is probably the most remarkable person ever to come along in the world of retail selling. Besides being the greatest retail salesperson ever, he is also one of the most gifted speakers you'll ever be in the presence of. Why? **JOE GIRARD has something to say.**

He always believed that working smart and being persistent could work wonders. His own life is proof positive of this. From the time he was a shoeshine boy and a newsboy growing up on Detroit's lower east side, Joe developed a keen sense of "street smarts" that would shock the world when he finally put them to the test on the front lines of automotive retail selling.

After numerous jobs including dishwasher, delivery boy, stove assembler, and then a short-lived stint as a home-building contractor, his fortune would change, and, before long, *the whole world would know about it.*

Joe Girard joined a Chevrolet auto dealership in Eastpointe, Michigan, where he would spend the next 15 years as a new vehicle sales rep. He would go on to record an astounding and amazing career for the ages. To put it mildly, there has never been anything quite like JOE GIRARD before or since JOE GIRARD.

He has sold more retail big-ticket items, one at a time, than any other salesperson in any retail industry in history including houses, boats, motor homes, insurance, automobiles, etc.

His accomplishments are simply jaw-dropping. They include no fleet, wholesale, or used car or truck sales. In addition, Joe has never held a management position! **His unbelievable sales statistics* have still not been broken!**
For the record, this is Joe Girard:

>> Highest average number of retail vehicles sold in one day—6

>> Most new retail sales in one day—18

>> Most new retail sales in one month—174

>> Most new retail sales in one year—1,425

>> Most new retail vehicles ever sold in a 15-year career—13,001

>> Number-one retail vehicle salesperson—12 consecutive years

Joe's awards and recognitions are as impressive as his records. He was the recipient of the coveted Golden Plate Award from the American Academy of Achievement. He was also nominated for the prestigious Horatio Alger Award by Dr. Norman Vincent Peale, author of *The Power of Positive Thinking*, and the renowned world traveler and radio broadcaster, Lowell Thomas. For his achievements, Joe Girard was inducted into the Automotive Hall of Fame in Dearborn, Michigan—the only salesperson ever to receive this honor. He is listed in the *Guinness Book of World Records* as the **"World's Greatest Salesman."**

He remains one of the world's most electrifying motivational speakers and has an enviable portfolio of important clients including Harvard Business School, 3M, Brunswick Corporation, CBS Records, Allstate Insurance, Ford Motor Company, General Electric, General Motors, Hewlett-Packard, IBM, John Deere, Mary Kay Cosmetics, and Bell Canada, just to name a few.

---

* All statistics audited and confirmed by the accounting firm Deloitte & Touche. Audit available upon request.

Joe has authored four multimillion-selling books on sales leadership and self-improvement:

How to Sell Anything to Anybody

How to Sell Yourself

How to Close Every Sale

Mastering Your Way to the Top

www.joegirard.com

Tony Gibbs

With a background in radio broadcasting and corporate communications, Tony brings over 40 years of experience to this book. Specializing in automotive sales and marketing communications, he has written countless dealership product, sales, and service training and motivational programs. He has also written numerous speeches for senior executives at the highest leadership levels in both Ford Motor Company and General Motors. Tony has collaborated with Joe Girard on other key promotional programs for over 10 years.

Printed in the USA
CPSIA information can be obtained
at www.ICGtesting.com
JSHW010206071123
51567JS00018B/352